Literacy and Language
Handbook

3

Janey Pursglove and **Charlotte Raby**

Series developed by **Ruth Miskin**

OXFORD
UNIVERSITY PRESS

OXFORD
UNIVERSITY PRESS

Great Clarendon Street, Oxford, OX2 6DP,
United Kingdom

Oxford University Press is a department of the University of Oxford.
It furthers the University's objective of excellence in research, scholarship, and education
by publishing worldwide. Oxford is a registered trade mark
of Oxford University Press in the UK and in certain other countries.

British Library Cataloguing in Publication Data
Data available

ISBN: 978-0-19-833076-9

13

Paper used in the production of this book is a natural, recyclable product
made from wood grown in sustainable forests. The manufacturing process
conforms to the environmental regulations of the country of origin.

Printed in Great Britain by Ashford Colour Press

Acknowledgements

Cover illustration by Anaïs Goldemberg

Illustrations by: Anthony Browne; Mark Chambers; Ben Galbraith; Ross Collins;
Lizzie Finlay; Garry Parsons; Anaïs Goldemberg; Gwen Keraval; Korky Paul; Q2A;
Tony Ross; Jeanne Willis

Design by Q2A

INSPIRATIONAL SUPPORT FOR TEACHERS
For free professional development
videos from leading experts, plus other
resources and free eBooks, please go to
www.oxfordprimary.co.uk

HELPING YOU ENGAGE PARENTS
We have researched the most common concerns
and worries parents have about their children's
literacy and provide answers and support in
www.oxfordowl.co.uk

This site contains advice on how to share
a book, how to pronounce pure sounds,
how to encourage boys' reading, and much
more. We hope you will find the site
useful and recommend it to your parents.

Contents

Introduction

What is Literacy and Language?

Literacy and Language is a complete literacy programme for children in Years 2–6 (Primary 3–7). It is designed to stimulate and challenge children's thinking and create enthusiastic, lifelong readers and writers.

It provides explicit guidance for developing children's reading comprehension and writing composition with support for teaching grammar, vocabulary development, critical thinking and spoken language. It gives you all the support you need to teach outstanding, consistent literacy lessons every day, and to deliver the new National Curriculum confidently.

The core purpose of the programme is to ensure that children, as the National Curriculum aims state:

read easily, fluently and with good understanding

develop the habit of reading widely and often for both pleasure and information

acquire a wide vocabulary

use grammar correctly

appreciate our rich and varied literary heritage

write clearly, accurately and coherently, adapting their language and style in and for a range of contexts, purposes and audiences

use discussion in order to learn; they should be able to elaborate and explain clearly their understanding and ideas

are competent in the arts of speaking and listening, making formal presentations, demonstrating to others and participating in debate

Literacy and Language resources for each year:

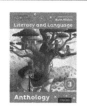				
an **Anthology** of complete stories, plays, poems and non-fiction texts	a **Pupils' Book** containing writing, grammar, comprehension and vocabulary activities related to the Anthology texts	a **Homework Book** providing further practice and consolidation of grammar points and writing tasks	**Software** with a wide variety of teacher-led activities and teacher support, for use on an interactive whiteboard	a **Handbook** giving clear day-by-day lesson plans for each Unit

Resources

Anthology

Literacy and Language is based on Anthologies of carefully chosen complete stories, plays, poems and non-fiction texts by leading children's authors including Michael Morpurgo, Jeremy Strong, Roger McGough, Geraldine McCaughrean, Jamila Gavin, Roy Apps and Susan Price.

The range of stories, plays, poems and non-fiction texts in *Literacy and Language* provide an opportunity for children to study texts which are absorbing, challenging and deep enough to dive into while being accessible to all children.

The children's increasing familiarity with a wide range of stories, plays, poems and non-fiction texts will generate a desire for more reading for pleasure. Wider reading lists are provided for every Unit.

All the texts in the Anthology are complete and are just the right length for children to read during the lesson and to develop reading stamina.

All the fiction and non-fiction texts include rarer vocabulary, which the children explore through Word power activities prior to reading the text.

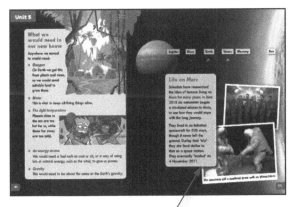

Each non-fiction text is a model of a particular form with a clear purpose, aimed at a specific audience. The high-interest, often humorous non-fiction texts provide further stimulus for reading widely and often.

Pupils' Book

Lively activities in the Pupils' Book develop children's writing, grammar, comprehension and vocabulary skills. The activities are linked to the Anthology texts and help children consolidate and apply what they are learning.

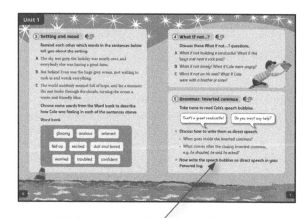

Each Unit has **activities** on **'Power words'** – ambitious words to enhance children's spoken vocabulary and ultimately their vocabulary for writing.

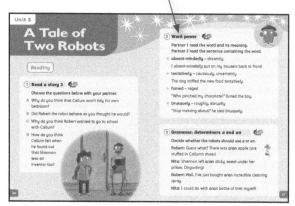

Grammar is taught in context and through writing to make it meaningful for children.

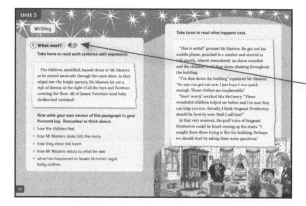

Partner work is embedded in the programme – many of the activities are rooted in discussion, which helps to develop children's spoken English.

Homework Book

The Homework Book contains weekly activities which allow children to practise and embed the grammar, writing and other language and literacy skills they have learnt in the lessons.

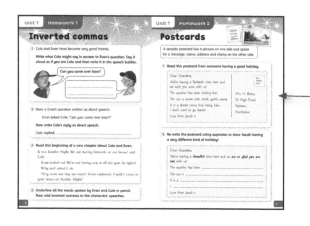

The activities are accessible and engaging, with age-appropriate glossaries and information boxes to ensure children can work independently at home.

Software

The Software is integral to the programme and is used for whole class teaching. It contains a range of resources to support your teaching.

There are fully illustrated texts, including stories, plays, poems and non-fiction texts from the Anthology, to display and explore as a class.

Audio and video clips are used to introduce drama activities or stimulate discussion.

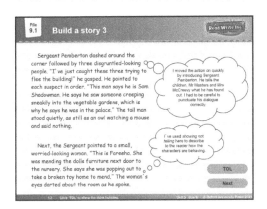

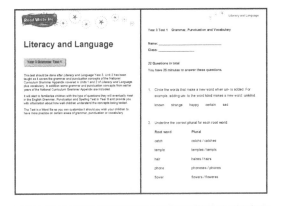

There are **modelled writing scripts** for the teacher to show how a text is built up, including how to 'Think out loud' to show children how to develop ideas.

A **Grammar Bank** gives teachers clear explanations about every aspect of grammar in the new National Curriculum and practice tests for children (see p.9).

Files include:

- video, audio performances of the poems and plays, radio interviews, music and images
- drag and drop language activities
- writing plans which can be printed out for class use
- 'Think out loud' teacher scripts for modelled writing
- 'Power words' for classroom display
- ready-prepared 'Write a story' texts for modelled writing
- editable timetables.

The Software booklet provides more detailed information about the features of the Software.

All this support makes it possible for you to teach an outstanding literacy lesson every day.

Teaching Handbook

Teachers are given comprehensive, structured support from the detailed day-by-day lesson plans in the Teaching Handbook and timetables.

> Overview timetables are provided in the Teaching Handbook and as editable files on the Software.

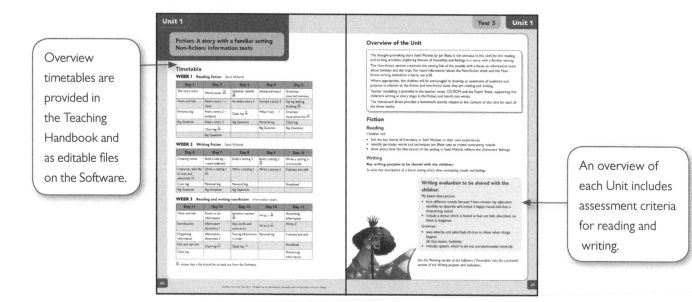

> An overview of each Unit includes assessment criteria for reading and writing.

> Lesson plans give detailed guidance for each activity.

> Activities are clearly matched to the new National Curriculum.

> Children write every day, building up ideas, planning, developing longer pieces of writing, then evaluating, editing and proofreading their work.

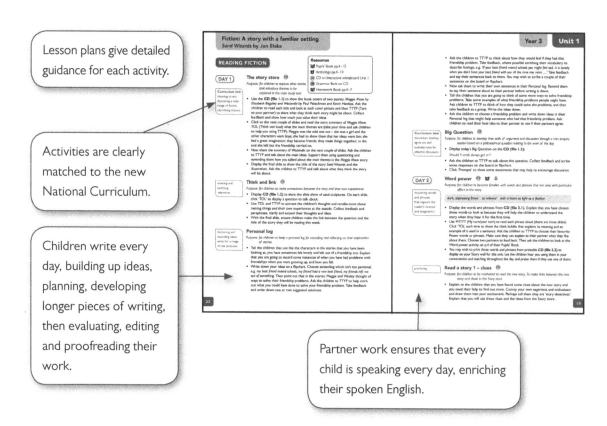

> Partner work ensures that every child is speaking every day, enriching their spoken English.

What will children be taught?

Comprehension skills

At the heart of *Literacy and Language* is the enjoyment of and engagement with a variety of texts. Children are encouraged to take their own meaning from each text, becoming independent and critical thinkers. Comprehension activities are designed to help children to infer, summarise, question, clarify, predict and argue a point of view. The children also make connections between texts and their own experiences. The programme approach integrates reading, writing, thinking, and spoken language in all activities, to ensure the daily development of children's comprehension and wider literacy skills.

Grammar

Children are taught the importance of using grammar correctly, so they can communicate clearly and convey their meaning effectively. Comprehensive guidance is provided for teachers, supported by engaging Software, Pupils' Book and Homework Book activities.

Children meet examples of the grammar point they will study in the context of the story, playscript, poem or non-fiction text in the Anthology. The teacher then explains the grammar concept to the children, often using the Software and an activity in the Pupils' Book. Children are also taught the grammatical terms. When the teacher models the writing process the grammar concept is included so that children can see how to use it in their writing. When children do their main writing task they are reminded to include the grammar point as it is listed in the evaluation criteria. Children consolidate their knowledge of the grammar concept through activities in the Homework Book.

Grammar Bank

A Grammar Bank on the Software provides teachers with explanations about every aspect of grammar in the new National Curriculum. It contains a detailed, cross-referenced glossary of grammar terminology with clear examples and 'test yourself' exercises for teachers, with answers included. There are also grammar tests for children that provide practice in the type of questions they will meet in the English Grammar, Punctuation and Spelling Test.

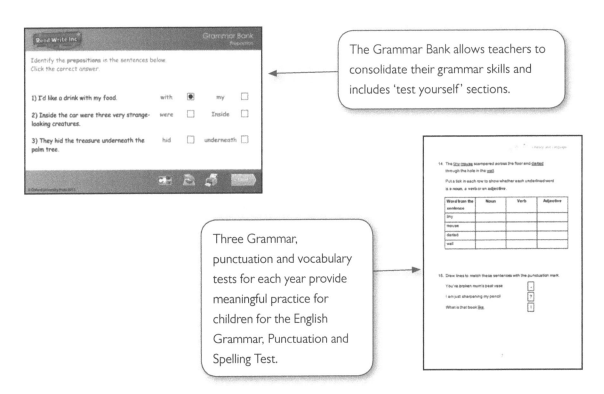

The Grammar Bank allows teachers to consolidate their grammar skills and includes 'test yourself' sections.

Three Grammar, punctuation and vocabulary tests for each year provide meaningful practice for children for the English Grammar, Punctuation and Spelling Test.

Writing

Daily writing is at the heart of *Literacy and Language*. Alongside the main, extended writing activities, opportunities are taken every day to create shorter pieces of writing. This allows children to focus on very specific skills, build up their confidence and stamina for writing, and develop their understanding of audience and purpose.

As the new National Curriculum recommends, children are shown the process of writing. Using the resources for modelled writing and 'Thinking out loud', you can show what is involved in being a writer: making choices, alterations and additions while monitoring for sense and meaning. This de-mystifies the writing process for children while demonstrating the 'magic' of creating different effects with language. Writing in action shows children the power of language.

What they read, talk about and see through teacher modelling encourages children to experiment with language to express their thoughts and ideas accurately and independently. Most importantly, daily writing opportunities help children to develop a belief in themselves as writers.

Vocabulary development

The greater the children's vocabulary and the complexity of the language they hear and read, the richer their writing will be. The stories, plays, poems and non-fiction texts in the programme all include ambitious vocabulary. Before children read the texts, they are taught the meanings of more challenging words – both in the context of the story and in real life situations. The teacher and children use the vocabulary throughout the lesson, but also through the week, until the words become familiar. These new words and phrases are displayed and collected from one week to the next, keeping the favourite and most useful words displayed throughout the programme.

Spoken language

The new National Curriculum places huge emphasis upon spoken language. It states, 'The quality of and variety of language that pupils hear and speak are vital for developing their vocabulary, grammar and their understanding for reading and writing.'

Teaching children to articulate their thoughts and ideas out loud and to communicate what they know and understand is critical to the success of *Literacy and Language*.

Children are taught to orally rehearse what they will write before putting pen to paper.

Teachers 'Think out loud' to show children what is involved in becoming an effective reader and writer. You can show children how you clarify and modify your understanding of what you read – how you infer and predict; build pictures in your mind; identify what's important; summarise key points; and importantly, persevere when things get tricky. In the same way, children are expected to 'Think out loud' with a partner to check their own understanding so their thinking is made clear to themselves as well as to you.

Literacy and Language uses carefully constructed partner work to make this possible. *Read Write Inc.* partner work is pacey, structured and meaningful – it keeps the children engaged throughout the lesson. Children answer every question with a partner, comment on each other's ideas, clarify each other's thinking, and build upon each other's thoughts and ideas. The teacher listens in carefully, selects children to give feedback and then selects others to build upon what they say. The teacher asks questions to take their thinking further and clears up any misconceptions.

Spelling

Read Write Inc. Spelling covers the National Curriculum spelling requirements and can be used alongside *Literacy and Language*.

How does the programme work?

Literacy and Language comprises six Units of work per year group. The Units are designed to be used over three weeks, but can also be used more flexibly, e.g. over a longer period if necessary as there is ample material and stimulus in the programme to extend tasks.

Whilst all literacy skills are developed throughout the programme, each week has a *particular* focus:

- Week 1 Reading fiction
- Week 2 Writing fiction
- Week 3 Reading and writing non-fiction

Children write every day in their Personal log (notebook) so that writing becomes a habit. They record their thoughts, ideas, and reactions to the text, often as mind maps and story maps – some of which they will draw on for extended writing activities in Weeks 2 and 3.

Grammar activities are woven into the programme on the Software and in the Pupils' Book. In addition, the Homework Book provides an opportunity for children to consolidate and practise their grammar, writing and other literacy skills at home.

Thinking and discussion skills are practised through a daily 'Big Question' which is a philosophical question that children debate so that their spoken language is developed every day.

Week 1: Reading fiction

The story store
The main story (or poem or playscript) the children study in each Unit is introduced via a brief discussion of other texts containing similar themes, some of which will be familiar to most children. Summaries of these texts are provided in the Story store on the Software. This activity helps children to make connections between texts and their own experiences.

Read a story 1, 2 and 3
Literacy and Language uses a three layers of text approach to teaching reading and writing. Children are introduced to the text via Read a story 1, 2 and 3.

Read a story 1 – clues introduces the children to the characters, setting, and plot through a series of image and audio clues, which you can explore by 'Thinking out loud' to make predictions about the story and build an idea of the 'bare bones' of the plot in the children's minds. This allows all children to access the basic story straight away. The ending is never revealed at this stage to ensure the children are motivated to want to read the full story.

Read a story 2 – evidence gives the children more information about the characters, setting and plot. This shows children how language can be used to change or develop readers' understanding of texts.

Being introduced to the text through Read a story 1 – clues and Read a story 2 – evidence first means that when the full story is revealed in Read a story 3, which is in the Anthology, the children can focus all their attention on the subtleties, nuances and their own interpretations of the text. The staged and guided access into the story means that children who need most support are undaunted by a challenging text and can immerse themselves in the world of the story as successfully as the children who need least support.

Week 2: Writing fiction

Build a story 1, 2 and 3
Having explored a text through three layers of meaning, from its simplest level to its most complex, children then see a new text being composed through the planning, oral rehearsing,

drafting and editing stages. The teacher shows how a story is 'built up' via three layers of development (Build a story 1, 2 and 3). Using the pre-prepared resources, you are supported in the role of a writer as you model the composition of a text. This modelled writing deepens children's understanding of the writing process and enables them to compose confidently themselves.

Write a story 1, 2 and 3
With your support, the children then mirror the process you have modelled, drafting and revising so that they write ambitiously and accurately as they compose their own extended piece of writing.

The Software provides two versions of a story being written – Write a story 1 and Write a story 2. Through drama activities, teacher modelling and partner work, children build on these story frameworks, adding their own ideas, developing sentences and using them as models for planning their own plots, structures and characters. These prepare children to write the full story – Write a story 3.

Week 3: Reading and writing non-fiction

The fiction and non-fiction texts in each Unit are linked via one of the 'Big Questions' that children debated in the fiction weeks. Children explore examples of the non-fiction text type, focusing on audience, purpose, form and style through Deconstruction 1, 2 and 3 activities which are designed to reveal the conventions of specific text types. Then they use what they have learnt to plan and draft their own pieces of writing, with an audience in mind, through Write a… 1 and 2 (discussion text/explanation text/instruction text, etc. depending on the text type). A final piece is then written (Write a… 3) presented and evaluated through self and peer assessment.

Core activities

The core activities encourage children to engage fully with the text as they explore character, motivation, settings and themes.

Word power
Powerful, evocative vocabulary is explained and explored before children encounter it in the story, play, poem or non-fiction text. Teachers and children are also encouraged to use the 'Power words' outside the context of the story to ensure they become part of the children's own vocabulary store.

Think and link
Used at different points in the programme, this ensures that children question what they are reading and connect it to their wider reading, own experiences and current understanding of the world.

What if not…?
An opportunity for children to speculate on how a story would change if the writer altered any one aspect of character, plot or setting, developing their awareness of how one is affected by the other, e.g. in *Beauty and the Beast*, we ask 'What if not *a handsome prince*? What if the Beast had turned into *a frog* when Beauty kissed him?'

Build a sentence
Build a sentence is used to build a vivid, engaging description. The starting point is often a single word or a short phrase which is chosen because it is particularly powerful or unusual. The activity is used, with My turn/Your turn, to build up a sentence from a simple fragment to an ambitious, complex sentence that provides children with a model of good writing in microcosm. Teachers model making choices out loud, making changes and improvements, and repeating their sentence to themselves to ensure they can remember it. Sentences can be built up out loud, or written down.

Jump in

The purpose of Jump in is to help children remember vocabulary and phrases from the story. Jump in is used in *Literacy and Language* on subsequent readings of the fiction texts, to help children remember and assimilate the 'Power words' and 'Special phrases'. Once they get to know the story, ask them to join in the reading of the words in bold. Exaggerate particular words and phrases and use actions and facial expressions to help.

Class and Personal logs

Children write in a Personal log (notebook) to:

* record responses to what they have read, thought and talked about
* experiment with vocabulary and text structures
* make notes, mind and story maps, diagrams and plans
* collect and paste related artefacts – tickets, photos, leaflets and drawings from home.

Big Question

A 'Big Question' is asked at the end of Days 1–8 and discussion should take about 10 minutes. These questions explore an idea linked to an aspect of the text covered that day, e.g. after thinking about the themes of friendship in the story *Sand Wizards* the children explore the question 'Should friends always get on?' The aim of the Big Question is to develop spoken language and argument skills. Children learn to justify ideas with reasons, negotiate, evaluate and build on the ideas of others, select the appropriate register for effective communication, as well as think in a deeper way about the more abstract issues that come from the text. Children are encouraged to express their opinions and enjoy a context in which there may be no right or wrong answers, just their own carefully considered opinions.

On Day 11 the non-fiction text is introduced through a brief re-examination of one of the Big Questions already discussed in the Fiction weeks, helping children to make links between their own ideas and contextualising the new non-fiction text. For example, in Unit 5 children explore clues and suspense in mystery stories and then discuss the Big Question 'Can an answer ever be the final one?' This is briefly revisited on Day 11 when introducing a non-chronological report about whether humans could ever live on another planet, such as Mars.

Picture Books in Year 2

The same concepts and structures are used in *Literacy and Language* across Years 2–6. In Year 2, however, the Story store is enhanced by the use of high quality picture books as an introduction to the themes to be explored in the Anthology story, play or poem.

Authors and illustrators include Tony Ross, Anthony Browne, Jeanne Willis and Korky Paul.

Differentiation – guided assistance

It has been assumed that children in the *Literacy and Language* groups will all be fluent readers but not necessarily working at the same comprehension level. Differentiation is achieved by the amount of support pupils need in order to learn something new. The guidance in *Literacy and Language* ensures that children who need least support receive the necessary challenge and that others receive the necessary assistance to understand the texts they read and to write confidently.

The range of teaching and learning strategies embedded within the *Literacy and Language* resources allows *Literacy and Language* teachers to become skilful at ensuring that all children develop their ability to understand the texts they read, use the spoken word confidently and become accomplished writers.

Teachers support and challenge the children by:

- developing comprehension using the three layers of text approach for reading, allowing access to engaging and challenging texts for all children
- modelling your thought processes in planning for writing and editing using 'Think out loud' and the three layers of text approach for writing
- preparing children for writing using oral rehearsal
- providing differentiated writing frames where necessary
- asking and encouraging children to ask questions, with an emphasis on allowing thinking and talking time
- using partner and small group work developed to a high level to provide peer support and challenge
- encouraging use of the Personal logs to enrich and extend children's thinking, providing a 'safe' place for recording thoughts and ideas and to experiment with short pieces of writing
- using Challenge activities in Years 5 and 6 for class extension work.

Assessment and marking

Assessment is integral to the whole *Literacy and Language* programme. Partner discussion helps teachers assess what and how children are learning throughout the lesson.

The specific focus for both reading and writing is set out at the beginning of each Unit, along with the key purpose and evaluation criteria for children's main writing composition. Each set of partners is provided with a copy of the writing Evaluation criteria (see the Planning section of the Software, and navigate to the 'Timetables' tab for these) at the start of the writing process and this is used as a guide for editing and evaluating their own and their partner's work. The criteria are included in the Pupils' Book for selected Units, and as PowerPoints on the Software, to show that they are integral to the writing process. They also form the basis for the teacher's marking. Teachers are encouraged to mark the children's work thoroughly and give advice on their next steps based upon the Evaluation criteria.

Commenting on Personal logs

Teachers explain that the Personal log is an important part of being a writer – it is to a writer what a sketch book is to an artist. The children know that the logs will not be 'marked' in the same way as their exercise books. Teachers read the children's notes and ideas and respond with thoughtful notes and suggestions. These should be written in pencil, not pen; it will be like a dialogue on paper. Children should be aware that their privacy will be respected and that ideas from their Personal log will not be shared with others without their permission. Although the Personal log is for notes and ideas, it should be stressed that this book is special – it is not a rough book or jotter. Children can leave the front page empty so that, at the end of the year, they can make a contents page for the year's work.

Class logs

Class logs are used in Years 2 and 3 to demonstrate how to keep a Personal log, as well as to collect combined responses from the class. The teacher writes some of the most pertinent ideas in the log and sticks in photocopies of children's writing and pictures they collect. The Class log is displayed in a place where children can read it at other points of the school day. A blank page is left at the start to create a contents page.

How do you get started?

Book training

Ruth Miskin Training provides a one- or two-day in-school training course or a one-day central training course. A knowledgeable and experienced trainer ensures you can teach the new National Curriculum confidently, using *Literacy and Language*. Please note: *Literacy and Language* should be taught by qualified teachers.

Appoint the *Literacy and Language* leader. Choose a confident and organised teacher to meet the other teachers every week for 20 minutes to discuss one particular aspect of *Literacy and Language*, demonstrate lessons to teachers, observe other teachers, evaluate children's progress and teachers' marking.

Training can be booked at: www.ruthmiskintraining.com

How does the programme fit with Read Write Inc. Phonics?

As soon as children have completed *Read Write Inc. Phonics*, or are reading at NC Level 2a, they are ready to start *Literacy and Language*. Children who finish *Read Write Inc. Phonics* during Year 2 join a Year 2 *Literacy and Language* class. Children who finish in Year 3 join a Year 3 *Literacy and Language* class, and so on. We develop the same teaching strategies and principles used in *Read Write Inc. Phonics*.

Full participation: this is fundamental to *Literacy and Language*. Teachers use 'Think out loud' to show the children how to analyse, plan and organise their ideas. 'My turn/Your turn' is also used to practise key activities and, crucially, partner work ensures that all children participate in the whole lesson.

Positive teaching: children learn at a much faster pace in an assertive and positive climate. They talk more readily in an atmosphere free from anger and tension. Praise for effective partner work is crucial.

Pace: each Unit has been planned to take three weeks. However, teachers might choose to add in extra time for some activities. You may also want to plan time for children to present and publish some of their final compositions.

Purpose: every part of the lesson has a very clear purpose. Please read the explanation behind the core activities on p.12. It is important to make the purpose of each activity transparent and easy to understand using child-friendly language.

Passion: this is a very supportive and detailed programme, which is why it works so well. However, it is the energy, enthusiasm and passion that teachers put into the lessons that bring the teaching and learning to life. Passionate teaching has impact.

Setting up Literacy and Language in your classroom

Timetable 70 minutes for *Literacy and Language* lessons. We also recommend that schools plan for an additional 20 minutes for Storytime every day. Please see the Ruth Miskin Training School Portal for suggested stories and poems to read to children. In the Overview chart on pp.18–19, there are also suggestions for stories and books for wider reading which will link to the themes and genres explored in the Units.

Management signals

Use these signals to ensure teaching is effective and consistent throughout the school.

The 'stop' signal: when all children are engaged in partner work, you need to be able to get their attention quickly and easily without raising your voice. Hold your hand in the air and do not talk whilst it is raised. When children see the signal they should finish what they are saying and raise one hand in response. Do not start talking until everyone has returned the signal and you have lowered your hand.

'My turn/Your turn' signal (MT/YT): there are times when you will need children to copy what you do. *My turn:* touch your chest with your palm when it's your turn. *Your turn:* open your palm to children when it's their turn.

The 'Turn to your partner' signal (TTYP): before you ask a question, tap two fingers together to warn children they will need to turn to their partners to answer. Explain that the 'hands up' system for answering questions will not be used. Ask children to put one hand on their head if they need clarification or have a question to ask.

The 'Perfect partner position': partners should sit side-by-side and shoulder-to-shoulder. (If they face each other the noise level increases.) Number the partners 1 and 2. Children keep the same number for the duration of the whole Unit. See the Planning section of the Software and navigate to the 'Extras' tab for further guidance on choosing partners, and activities to ensure partners work effectively together.

Planning and preparation

All the planning is ready for you to use. However, a thorough understanding of the programme's multi-layered and integrated approach to teaching fiction, non-fiction and grammar is vital. The more prepared you are, the more successful your children will be.

First, gain a thorough overview of the whole Unit. Read the story and non-fiction texts in the Anthology, followed by the teachers' notes in the Handbook, and the activities in the Pupils' Book and Software. You will see how the individual layers unfold; how the reading activities feed into the writing and how the 'Big Questions' weave together the fiction and non-fiction texts. Each activity builds upon the next.

Study the timetable at the beginning of each Unit – it provides an overview of the activities for each day and shows when you need to print out any files from the Software such as evaluation sheets, modelled writing prompts, words for display, etc.

Prepare for your lessons using the teaching notes for the Unit. You could also use and adapt the flexible planning sheets on the Software.

Organising discussion

Setting ground rules for discussion
The ground rules for discussion should inform the whole school policy on teaching and learning so they become fundamental to every lesson in every curriculum area. Children should be taught, explicitly, the rules for working in a group or with a partner and take part in regular

evaluations of what makes for effective discussion – see the Planning section of the Software, and navigate to the 'Extras' tab for the Effective discussion poster. Although the rules are similar for all ages, children's responses increase in complexity and sophistication year-by-year.

Display the Effective discussion poster in a prominent position. Praise the children for specific behaviour when partners co-operate successfully.

Short answers
Explain to the children that you will sometimes require a one- or two-word answer to questions – use a finger and thumb to show 'small'. This action tells partners to turn back to you quickly once they have said their answer to their partner.

One, two, three: if there is only one answer to the question, say 'One, two, three,' and ask children to call out the answer together.

Popcorn: if there are lots of different one-word answers use Popcorn – children call out their answers in the pauses between other answers.

Wave: sweep your arm across the room in a wave. Children call out their answer as your arm sweeps over them.

Longer answers to explain why
Ask a question, then ask partners to TTYP (Turn to your partner). Listen in to different partnerships each time, sometimes building on their ideas. Do not get too involved with one partnership as it is important to observe how well all sets of partners work together – particularly in the early days. Do not give children too long to answer or let the discussion tail off. Importantly, make sure children carry on talking until you raise your hand to stop. It is very disruptive to discussion when children raise their hands/show thumbs or use any other signal to show that they have an answer ready. Select partnerships with helpful contributions to feed back to the group or do this on their behalf.

In-depth answers to consider different viewpoints, challenge claims politely, negotiate an agreement
As above but go backwards and forwards, asking other partnerships to build on the contributions of others.

Overview chart

Unit	Unit 1	Unit 2	Unit 3	
Main grammar focus for the Unit	Adverbs and adverbials Inverted commas Headings and subheadings	Adverbs of time	Determiners *a* and *an* Conjunctions Adverbs and adverbials	
Fiction text	*Sand Wizards* by Jon Blake (A story with a familiar setting)	*A Tune of Lies* by Lou Kuenzler (A playscript)	*A Tale of Two Robots* by Roy Apps (A science fiction/fantasy story)	
Focus	This Unit explores the themes of friendship and feelings through the study of an evocative story set at the seaside. Children explore the changing moods of the main characters and how these are reflected in the setting. In the writing week, children build ideas about setting and character and then write descriptions of two contrasting beach settings, from a first-person narrator's point of view.	In this Unit children study a playscript, *A Tune of Lies* by Lou Kuenzler. They explore the key themes in the playscript of friendship and lying and the techniques typical of the genre. In the writing week, children develop ideas for an extended scene for the play, using what they know about the characters to develop convincing actions and dialogue for them.	This humorous story introduces a science fiction element into a familiar setting. Children will be encouraged to develop empathetic responses to characters and situations and an awareness of different points of view. They write a new episode for the story about a new adventure for the robots, during which they decide to go on a day out.	
Suggestions for wider reading	Stories with a familiar setting (seaside) *Katie Morag books* – Mairi Hedderwick *Buried Alive* – Jacqueline Wilson *The Shrimp* – Emily Smith *School According to Humphrey* – Betty G. Birney *Judy Moody* – Megan McDonald *A Villain's Night Out* – Margaret Mahy	*Pippi Longstocking* – Astrid Lindgren *Sabine* – Tim Kennemore *Matilda* – Roald Dahl *The Marble Crusher* – Michael Morpurgo *Stig of the Dump* – Clive King	*Space Race* – Malorie Blackman *Letters from an Alien Schoolboy* – Ros Asquith *Dotty Inventions and Some Real Ones Too* – Roger McGough *How Dogs Really Work* – Alan Snow *Wendel's Workshop* – Chris Riddell *Alienography: Or: How To Spot an Alien Invasion and What To Do About It* – Chris Riddell & Paul Stewart	
Non-fiction text	'Your A to Z Holiday Guide' 'Which Holiday?' (Information texts)	'How to Make a One-string Guitar' (An instruction text)	'Nose in a Book or Eyes on the Game?' 'How Long Should Break Be?' (Discussion texts)	
Focus	The Non-fiction week is linked to *Sand Wizards* through the seaside setting. Children explore the features of different information texts, using two website texts about holidays as the main focus. They think about how features of the information text, such as alphabetical order and headings, make them clear and engaging for the reader. They draw on what they have learnt to write their own entry for a class A to Z guide.	This Non-fiction week continues the link of music with a focus on instruction texts about making musical instruments. Children explore examples of instruction texts and think about what works well and how they can be improved, before using what they have learnt to write an effective instruction text of their own.	Children's understanding of discussion texts, fact and opinion is developed through the exploration of two discussion texts on subjects that will be familiar to children. They then write their own discussion text and take part in a class debate.	

Unit 4	Unit 5	Unit 6
Prefixes	Adverbs and word families Sentences Perfect tense	Prepositions Paragraphs
'Water-cycle' by Andrew Fusek Peters (A poem)	*Smash and Grab!* by John Dougherty (A mystery story)	*The Enchantress of the Sands* by Jamila Gavin (A folktale)
Children have fun with word play and imagery, exploring a range of short tongue twisters, riddles, nonsense poems and a longer performance poem. Children are given an opportunity to learn a short section of the poem and enjoy the experience of performing it in a dramatic way. They write their own poem, experimenting with water imagery and unusual combinations of words.	In this Unit children explore how authors create mystery and suspense in mystery stories. They use similar techniques to write their own dramatic and compelling mystery story.	This Unit explores folktales, using *The Enchantress of the Sands* and other stories from a variety cultures to explore the key features, settings, and dramatic language used in this genre. Children then draw on what they have learnt to write their own folktale in a new setting.
Tongue twisters, nonsense poems and riddles *The Works* – chosen by Paul Cookson *The Works 4* – chosen by Pie Corbett and Gaby Morgan *We Couldn't Provide Fish Thumbs* – James Berry *Mustard Custard Grumble Belly and Gravy* – Michael Rosen and Quentin Blake *Funky Chickens* – Benjamin Zephaniah *The Stinky Cheese Man and Other Fairly Stupid Tales* – Jon Scieszka	*Who Pushed Humpty Dumpty?: And Other Notorious Nursery Tale Mysteries* – David Levinthal and John Nickle *Ruby Redfort books* – Lauren Child *Dead Man's Cove (Laura Marlin Mysteries)* – Lauren St John *The Diamond Brothers Mysteries* – Anthony Horowitz *Grk and the Hot Dog Trail* – Joshua Doder *Murder & Chips (A Jiggy McCue Story)* – Michael Lawrence	*Grandpa Chatterji* and *Grandpa's Indian Summer* - Jamila Gavin *Folk Tales From Africa: The Baboons Who Went This Way And That* – Alexander McCall Smith *Where Are You Going Manyoni?* – Catherine Stock *Folktales from Africa: The Girl Who Married a Lion (Illustrated Children's Edition)* – Alexander McCall Smith *Mufaro's Beautiful Daughters* – John Steptoe *The Butterfly Lion* – Michael Morpurgo *The Gift of the Sun* – Dianne Stuart and Jude Daly *S is for South Africa* – Beverly Naidoo *The Great Tug of War* – Beverley Naidoo and Piet Grobler *Botswana* – Sioned V. Hughes *The Great Cake Mystery: Precious Ramotswe's Very First Case* – Alexander McCall Smith *Anna Hibiscus stories* – Atinuke
'Where Does Water Come From?' (An explanation text)	'Wanted: A New Planet!' (A non-chronological report)	'Jamila Gavin – Biography' 'Jamila Gavin – Autobiography' (A biography and autobiography)
This Non-fiction week is linked to the fiction through the scientific subject of the water-cycle and will develop the children's understanding of the language features of explanation texts in written and spoken forms.	Children's understanding of non-chronological reports is developed in this week. They will identify key features of this text type and, with support, write their own non-chronological report about space.	Children compare an autobiography and a biography about Jamila Gavin, the author of *The Enchantress of the Sands*. They then use audio and written sources to write biographies for a website of stories from people sharing their experiences of moving from one country to another.

Fiction: A story with a familiar setting
Non-fiction: Information texts

Timetable

WEEK 1   **Reading fiction**   *Sand Wizards*

Day 1	Day 2	Day 3	Day 4	Day 5
The story store	Word power 🖨	Grammar: adverbs 🖨	Setting and mood	Grammar: inverted commas
Think and link	Read a story 1 – clues	Re-read a story 3	Re-read a story 3	Saying, feeling, thinking 🖨
Personal log	Read a story 2 – evidence	Class log 🖨	What if not . . .?	Dramatic reconstruction 🖨
Big Question	Read a story 3	Big Question	Personal log	Class log
	Class log 🖨		Big Question	Big Question
	Big Question			

WEEK 2   **Writing fiction**   *Sand Wizards*

Day 6	Day 7	Day 8	Day 9	Day 10
Creating mood	Build a setting 1 – word collection	Build a setting 2	Build a setting 3 🖨	Write a setting 3 (continued)
Grammar: adverbs of time and adverbials 🖨	Write a setting 1 🖨	Write a setting 2	Write a setting 3	Evaluate and edit
Class log	Personal log	Personal log		Proofread
Big Question	Big Question	Big Question		

WEEK 3   **Reading and writing non-fiction**   Information texts

Day 11	Day 12	Day 13	Day 14	Day 15
Think and link	Zoom in on information	Sentence starters 🖨	Write 1 🖨	Presenting information
Introduction	Information detectives 1	Key words and summaries	Write 2 🖨	Write 3
Organising information	Information detectives 2	Putting information in order	Personal log	Evaluate and edit
Fact and opinion	Class log 🖨	Class log 🖨		Proofread
Class log				Presenting information

🖨: shows that a file should be printed out from the Software.

Overview of the Unit

The thought-provoking story *Sand Wizards* by Jon Blake is the stimulus in this Unit for the reading and writing activities, exploring themes of friendship and feelings in a story with a familiar setting.

The Non-fiction week continues the setting link of the seaside with a focus on information texts about holidays and day trips. For more information about the Non-fiction week and the Non-fiction writing evaluation criteria, see p.36.

Where appropriate, the children will be encouraged to develop an awareness of audience and purpose in relation to the fiction and non-fiction texts they are reading and writing.

Teacher modelling is provided in the teaching notes, Software and the Pupils' Book, supporting the children's writing at every stage in the Fiction and Non-fiction weeks.

The Homework Book provides a homework activity related to the content of this Unit for each of the three weeks.

Fiction

Reading

Children will:

- link the key theme of friendship in *Sand Wizards* to their own experiences
- identify particular words and techniques Jon Blake uses to create contrasting moods
- think about how the description of the setting in *Sand Wizards* reflects the characters' feelings.

Writing

Key writing purpose to be shared with the children:

To write two descriptions of a beach setting which show contrasting moods and feelings.

Writing evaluation to be shared with the children

My beach descriptions:

- have different moods because I have chosen my adjectives carefully to describe and create a happy mood and then a threatening mood
- include a threat which is hinted at but not fully described, so there is suspense.

Grammar:

- uses adverbs and adverbials of time to show when things happen *(At that instant, Suddenly)*
- includes speech, which is set out and punctuated correctly.

See the Planning section of the Software ('Timetables' tab) for a printable version of the Writing purpose and evaluation.

Fiction: A story with a familiar setting
Sand Wizards by Jon Blake

READING FICTION

Resources

- **PB** Pupils' Book pp.4–15
- **A** Anthology pp.4–19
- **CD** CD on Interactive whiteboard Unit 1
- **GB** Grammar Bank on CD
- **HB** Homework Book pp.4–7

DAY 1

Curriculum link:
listening to and discussing a wide range of fiction, identifying themes

The story store **CD**

Purpose: for children to explore other stories that introduce themes to be explored in the main study text

- Use **CD (file 1.1)** to show the book covers of two stories: *Meggie Moon* by Elizabeth Baguley and *Weslandia* by Paul Fleischman and Kevin Hawkes. Ask the children to read each title and look at each cover picture and then TTYP (Turn to your partner) to share what they think each story might be about. Collect feedback and show how much you value their ideas.
- Click to the next couple of slides and read the story summary of *Meggie Moon*. TOL (Think out loud) about what the main themes are (take your time and ask children to help you using TTYP): Meggie was the odd one out – she was a girl and the other characters were boys; she had to show them that her ideas were fun; she had a great imagination; they became friends; they made things together; in the end she left but the friendship carried on.
- Now share the summary of *Weslandia* on the next couple of slides. Ask the children to TTYP and talk about the main ideas. Support them using questioning and reminding them how you talked about the main themes in the *Meggie Moon* story.
- Display the final slide to show the title of the story *Sand Wizards* and the illustration. Ask the children to TTYP and talk about what they think the story will be about.

drawing and justifying inferences

Think and link **CD**

Purpose: for children to make connections between the story and their own experiences

- Display **CD (file 1.2)** to show the slide show of sand sculptures. On each slide, click 'TOL' to display a question to talk about.
- Use TOL and TTYP to activate the children's thoughts and recollections about making things and their own experiences at the seaside. Collect feedback and paraphrase, clarify and extend their thoughts and ideas.
- With the final slide, ensure children make the link between the question and the title of the story they will be reading this week.

discussing and recording ideas; write for a range of real purposes

Personal log

Purpose: for children to keep a personal log for recording and reflecting on their exploration of stories

- Tell the children that just like the characters in the stories that you have been looking at, you have sometimes felt lonely and left out of a friendship too. Explain that you are going to record some instances of when you have had problems with friendships when you were growing up, and how you felt.
- Write down your ideas on a flipchart. Choose something which isn't too personal, e.g. *my best friend moved schools, my friend had a new best friend, my friends left me out of something*. Then point out that in the stories, Meggie and Wesley thought of ways to solve their friendship problems. Ask the children to TTYP to help work out what you could have done to solve your friendship problem. Take feedback and write down one or two suggested solutions.

- Ask the children to TTYP to think about how they would feel if they had that friendship problem. Take feedback, where possible enriching their vocabulary to describe feelings, e.g. *'If your best friend moved schools you might feel sad. It is lonely when you don't have your best friend with you all the time any more ...'* Take feedback and say their sentences back to them. You may wish to scribe a couple of their sentences on the board or flipchart.
- Now ask them to write their own sentences in their Personal log. Remind them to say their sentence aloud to their partner before writing it down.
- Tell the children that you are going to think of some more ways to solve friendship problems. Take some examples of what friendship problems people might have. Ask children to TTYP to think of how they could solve the problems, and then take feedback as a group. Write the ideas down.
- Ask the children to choose a friendship problem and write down ideas in their Personal log that might help someone who had that friendship problem. Ask children to read their best idea to their partner to see if their partners agree.

Curriculum link: discussion; develop, agree on, and evaluate rules for effective discussion

Big Question

Purpose: for children to develop their skills of argument and discussion through a mini enquiry session based on a philosophical question relating to the work of the day

- Display today's Big Question on **CD (file 1.3)**:

  Should friends always get on?

- Ask the children to TTYP to talk about this question. Collect feedback and scribe some responses on the board or flipchart.
- Click 'Prompts' to show some statements that may help to encourage discussion.

DAY 2

discussing words and phrases that capture the reader's interest and imagination

Word power

Purpose: for children to become familiar with words and phrases that are used with particular effect in the story

> *dark, depressing frown   so relieved   with a heart as light as a feather*

- Display the words and phrases from **CD (file 2.1)**. Explain that you have chosen these words to look at because they will help the children to understand the story when they hear it for the first time.
- Use MT/YT (My turn/your turn) to read each phrase aloud (there are three slides). Click 'TOL' each time to show the think bubble that explains its meaning and an example of it used in a sentence. Ask the children to TTYP to choose their favourite Power words or phrases. Make sure they can explain to their partner what they like about them. Choose two partners to feed back. Then ask the children to look at the Word power activity on p.4 of their Pupils' Book.
- You may wish to print these words and phrases from printable **CD (file 2.2)** to display on your Story wall for this Unit. Let the children hear you using them in your conversation and teaching throughout the day and praise them if they use one of them.

predicting

Read a story 1 – clues

Purpose: for children to be motivated to read the new story. To make links between the new story and those in the Story store

- Explain to the children that you have found some clues about the new story and you need their help to find out more. Convey your own eagerness and enthusiasm and draw them into your excitement. Perhaps tell them they are 'story detectives'. Explain that you will use these clues and the ideas from the Story store.

Fiction: A story with a familiar setting

- Display **CD (file 2.3)** and explain that every time you click, you will see a clue. Click 'Reveal' to reveal each clue. (Note that there are two clues on the first slide and four on the second.) After each clue appears, ask the children to TTYP and talk about what it is or shows and how it might relate to the story.

Curriculum link: predicting, identifying how language, structure, and presentation contribute to meaning

Read a story 2 – evidence 🄲🄳

Purpose: for children to hear more about the new story before they hear the full version, and to make links with their own experiences and make predictions

- Tell the children that more evidence has come to light about the story. Display **CD (file 2.4)** to show the evidence (a postcard).
- Click 'Audio 1' to hear the contents read out. Ask the children to TTYP to make a prediction about the story.
- Click on 'Audio 2' to hear a question about the postcard and the story. Invite suggestions and ideas from the children in response to the questions posed in 'Audio 2'.

checking that the text makes sense, asking questions, drawing inferences

Read a story 3   (teacher only)

Purpose: for children to hear and enjoy the full version of the story for the first time

- Tell the children that they are now going to hear the whole story for the first time. TOL about which parts you can't wait to hear about. Ask the children to TTYP to share what they are looking forward to in the story.
- Say that you need to switch your Storyteller voice on! Make it a special moment as if you are getting ready for a performance. Read aloud to the children the full story from the Anthology pp.4–12 with great enjoyment, enthusiasm and appropriate intonation to convey meaning and impact.
- At the end of the story, ask the children to look at the Read a story 3 activity on p.5 in their Pupils' Book. Guide them as they TTYP to talk about the questions and feed back to the class.

participate in discussions taking turns to listen to what others say

Class log 🄲🄳 📄

Purpose: for children to share the process of keeping a class reading, writing and thinking log to record responses to texts and activities in a variety of forms

- Before the lesson, you may want to make a collection of seaside realia to display/ stick in the Class log.
- Remind the children of the first piece of evidence from the story: a postcard from the seaside. Ask the children to TTYP and talk about the setting of the story. Take feedback and use additional questions and TTYP to get more details about the setting and scribe these.
- When you have got enough details written down, build one or two sentences aloud to describe the seaside. Use MT/YT to compose your final sentence or sentences and then write them into your Class log.
- Show the children the different pictures of the seaside settings on **CD (file 2.5)**. Ask them to TTYP and talk about which one they think fits the setting of the story best. You may wish to print it out and stick it in the Class log beneath the descriptive sentence.
- If appropriate, tell the children that you have some extra seaside things to stick in the Class log and put on the story table. Tell them if they have any relevant materials that they should bring them in too.

Curriculum link: discussion; develop, agree on, and evaluate rules for effective discussion

Big Question

Purpose: for children to develop their skills of argument and discussion through a mini enquiry session based on a philosophical question relating to the work of the day

- Display today's Big Question on **CD (file 2.6)**:

  Can you tell what people are feeling?

- Follow the process as explained on Day 1.

DAY 3

Year 3 Grammar adverbs

Grammar: adverbs

Purpose: for children to learn the meaning of specific vocabulary used in the story and increase their knowledge of how adverbs can change the meaning of verbs

- Tell the children that there were some words in the story they heard yesterday that the writer of the story had chosen because they were powerful. They are four verbs in the past tense: *tramped, clambered, smashed* and *searched*. You may wish to write these on the board or flipchart.

- Look at the words with the children and make sure they understand their meaning. You may need to mime *tramped* and *clambered*.

- Display the first screen on **CD (file 3.1)**. Move the adverb *wearily* alongside *tramped* and explain that the writer put this adverb with the verb to show us exactly how Cole was moving – it is an adverb of manner. Explain that *tramped* means that Cole moved heavily and noisily and *wearily* means that he looked tired when he did move, as if it was really hard work to move at all. Emphasise how putting the two words together gives us a really good picture of how Cole moved.

- Ask the children to mime *tramping wearily*. They can mime the movement with their bodies and fingers whilst they say the words, without actually getting out of their seats. Use special emphasis for the adverb *wearily*.

- Use drag and drop to substitute other adverbs to go with the verb *tramped* and use MY/YT to read it aloud after each substitution. Make sure the children understand each phrase. Ask the children to mime the movement each time.

- Move through the screens and do the same with the other verbs and adverbs. Make sure the children can see how the adverb tells us more about the way the person is doing the verb, e.g. '*We know that the character is tramping but we don't know how they are tramping. The adverb tells us exactly how – there is a difference between tramping wearily and tramping angrily.*'

- You may wish to print these words and the adverbs from the printable **CD (file 3.2)** to display on your Story wall for this unit. Let the children hear you using these words in your conversation and teaching throughout the day and praise them if they use them.

- This is an introduction to adverbs in context – there are more activities to clarify the meaning and correct use of adverbs in the following Units.

checking that the text makes sense, asking questions, drawing inferences

Re-read a story 3

Purpose: for children to gain a deeper understanding of the story and to see the text for the first time

- Ask the children to read aloud with their partners the story on Anthology pp.4–12. They should read alternate sections each, and ensure they use expression and intonation to convey meaning and impact to their partner. Explain that you will be listening in and looking out for particularly good reading.

- For some groups, you may wish to read aloud to the children first as they follow the text in their own copy so that they can 'Jump in' (see Introduction p.13) to say the Power words or phrases.

Curriculum link:
identifying themes

Class log

Purpose: for children to share the process of keeping a class reading, writing and thinking log to record responses to texts and activities in a variety of forms

- Show the children the word cloud generated from the words in the story on **CD (file 3.3)**.
- Ask them to TTYP and think about what they feel are the most important themes in the story. Then ask them to TTYP and say whether these themes are reflected in the word cloud. Collect feedback using a Wave (see Introduction p.17).
- Work together to make a new word cloud, ensuring that the children are happy that the most important words and themes are in the word cloud. (Note that there are various ways of creating word clouds, e.g. through the website http://www.wordle.net.) Print off the word cloud from **CD (file 3.4)**, or your own, and paste it into the Class log.

discussion; develop, agree on, and evaluate rules for effective discussion

Big Question

Purpose: for children to develop their skills of argument and discussion through a mini enquiry session based on a philosophical question relating to the work of the day

- Display today's Big Question on **CD (file 3.5)**:

  What's more important – what you say or what you do?

- Follow the process as explained on Day 1.

DAY 4

discussing words and phrases that capture the reader's interest and imagination

Setting and mood

Purpose: for children to understand how certain words create atmosphere and mood and to identify what mood the author is creating

- Display the first screen on **CD (file 4.1)** which shows three text extracts, each of which contains a different description of the seaside setting. Read the three sentences using MT/YT and ask the children to TTYP and talk about how the three different sentences made them feel and why. Take feedback.
- Go to the next screen to focus on the first sentence. Explain that the writer is using the setting to create mood and the mood he is creating reflects how Cole is feeling.
- Draw attention to the word *grey* and point out the two words the writer could have chosen instead below the sentence. Drag and drop the different words into the sentence and use MT/YT to share each new sentence. Each time, ask the children whether they think the mood of the sentence has changed and if so, how.
- Click on to the next screen and show the words the writer could have chosen instead of *wreck*. Repeat the process as before for this and the next screen.
- Go back to the first sentence. Point to the word *grey*. Ask the children to TTYP and talk about how this word relates to Cole's emotions. Take feedback and check they have come up with words such as *gloomy, fed up* and *dull and bored*.
- Now ask the children to look at the Setting and mood activity on p.6 of their Pupils' Book. Guide them as they TTYP to talk about the sentences and choose words to describe the mood of the setting and Cole's feelings.

checking that the text makes sense, asking questions, drawing inferences

Re-read a story 3

Purpose: for children to deepen their understanding and enjoyment of the story by increasing familiarity with the text

- Ask the children to look at *Sand Wizards* on pp.4–12 of their Anthology and to read the whole story silently to themselves.

- Tell them to read it again and take notes recording their responses to the prompts on **CD (file 4.2)** in their Personal log.
- When they have had enough time to read the story through twice and make their notes, ask the children to TTYP to share what they have noticed or asked. Take feedback and use their responses to guide the discussion and/or explanations for choices with the whole group. These may feed in to the next activity.

What if not . . . ? 📖

Curriculum link: drawing inferences, participate in discussion about books

Purpose: for children to consider how character, setting and plot affect each other

- Ask the children to look at the What if not...? questions in the Pupils' Book p.7. Model how you think out loud about the first What if not...? e.g. 'What if not *building a sandcastle? What if the boys had met near a rock pool?*'

  The sandcastle competition meant that the two boys could build something together, and working together helped Cole overcome his shyness. If they had met by the rock pool, I'm not sure if Cole would have stayed around to talk to Evan. But then maybe they would have worked together in a different way – for example saving someone from danger.

- Now ask the children to TTYP and talk about the other What if not...? questions. Collect feedback and develop answers.

Personal log 📖

recording ideas

Purpose: for children to keep a personal log for recording and reflecting on their exploration of stories

- Ask the children to choose one answer from the What if not . . .? activity in their Pupils' Book to write up in their Personal log.

Big Question ⓒⒹ

discussion; develop, agree on, and evaluate rules for effective discussion

Purpose: for children to develop their skills of argument and discussion through a mini enquiry session based on a philosophical question relating to the work of the day

- Display today's Big Question on **CD (file 4.3)**:

  Is it important to hide your feelings?

- Follow the process as explained on Day 1.

Grammar: inverted commas Ⓐ ⓒⒹ 📖 📕

(DAY 5)

Year 3 Grammar inverted commas; using and puctuating direct speech

Purpose: for children to develop their understanding of inverted commas and how to use them correctly

- Tell the children that they are going to focus on what is called direct speech.
- Explain that you are now going to be in role as Cole's mum from the *Sand Wizards* story when she sees the poster advertising the sandcastle competition. Pick one child to be Cole and stand in front of him as you say *'That will be perfect for you, Cole! Why don't you have a go?'* with appropriate emphasis and intonation to convey meaning.
- Ask 'Cole' to return to his partner. Now use MT/YT to say Cole's mum's speech again. Tell them to TTYP to say it once more. Explain that in real life, we know when someone is speaking directly to us because we can see and hear him or her speaking, but it is a bit trickier when written down, e.g. in a story such as *Sand Wizards*.
- Now ask them to TTYP to explain how the writer has shown us that Cole's mum is speaking. Collect feedback to check their awareness of the writer's use of inverted commas (speech marks). Revise or teach the punctuation mime for inverted commas (see the 'Extras' tab in the Planning section of the Software).

Now ask the children to say the whole text using punctuation mimes to indicate which part is direct speech.

- Now ask the children to look at the top of p.5 of the Anthology (fourth line down) and to TTYP to identify exactly what Cole's mum is saying. Tell them to read aloud her speech all together. Check that they omitted *she said*.
- Display **CD (file 5.1)** to show another example of direct speech from the story. Model reading it out to the children with the addition of the punctuation mime. Now ask them to read it aloud altogether along with the mime.
- Explain that it is quite easy to spot inverted commas when we are reading a story, but it is a bit trickier when we are writing direct speech ourselves. Click on 'Next' to show a character with a speech bubble. Say that a speech bubble makes it really easy for a writer to show which character is speaking and what they are saying.
- Tell them that if the speech were written in a story without a speech bubble, the writer would have to use inverted commas to show what was being said and to tell us who was speaking.
- Click on 'Next' again to show the speech punctuated with inverted commas. Use the punctuation mime as you read it aloud to the children. Click on 'Next' to show an explanation and use it and/or your own ideas to explain how the punctuation works.
- Tell the children that Evan's speeches had either a question mark or an exclamation mark at the end. Point out the fact that these punctuation marks are included inside the inverted commas because they are linked to how something is being said.
- Explain that if we didn't have a question mark or an exclamation mark, we would have to have a comma. Click on 'Next' to show an example.
- Now ask them to look at the Grammar: inverted commas activity on p.7 of their Pupils' Book. Explain the activity and ask them to complete it with their partners. Choose two or three children to share their answers. Ask them to clarify where necessary.

Homework Book p.4 provides further practice on inverted commas.

Curriculum link: inferring characters' feelings, thoughts and motives

Saying, feeling, thinking ⓒᴰ 🖨

Purpose: for children to develop empathetic responses to characters and situations

- Before the lesson, print a copy of the writing frames from **CD (file 5.4)** for each child.
- Use **CD (file 5.2)** to show pictures of the two main characters from the story and their speech bubbles. On the first screen, explain that the two speech bubbles show what Evan said in two different places in the story. Use MT/YT to read each speech bubble and then ask the children to TTYP to identify which part of the story it is from to contextualise the dialogue.
- Explain that sometimes what we say doesn't always directly match what we are really feeling and thinking. Point out the four think bubbles on the screen. Talk through them and ask the children to TTYP to decide which think bubble is the best match for each speech bubble.
- Collect feedback and talk through their answers to make sure they have made justifiable choices. Drag and drop the bubble to the right character.
- Click on the next screen and read the speech bubbles with the children, making sure they know where in the story each one occurs. Repeat the matching activity for Cole's speech and thoughts. You can print off the final answers to stick in your Class log.
- Display **CD (file 5.3).** Point out that on the first slide there is a picture of Cole's mother watching from her deckchair as Cole smashes up the castle. Point out the empty think bubble and ask the children to TTYP to decide what she might be thinking at that point.

- Take the children's feedback and model using some of their ideas in sentences (this can either be done orally or by typing into the think bubble).
- Now give each child a copy of the images and think bubbles from **CD (file 5.4)**. Ask them to write sentences to show what Cole's mum might be thinking. Make sure the children have come up with some ideas before writing their thinking sentences.
- On the next slide, talk about what the picture shows (Mum, watching Cole and Evan win the sandcastle competition, at the end of the story). Ask the children to TTYP and talk about what Cole's mother might be thinking at the end of the story and what she might say to Cole.
- Tell children to compose their sentence for what Mum might be thinking and saying, and then say them aloud to their partner, before writing.
- When they have finished, the children can then stick their writing frames into their Personal log.

Dramatic reconstruction

Purpose: for children to explore the difference between what characters say and what they are actually feeling and thinking, through dramatic reconstruction of part of the story

> **Curriculum link:**
> showing understanding through intonation, tone, volume and action

- Before the lesson, print out a script from **CD (file 5.5)** (there are two options to choose from) for each group of four children.
- Group the children into fours where possible, by joining together two sets of partners. Tell the children that they are going to act out the scene where Cole and Evan meet.
- Ask each group of four children to share out their parts:
  - One pair will be Evan and Cole and act out the meeting.
  - The other pair will be the 'inner voices' of Evan and Cole and will say what the characters are really thinking.
- Give each group a script from **CD (file 5.5)** and ask children to work together to read out the lines and think about what Evan and Cole are really thinking when they say each line (or when Cole says nothing!).
- They should then rehearse the scene, with one pair acting out being Cole and Evan and the other pair saying what the characters are really thinking. Remind the children who are acting out being Evan and Cole that they don't need to read the stage directions aloud – these are just to help them know what they should be doing. As the children act and rehearse, move through the room quietly, giving advice and encouraging feedback.
- Make sure that the children have time to watch each other's performances if they feel confident to do so.

Class log

> **justifying inferences with evidence**

Purpose: for children to share the process of keeping a class reading, writing and thinking log to record responses to texts and activities in a variety of forms

- Give each partnership two sticky notes. Tell them to TTYP to talk about and choose a character. Ask them to think of two words to describe how that character felt at two different points in the story. (You can specify which points in the story to focus on.)
- Ask them to write the name of the character and their feelings on their sticky notes and come up to the front to stick them in the Class log. Pick out a few sticky notes and ask the children to explain their choices. Make a display of the different feelings for each of the characters.

Fiction: A story with a familiar setting

Curriculum link: discussion; develop, agree on, and evaluate rules for effective discussion

Big Question

Purpose: for children to develop their skills of argument and discussion through a mini enquiry session based on a philosophical question relating to the work of the day

- Display today's Big Question on **CD (file 5.6)**:

  What is friendship?

- Follow the process as explained on Day 1.

WRITING FICTION

 DAY 6

building a varied and rich vocabulary

Creating mood

Purpose: for children to make connections with the language used in the story and the setting for their writing

- Explain to the children that they are going to be writing about a seaside setting like the one in the story *Sand Wizards*. Remind them how the writer, Jon Blake, changed the mood of the setting to reflect how Cole was feeling. Review this from the first week by displaying the three sentences they analysed on Day 4, on **CD (file 6.1)**. Ask the children to read the first sentence and then TTYP and talk about which words create the mood in that sentence. Take feedback and ask them to TTYP and say how they think Cole was feeling, then discuss their responses. Repeat for the other two sentences.
- Click onto the next screen to reveal two pictures and a variety of adjectives that describe the two settings. Model reading a word and dragging it onto the setting that you think it belongs to and explaining why you made that choice. Ask the children to TTYP and do the same for a few of the other words. Take feedback and build up the list of words on each picture.
- Now ask the children to do the activity in their Pupils' Book, using the words and underwater photos on p.8. Note that some of the words are the same as in the CD activity, but there are also some additional ones. After the children have finished, take feedback, and discuss and check their understanding of all the words.

Year 3 **Grammar** using adverbs to express time

Grammar: adverbs of time and adverbials

Purpose: for children to understand how words and phrases that relate to time can add tension to writing

- Tell the children that you have collected words that the writer has used to add tension and drama to *Sand Wizards* and that you think they will be useful later on when they write, to add tension and drama to their own work.
- Show the words and phrases on **CD (file 6.2)** and use MT/YT to read them out. Point out that in *Sand Wizards*, the author creates drama by contrasting the slow passing of time with sudden moments. Work with the children to drag and drop the phrases into the correct box (a few of these are extra options that are not in the story).
- Then navigate to the next screen to focus on adverbs and adverbials that signal time passing at different speeds. Choose one of the words or phrases and place it where you think it should go on the line of intensity (this shows the relative passing of time from slowest to quickest). Explain your decision.

- Now choose another word or phrase and ask the children to TTYP and decide where they think it should go. Take feedback and place it on the line of intensity. Repeat the process for the remaining words and phrases.
- Ask children to note three of the time words or phrases that they liked in their Personal log, noticing whether they show time moving quickly or slowly. The time words and phrases can be printed out for display, from **CD (file 6.3)**.

Class log

Purpose: for children to share the process of keeping a class reading, writing and thinking log to record responses to texts and activities in a variety of forms

- Show the children the image on **CD (file 6.4)** of the sharks. Use MT/YT to describe the picture, e.g. say that you think *'The sea is* not just *scary ... it is terrifying. / The sharks are* not just *frightening ... they are petrifying predators.'*
- Ask the children to TTYP and try their own Not just... descriptions for the sea and then the sharks. Show them how to use a thesaurus to help them think of effective words. Remind them of the words that they have been using today in the Creating mood activity, which should be displayed, to help them. Take feedback and scribe some of the best ideas into the Class log.

Big Question

Purpose: for children to develop their skills of argument and discussion through a mini enquiry session based on a philosophical question relating to the work of the day

- Display today's Big Question on **CD (file 6.5)**:

  Do words mean the same thing to everyone? *

- Follow the process as explained on Day 1.

  * This Big Question will be revisited on Day 11 – the first day of the Non-fiction week.

DAY 7

Build a setting 1 – word collection

Purpose: for children to see a setting grow through three stages of development and to see the first stage of word generation that will provide a model for their own initial ideas

- Tell the children that you are going to use the same setting as *Sand Wizards* to explore how to create mood by describing the setting. Show the image of a beach **CD (file 7.1)**. Remind the children of all the words they have explored so far and ask the children to TTYP to come up with three words to describe the beach in the picture. Then ask the children to TTYP and choose the best of their three words. Popcorn feedback (see Introduction p.17). Scribe some of the words onto the board or flipchart.
- Click on the ear icon to highlight it. Use TOL to say what you imagine you can hear when you look at the picture. For example: *'I can hear the happy shrieks of the children ... I'll improve that: the children's shrieks of excitement'.*
- Ask the children to TTYP and come up with a short description for one thing they imagine that they can hear when looking at the picture (this doesn't need to be a sentence). Take feedback and model improving the description using MT/YT. Scribe a few of the ideas onto the board or flipchart. Ask the children to write their idea into their Personal log.
- Repeat the process for the two remaining icons (legs: movement: *'children dashing in and out of the waves'*) and (hand: feel, as in touch: *'the hot sun and a warm breeze ...'*).
- Encourage the children to improve their descriptions. Keep your collection of words on the board or flipchart or key them into a new word file and print it out for display and future use.

Write a setting 1

Curriculum link:
composing
and rehearsing
sentences orally;
in narratives,
creating settings

Purpose: for children to explore using descriptive language to use in sentences

- Show the children your original description of what you 'heard' when you looked at the beach picture on **CD (file 7.2)** – *the children's shrieks of excitement.*
- Explain that you want to play with the words to make the description *the children's shrieks of excitement* even stronger and then make a full sentence by adding an opening and an ending. Show how you can drag and drop words and phrases into the text box to improve your original sentence. (Note that there are two alternative sentence beginnings and two alternative sentence endings.)
- TOL as you drag and drop words and phrases into the text box. Use MT/YT to practise the changes with the children. When you have finished, you can print out your final sentence.
- Display **CD (file 7.3)** which shows a description of some movement in the picture. Again, demonstrate how you can improve the phrase, choosing alternative words and adding a suitable sentence starter and ending.
- Now tell the children they are going to create and improve their own description. Give out copies of the printout from **CD (file 7.4)** and explain that it gives some short descriptions, some sentence starters and endings, and a bank of words to help them. This Word file can be edited for differentiation to reduce or increase the number of options given. Note that the children can use other words if they wish, and if they are suitable.
- Ask children to TTYP to share their sentences and discuss reasons for their choices.

Personal log

assessing the
effectiveness of
their own and
others' writing
and suggesting
improvements

Purpose: for children to keep a personal log for recording and reflecting on their exploration of stories

- Share some of the sentences that the children have built. Choose two to read out their sentences to the class. Choose one to scribe on the board and TOL as you focus on how it has been improved from the original descriptions.
- Ask the children to TTYP and discuss a change they could make to their own description to improve it even further. Then ask them to rewrite it in their Personal log.

Big Question

discussion;
develop, agree
on, and evaluate
rules for effective
discussion

Purpose: for children to develop their skills of argument and discussion through a mini enquiry session based on a philosophical question relating to the work of the day

- Display today's Big Question on **CD (file 7.5):**

  Which sense is most likely to bring back memories?

- Follow the process as explained on Day 1.

DAY 8

Build a setting 2

building a
varied and rich
vocabulary

Purpose: for children to see a setting grow through three stages of development and to see the second stage where they develop their ability to use language to describe what they observe

- Tell the children that they are going to see another aspect of the setting that has been hidden from them. Display **CD (file 8.1)** which shows a similar picture of the setting studied before, but there are two differences: the weather has changed (it looks overcast rather than sunny) and the picture is taken from further away (you can see more in the foreground). TOL as you describe what you see: *'The water seems darker, bottle green, mysterious, and there is a terrible shape in the water which no-one seems to see.'*

- Ask the children to TTYP and talk about what they see. Use every opportunity to develop their confidence and knowledge of language, e.g. draw attention to powerful, rare words they offer and to antonyms and synonyms.
- Say that you feel the mood of the picture has changed. The setting seems dangerous, sinister, worrying. Click 'Reveal' and model using words and phrases that create the atmospheres: *the darkened sea, the murky, bottle green ocean.*
- Ask the children to TTYP and think of one word or phrase they would use to describe the beach or sea now to help create its new mood. Take feedback and choose two favourite words or phrases from the options.
- Now remind them of the sentences they wrote yesterday about the children playing on the beach. Write one of them on your flipchart, and adapt it to suit the new mood, modelling how you are making choices to make the mood more threatening.
- Use MT/YT to share your final sentence with the children.

Write a setting 2

Purpose: for children to use descriptive language to change the mood of sentences

- Display your collection of mood words and phrases on **CD (file 8.2)**. (You may also have other words and phrases that you have collected from the past few days.) Remind the children that some of these words helped you transform your setting. Explain that you've also added some more words, and remind them how you transformed your sentence so that the mood became dangerous and threatening.
- Ask the children to find their sentences describing the beach in their Personal log. Tell them to use the mood words and phrases on p.9 of the Pupils' Book and any words and phrases they have seen or heard during this Unit to transform their own sentences so the mood becomes dangerous and threatening.

Curriculum link: composing and rehearsing sentences orally

Personal log

Purpose: for children to keep a personal log for recording and reflecting on their exploration of stories

- Ask children to TTYP and think of some threatening moments in other stories they have read, e.g. when Red Riding Hood is walking through the dark forest. Where did they take place? What happened? Ask them to record some and a detail that they remember (e.g. *Red Riding Hood wore a scarlet cape*) in their Personal log.

discussing and recording ideas

Big Question

Purpose: for children to develop their skills of argument and discussion through a mini enquiry session based on a philosophical question relating to the work of the day

- Display today's Big Question on **CD (file 8.3)**:
  What creates mood and atmosphere?
- Follow the process as explained on Day I.

discussion; develop, agree on, and evaluate rules for effective discussion

DAY 9

Build a setting 3

Purpose: for children to see a setting grow through three stages of development and to see the third stage of writing that will provide a model for their own paragraphs

- Tell the children that you have three sentences you really like, and you are going to make them into a description and use additional images to write a paragraph to describe the first setting. Display these on **CD (file 9.1)**. Say that you are choosing words to create a happy mood.

organising paragraphs around a theme; in narratives, creating settings

- Use the notes on the printable file **CD (file 9.2)** to help you model your setting paragraph. TOL as you explain and improve your sentences on a flipchart. Use MT/YT to share the final sentences. TOL as you model using inverted commas correctly, reminding children of their work on inverted commas on Day 5.
- Tell the children they can read 'your' final paragraphs on p.10 of their Pupils' Book (there may be some differences depending on which improvements you chose). Ask them to TTYP to read them a sentence at a time.
- Ask the children to TTYP to give you feedback about your setting. Ask: 'How would you describe the mood of this setting? Which are your favourite powerful words? Which words would you add to improve it?' Take feedback from the children and note any of their ideas for improvement.

Curriculum link:

creating settings, characters, plot; monitor whether their writing makes sense

Write a setting 3   PB

Purpose: for children to continue their writing about a setting using all the skills they have been exploring

- Tell the children that they are going to write their paragraph now using the ideas and descriptions they have started writing in their Personal log. Remind them of their three sentence ideas, the time words and phrases to show the speed of things happening and the mood words (Day 6) in their Pupils' Book pp.8–9 and the words and phrases you have collected as a class on the Setting display.
- Tell them that they need to weave their sentences into a description of the beach. Remind them that they should describe the people, children, waves, sun and overall setting and that the setting should have a happy, excited mood.
- The image of the beach is on p.11 of the Pupils' Book along with some prompts to help the children write their description.

DAY 10

creating settings, characters, plot; monitor whether their writing makes sense

Write a setting 3 (continued)   CD   PB

Purpose: for children to continue their writing, contrasting the second setting with the first

- Tell the children that you are going to use the first setting that you wrote as the basis of a new text describing a threatening or dangerous setting. Show the first slide on **CD (file 10.1)**. Read it to the children to remind them of the setting. Then click on the next slide and read the new text. Draw their attention to the sentence: 'At that instant, I saw a shadow lurking just ahead of them.' Explain this is how you introduced the menace of the shark – without mentioning what it was.
- Click 'Highlights' to show which parts of the text have been changed. TOL as you explain which words have been changed and what effect they have.
- Show the children the whole extract on p.12 of the Pupils' Book along with the picture. Tell them to TTYP to talk about the questions. Take feedback and ensure the children understand how the changes in the description of the setting have altered the mood of the story.
- Tell the children they are now ready to write their own paragraph to describe the second setting, which has a dangerous, threatening mood. Show the children the sentence prompts that will help them write their description, on p.13 of the Pupils' Book. They should write in their writing books.

assessing the effectiveness of their own and others' writing

Evaluate and edit   CD

Purpose: for children to evaluate their own and their partner's work against specific criteria and then discuss how they could improve their work

- Display **CD (file 10.2)** to show the evaluation prompts and read them together using MT/YT.

- As a model, select an example of work where the writing has met the criteria, and share this with the other children, explaining why it works well.
- Tell the children to take turns to read their partner's writing in pairs and discuss together how well each piece of writing has met the criteria.
- Ask children to discuss at least two changes they could make to improve their work.

Curriculum link: proofread for spelling and punctuation errors

Proofread

Purpose: for children to proofread their work and make changes to improve the accuracy of their grammar, punctuation and spelling

- Now ask children to proofread their work. If you have noticed that several children need to improve on a particular aspect of spelling, grammar or punctuation, use this as a focus for the Proofread activity. Write an example which includes common errors from the children's writing and use this as a model.
- The children should always be checking for standard use of punctuation and correct spelling of common exception words.
- The following points would be relevant as the particular focus for this Unit:
  - using inverted commas correctly
  - using capital letters, commas and full stops to structure clear sentences
  - checking spelling of ambitious vocabulary choices (i.e. those borrowed from the Pupils' Book or Anthology text)
  - checking their spelling of high-frequency words and phrases such as *suddenly, after a while* (they can find many of these in the Anthology text).

Further activity

- Publish: ask the children to type up their settings, making any changes from the Evaluate and edit and Proofread activities.

Information texts

READING AND WRITING NON-FICTION

The Non-fiction section continues the setting link of the seaside with a focus on information texts about holidays and day trips. Note: if you feel that some children may not have a lot of experience of holidays, you could focus on a local area of interest and make this an 'A to Z day trips guide' or 'A to Z class trips guide'.

See p.20 for the daily timetable for the Non-fiction week.

Non-fiction

Reading

Children will:

- notice key features of information texts (e.g. *headings, subheadings, captions*) and think about how these make the texts clear and informative
- use mind maps and summarise information
- consider the difference between general information and specific information and think about why both can be useful
- notice how information is organised and experiment with ordering in different ways, e.g. *alphabetically* or *by popularity*.

Writing

Key writing purpose to be shared with the children:

To write an entry for an A to Z travel guide that gives the reader clear, useful and interesting information.

Writing evaluation to be shared with the children

My A to Z entry:

- gives useful information to the reader, e.g. *about places to go, activities to do, where to stay*
- lays out the text clearly to make it easy for the reader to find information

Grammar:

- includes a variety of sentence starters to engage the reader.

See the Planning section of the Software ('Timetables' tab) for a printable version of the Writing purpose and evaluation.

Curriculum link: understanding and explaining the meaning of words in context

Think and link (CD)

Purpose: for children to become interested in information texts via one of the Big Questions they have explored

- Display the Big Question from Day 6 on **CD (file 6.5)**:

Do words mean the same thing to everyone?

- Ask the children to TTYP to recall some of what they talked about before for this Big Question and take feedback. Remind the children that we need to know the context of a word to understand its meaning and that sometimes words have more than one meaning.

- Show the children the slide show on **CD (file 11.1)** of homophones and homographs. (Note that homophones are words that sound the same but have different meanings, origins or spellings; homographs are words that are spelt the same but are not necessarily pronounced the same and have different meanings and origins.) Talk about how the meaning becomes clear from how the words are used or from the information given about them.

- As you show each slide ask the children to TTYP and talk about how they could remember the different meanings of the words.

- Tell the children that the best way to work out a word is often through context, and this is usually how we decide the meaning of unfamiliar words that we read. Sometimes you have enough information from the context, but sometimes you may need to look for more information from different sources – and in this case, a dictionary, thesaurus or encyclopaedia may be useful.

reading for a range of purposes

Introduction

Purpose: for children to understand why we read information texts

- Tell the children that there are many ways of finding information. Remind them that dictionaries and thesauruses give us information about words and they are organised in alphabetical order to help the reader locate the word they need.

- Ask the children to TTYP and talk about any other information texts that they know. Take feedback. Write a list of types of information texts to go up on an Information texts display, e.g. posters, leaflets, brochures, encyclopaedias, non-fiction books, Internet sites.

- Tell the children that information texts give the reader information to help them understand a topic. This information may include diagrams, maps and photographs as well as written text, including general and specific information. Explain that they will be writing an A to Z of holidays giving information to people who want help in choosing a holiday.

learn the conventions of different types of writing such as the use of presentational devices

Organising information

Purpose: for children to understand how information texts are organised to be clear, engaging and helpful

- Click on **CD (file 11.2)** and ask the children to turn to pp.13–15 of their Anthology. Explain that the Anthology text is called 'Your A to Z Holiday Guide' and sections of it are reproduced on two slides on screen. Display the first slide and draw children's attention to the labels on the screen, which relate to organisational features of information texts.

- Read each label and ask the children to TTYP and decide where on the page an example of each organisational feature can be found. Share their responses and use your whiteboard tools to draw a line from the label to the correct place in the extract.

- As you do this, at relevant points, ask the children to TTYP and discuss *why they think the features you are discussing are included in the text*, e.g. *'Why do you think there are pictures? (to help show what something looks like; because they are engaging to the reader and break up the text); Why do you think the author included sub-headings? (to make it easier to find information that they want)'*
- Move on to the second screen which displays another extract of the information text and repeat the process.
- Ask the children to read the full text in the Anthology keeping an eye out for key features of organisation that they can spot – you can display **CD (file 11.3)** if the children need a reminder of these when reading (this list includes some additional features to those discussed in the previous activity). Take feedback asking them to explain what the effect of the feature was, e.g. *There was a photo here, and this was interesting and helped me imagine what Dartmoor is like or There was a subheading here, so I knew the section was all about Edinburgh.*

Curriculum link:
retrieve information from non-fiction

Fact and opinion

Purpose: for children to understand the difference between fact and opinion, and think about why they are useful to a reader

- Remind children that a fact is something that can be proved to be true, unlike an opinion which can differ from person to person.
- Display **CD (file 11.4)** and ask children to TTYP and discuss which three statements are facts and which are opinions. (The statements are adapted from the Anthology text).
- Point out that sometimes it's easy to identify opinions because the person giving them starts with *I think*, but at other times it's harder because they state an opinion as if it were a fact, e.g. *'You can't go into the countryside without having a cream tea'* sounds like a fact but is really an opinion.
- Ask the children to TTYP and find some more opinions in the 'Your A to Z Holiday Guide' text (pp.13–15), and discuss whether facts or opinions provide more useful information. There are no right answers here – point out that when choosing a holiday, you might want to know facts about the place *and* opinions, because they both provide different types of information.

retrieve and record information

Class log

Collect and bring in travel brochures, maps or tourist information leaflets for your area, to help the children with this activity.

Purpose: for children to share the process of keeping a class reading, writing and thinking log to record responses to texts and activities in a variety of forms

- Show the children the different holiday information sources you have brought in. As you reveal each item, ask them to TTYP and talk about how it could help someone choose a holiday.
- Ask the children: *'What do we know about holidays?'* Explain that you will be writing a guide to holidays this week and this is the first step in writing – gathering up all the ideas and knowledge. They should think about holidays or days out they have been on for ideas.
- Draw up a mind map on the board or a flipchart. In the central panel write *What we know about holidays*. Ask the children to TTYP to talk about holidays. Scribe their ideas onto the mind map and display it or put in the Class log.

- Ask the children to bring in anything that has information about holiday destinations or days out. Explain that this information could be about the local area or local activities that they like doing. It could be pictures, brochures, pages from the Internet, maps, etc.

DAY 12

Zoom in on information

Purpose: for children to explore general and specific information, thinking about why both might be helpful in different ways

Curriculum link:
retrieve information from non-fiction

- Remind the children that most information texts give a mix of specific information and general information. If necessary, give them an example of specific information which relates to a particular place, person or event, e.g. *'Our school is in the village/town/city of ...'*. Then give an example of some general information which does not include any particular names, e.g. *'In most schools children can choose whether to have a school dinner or a packed lunch.'* Invite children to think of their own examples of specific information or general information and discuss why both types of information can be useful.
- Ask the children to take turns to read the text on pp.16–19 of the Anthology. It is an information text on a website about different types of holidays.
- Use MT/YT to share a sentence that gives general information about one type of holiday, e.g. *'Most holiday parks are at seaside resorts.'* Point out that this sentence gives us information about holiday parks in general. The word *most* shows that it is referring to lots of parks, rather than any one in particular.
- Remind children that general information is really useful for giving us a broad overview of something. Specific information is useful when we want to know more about a *particular* thing or place.
- Display **CD (file 12.1)** and model sorting the first sentence into either the General information or Specific information columns. (Note that not all the sentences are from the Anthology text.) Now ask the children to TTYP to look at each example and use a Choral response to decide which column to place them in.
- Ask the children to TTYP: which information would be more helpful when choosing a holiday or trip? Take feedback and explore the idea that it might depend on whether you are just thinking generally about where to go or what to do (i.e. *beach, camping, city*) or looking at actually arranging a visit to a particular place.
- Tell the children to read the sentences on p.14 of the Pupils' Book and TTYP to decide which sentences give general information and which give specific information. (Note that not all the sentences are from the Anthology text). Move around the room listening and supporting children as necessary. Take feedback.
- Go back to the text in the Anthology (on pp.16–19) and explain that information texts sometimes give advice too. When they give advice, they often address the reader as *you*. Use MT/YT to focus on the example 'You may want to limit your stay to just a few days.' Ask the children to TTYP and talk about what other advice this text gives. Take feedback and ensure the children have identified some advice, e.g. *'You'll need to pack some waterproof clothes'* and *'Make sure you pack your sun cream'*.

Information detectives 1

Purpose: for children to decide what information they should include in their writing, and how information could be grouped to make it clearer

using simple organisational devices such as headings and subheadings

- Explain to the children that you are going to go back to the information text you looked at earlier, which was the 'A to Z Holiday Guide' (pp.13–15). Remind them that information texts are written to give answers to questions that a reader might have. For example, if a reader wants to know what sort of holiday to go on, they might look up the different types of holiday on a website or in an A to Z Holiday Guide.

- Tell them that together, you are going to draw up a list of questions about holidays that a reader looking for information about a holiday might want answers to in an information text. Remind the children of good words to start questions with: what, where, when and how.
- Ask the children to TTYP and think of a question about holidays, starting with one of the above question words. Take feedback and scribe the questions onto a flipchart as a list. Ensure that there are a variety of questions that fall into each of the categories listed below. If the children do not come up with them, use TOL to add some additional questions.
- Work with the children to group the questions into headings, for example, questions about: *what you could do on holiday, what things you need for different types of holidays, places to visit, how to travel to holiday destinations.*
- Draw a mind map with the title *Information about holidays* in the central panel. Draw seven large circles radiating out from the centre, each with a different heading: *Travel, Equipment/Clothes, Accommodation, Food, Activities, Places to visit, Types of holiday.* Use MT/YT to go through the headings and ensure the children understand what each one means. Make it clear that these headings are a way of summarising the groups of questions they came up with.
- Ask the children to turn to pp.13–15 in their Anthology, which shows the 'A to Z Holiday Guide'. Model how to decide which entry in the A to Z goes under which heading on the mind map. Some might go under more than one heading, e.g. TOL: '*Camping is a type of holiday – I'm going to put* camping *under Holiday type and Accommodation because a tent is a type of accommodation.*'
- Ask the children to TTYP, choose another heading and decide which heading they go under. Take feedback and write key words and phrases under each heading.
- Ask children to TTYP and remind each other why it is useful to group information under headings (i.e. *so that a reader looking for information about a certain thing knows where to look*).

<table>
<tr><td>

Curriculum link:
using simple organisational devices such as headings and subheadings; know what information they need to know before they begin

</td></tr>
</table>

Information detectives 2 🅰 🅷🅱

Purpose: for children to practise organising information in a way that is helpful, by planning headings and subheadings for an information text

- Display your mind map with the same headings as before, i.e. *Travel, Accommodation, Activities.* Explain to the children that you will be using this to help plan what other information could go in the 'A to Z Holiday Guide'.
- Remind them of the entries that they looked at previously, that are already in the Holiday Guide. Tell them that they are going to think up some new entries for the text, and they need to decide which heading they would go under on the mind map. Use MT/YT and TOL to model how to do this, e.g. '*I could include an entry about a theme park, as that's somewhere people sometimes visit on holiday, so that would go under the heading Places to visit or maybe Activities.*'
- Ask the children to TTYP and talk about a possible new entry. It could be an activity, a place to visit, a type of holiday, food that you might eat on holiday, etc. Remind them that they need to decide which heading the entry would go under in the mind map. Take feedback and scribe some examples on the mind map under the appropriate heading.

<table>
<tr><td>

Year 3 Grammar
headings and subheadings to aid presentation

</td></tr>
</table>

Headings and subheadings

- Ensure the children's understanding of headings and subheadings is secure.
- Remind the children that some entries in the 'A to Z Holiday Guide' had subheadings Refer them back to p.13 in the Anthology if necessary. Look at the examples on the mind map and ask the children if they can think of any subheadings for any of

the examples. TOL to model how to approach this, e.g. *'Under* Theme park, *I could include information about theme park characters, and theme park rides. These would be subheadings where I could give more information.'*

- Ask the children to TTYP and decide on one or two subheadings for one of the entries on the mind map. Take feedback and scribe some of the best examples on the mind map, e.g. *ice cream* could have the subheading *flavours* (chocolate, mint, butterscotch) and *types* (single cone, tubs, lollipops, branded products). Save your mind map for use in the next activity.

Homework Book p.6 provides further practice on headings and subheadings.

<table>
<tr><td>**Curriculum link:** discussing reference books</td></tr>
</table>

Class log

Purpose: for children to share the process of keeping a class reading, writing and thinking log to record responses to texts and activities in a variety of forms

- Before the lesson, print a copy of the Alphabetical organiser from **CD (file 12.2)** for each pair of children.
- Remind the children that often readers do not have time to read a big chunk of information like a whole book, so they just want to be able to pick out the bit of information that they are interested in or need to know, e.g. if they are looking for the definition of a word they want to just find that word, rather than reading a whole dictionary! This is why some information texts are arranged alphabetically – it makes it easy for a reader to locate quickly the particular information they are looking for.
- If necessary, refresh their memories of alphabetical order by calling out a letter and asking children to TTYP to tell their partner the next letter of the alphabet, then taking feedback.
- Display the mind map with the suggested headings and subheadings that you compiled with the children. Explain that as a class, you are going to organise these new headings and subheadings into alphabetical order. This would make it easier for someone looking for information about one thing, such as accommodation, to find that information quickly.
- Give the children copies of the Alphabetical organiser printed off from **CD (file 12.2)**. Model choosing one of the headings from the mind map and deciding where it should go on the organiser, using TOL, e.g. *'Ice cream, now that starts with an "i", so that slots under the section heading "I"'.*
- Ask the children to choose an entry on the mind map and TTYP to talk about where it should go. Take feedback until you have used up the ideas on the mind maps. Try to ensure that there are at least two entries that begin with the same letter, so children have to look at the second letter in each word to decide on the correct alphabetical order. Stick the Alphabetical organiser in the Class log.

DAY 13

<table>
<tr><td>discussing writing in order to learn from its structure, grammar and vocabulary</td></tr>
</table>

Sentence starters

Purpose: for children to identify a variety of sentence starters and think about why writers use them

- Ask the children to take turns reading each paragraph of the website information text on pp.16–19 of their Anthology, looking carefully at how the sentences start. Explain that you want them to find three different ways in which the writer has started sentences. Collect the children's feedback and note their ideas on a flipchart.
- Display the first few paragraphs of the website text **CD (file 13.1)** and click on 'TOL' to show the start of the first sentence, which is a question. (What's your ideal holiday?) and the TOL bubble for it. Ask the children to find another question sentence starter in the text. Take feedback.

- Repeat this for all the sentence starters, which will be highlighted when you click 'TOL' (there are three on the first screen, and three on the second screen).
- Print out a list of different types of sentence starters on **CD (file 13.2)** for display so the children can use them in their writing later on.

Curriculum link:
identifying main ideas drawn from more than one paragraph and summarising these

Key words and summaries 🅐 ⓒ

Purpose: for children to take notes from an information text and summarise the information

- Now ask the children to look again at p.16 in their Anthology. Ask them to read the text together then TTYP to discuss what each paragraph is about. Take feedback. Draw out that the first few sentences below the main heading act as an introduction, explaining that the information text is designed to help people decide on what sort of holiday might suit them. The first and second paragraphs are specifically about the good things about a camping holiday (pluses), and the third is about the possible disadvantages (the minuses).
- Display the paragraph about camping on **CD (file 13.3)** and ask the children to TTYP and decide which of the words helped them know what the paragraph was about. Take feedback.
- Explain that these words are *key words* as they tell us the main information in a text. Click 'Highlights' to show your chosen key words. (Note that other key words could also be selected, depending on what interests the reader most!)
- TOL as you compose a sentence or two summarising the main pluses and minuses of camping using some or all of the key words chosen. Use MT/YT to share the sentence with the children. Scribe a key plus and minus sentence on the flipchart, e.g. *Camping could be an ideal family holiday as there are many family campsites in the countryside. However the British weather can be unpredictable so you may need waterproof clothes.*
- Repeat for a key plus and minus sentence about city breaks, on the next slide.
- Ask the children to take turns to read Anthology p.18, about sun, sea and sand, with their partner. Tell them to note down some key words. Ask them to orally compose a summarising sentence or two about the positive and negatives of beach holidays. Take feedback and ask the children to write their final summarising sentences in their writing book.

discussing and recording ideas

Putting information in order ⓒ 🅿🅑

Purpose: for children to take notes independently, summarise the main ideas and make decisions about preferences

- Display the list of five seaside resorts on **CD (file 13.4).** Explain that this is information linked to the website about different holidays, but the developers are still working on this text. They have decided that instead of listing these alphabetically, they will display them in order of popularity. They need to display the top five resorts in order of popularity (with the best at the top of the list). You, as a class, are going to help them.
- Explain that first you need to look carefully at each resort and decide what are the good things about it (the pluses), and what are the bad things (the minuses). Use MT/YT to read the first entry. Ask the children to TTYP and decide what are the good things and the bad things about the resort. Take feedback and scribe the resort name, pluses and minuses onto a flipchart.
- Tell the children to turn to p.15 of the Pupils' Book and take turns to read each entry. Then TTYP to talk about the pluses and minuses of each resort. Tell them to note good and bad things about each resort in their Personal log.

- When they have made their notes ask each pair to TTYP to decide on the three resorts that they think are the best. Give their favourite 3 points, the second 2 points and the third 1 point. Note that if you wish to extend this activity for children who need more challenge, the **CD (file 13.5)** lists ten resorts rather than just five.

Class log

Purpose: for children to share the process of keeping a class reading, writing and thinking log to record responses to texts and activities in a variety of forms

- Display the **CD (file 13.6)**. Tell the children that together you are going to write the webpage by putting the resorts in order and introducing them with some text, explaining the order.
- List the resorts on a flipchart. Ask the children to feed back their three best resorts in turn and give each resort mentioned the relevant number of points. Add up the points for each resort and write the total next to each resort.
- Ask the children which are the most popular resorts (i.e. which have the most points). On **CD (file 13.6)** add a number along the side, from one to five, to show the order of popularity.
- Tell the children that you now need to write an introductory sentence for the page so the reader can know how you made your choices. There is a space for this at the top of the slide. Ask the children to TTYP and tell their partner how they made their decisions. Take feedback.
- Tell the children that together you are going to create an introductory sentence. TOL as you build up an opening sentence. For example *'These are the five resorts in order of popularity, which have been chosen by class X. First we…'* Use MT/YT to build and improve the sentences and then type them into the text box.
- When you are happy with the list of resorts in order of popularity, and the introductory sentence, print them off and stick them in the Class log.

Write 1

Purpose: for children to participate in shared writing of part of an information text

- Note that you will need to print off **CD (file 14.2)** for your reference before the start of this lesson.
- Remind the children that they have looked at lots of different ways to organise information about holidays to make it easy for the reader to find what they are looking for, e.g. *alphabetically, using popularity ratings, and using headings and subheadings*. They have also looked at different types of information that a reader might want to know about when choosing a holiday – specific information, general information, advice, and opinions. Tell the children that they are going to help you to write the entry for F in the 'A to Z Holiday Guide'. It will be a fun and informative entry that will give information to the reader, as well as engage and entertain them. Open **CD (file 14.1)**. Explain that you will use these notes to write the entries in full. Ask the children for ideas for things to do with holidays beginning with 'F'. Add these to the box under Note 1 (ensure that *fishing* and *friends* are included as ideas, as you will need these below).
- Click 'Reveal' to show the ideas you have chosen to write about in more detail (*fishing* and *friends*) then navigate to the next screen and click 'Reveal' to show more detailed notes. Ask children to TTYP to think of ideas for *friends*. Take feedback and add notes to the space under the heading.
- Use the model script on **CD (file 14.2)** to build your notes about fishing into a complete script on your board or flipchart. Then ask the children to TTYP and evaluate your entry: does it include enough information, is it easy to understand?

Collect feedback and make a few changes based on the children's evaluations and/ or your own ideas.

- Now ask the children to TTYP and to work together to create some sentences orally about *friends* and then write them into their Personal log. Choose two or three to share their sentences with the rest of the class.

Curriculum link: progressively building a varied and rich vocabulary and an increasing range of sentence structures

Write 2

Purpose: for children to write their information text independently

- Tell the children that they are now going to write their own information text entry. Give each set of partners a letter from G to Z (you may wish to omit some harder letters, e.g. J and Z) and a copy of the note-maker template from **CD (file 14.3)**. Explain that the children should work together to write notes about their ideas into the note-maker template. You may want to write the ideas on the note-maker for some children.
- Remind the children about some of the different sentence starters for information texts you looked at.
- Display the **CD (file 14.4)** which gives children some Top Tips for writing a holiday information text. Tell them to develop their entries from their notes together, referring to the Top Tips. Guide the children through the process of writing as independently as possible but give support where necessary.

discussing and recording ideas

Personal log

Purpose: for children to keep a personal reading, writing and thinking log to record thoughts and ideas for their own writing

- Remind the children that the Anthology entries about holidays they read had images to engage the reader and give them more information. Ask the children to TTYP and discuss what images would enhance their texts.
- Ask them to select their two best ideas and write a description in their Personal log of what the images would be and why it would be useful to include them.

DAY 15

Presenting information

using simple organisational devices

Purpose: for children to explore a variety of ways to organise their information text

- Ask the children to look again at the 'A to Z Holiday Guide' in their Anthology pp.13–15. Draw their attention to the presentational features of the text, such as the headings, subheadings, photographs, map and captions. Ask them to TTYP and talk about which of these presentation features they would like to use with their entry.
- Display **CD (file 15.1)** and explain that it is a rough outline for the presentation of your 'A to Z Holiday Guide' entry with some extra entries for F included. Click 'Complete' to show the children how you would fill in the outline, to plan the presentation of your F entries.
- Ask the children to use their Personal log to extend their notes about how they want to present their entry on the page, including headings, subheadings, pictures and captions.

using simple organisational devices; organising paragraphs around a theme

Write 3

Purpose: for children to publish their information text

- Tell the children that they have everything they need to publish their entry in the 'A to Z Holiday Guide'. Remind them to use the ideas for pictures, headings, etc. from their Personal log to make it attractive and easy to use. They should present it on a sheet of A3 or A4 paper.

Evaluate and edit

> Curriculum link: assessing the effectiveness of their own and others' writing

Purpose: for children to evaluate their own and their partner's work against specific criteria and then discuss how they could improve their work

- Display **CD (file 15.2)** to show the evaluation prompts and read them together using MT/YT.
- As a model, select an example of work where the writing has met the criteria, and share this with the other children, explaining why it works well.
- Tell the children to take turns to read their partner's writing in pairs and discuss together how well each piece of writing has met the criteria.
- Ask children to discuss at least two changes they could make to improve their work.

Proofread

> proofread for spelling and punctuation errors

Purpose: for children to proofread their work and make changes to improve the accuracy of their grammar, punctuation and spelling

- Now ask children to proofread their work. If you have noticed that several children need to improve on a particular aspect of spelling, grammar or punctuation, use this as a focus for the Proofread activity. Write an example which includes common errors from the children's writing and use this as a model.
- The children should always be checking for standard use of punctuation and correct spelling of common exception words.
- The following points would be relevant as the particular focus for this Unit:
  - checking questions are correctly punctuated
  - using the conditional tense correctly
  - using the imperative form of verbs for tips and advice.

Presenting information

> read aloud their own writing to a group

Purpose: for children to work together to organise their entries in a class information text

- Sets of partners will now have an entry for the class A to Z Guide on A3 or A4 paper.
- Remind the children that you could organise the entries in several different ways, but as yours is an A to Z Guide, you will organise them alphabetically.
- Call out letters and ask the children to stand in alphabetical order with their entries.
- Then join sets of partners to make groups of four. Ask children to present their entries to each other.
- You may wish to display the entries together, in order, to make a class A to Z Guide.

Fiction: Playscripts
Non-fiction: Instruction texts

Timetable

WEEK I Reading fiction *A Tune of Lies*

Day I	Day 2	Day 3	Day 4	Day 5
The story store	Playscript language 🖥	Word power 2 🖥	Not just…	Word power 3 🖥
Word power I 🖥	Read a playscript I – clues	Re-read a playscript 3	Explore stage directions	Most powerful and most important?
Personal log	Read a playscript 2 – evidence	Quiz the character	Grow a setting	Feelings map 🖥
Big Question	Read a playscript 3	Class log	Personal log	Class log
	Class log	Big Question	Big Question	Big Question
	Big Question			

WEEK 2 Writing fiction *A Tune of Lies*

Day 6	Day 7	Day 8	Day 9	Day 10
What if not…?	Build a scene	Build a script 2 🖥	Build a script 3 🖥	Special effects
Voices 🖥	Build a script I	Write a script 2	Write a script 3	Evaluate and edit
Step into the script	Write a script I	Class log		Proofread
Personal log 🖥	Personal log	Big Question		Act a script
Big Question	Big Question			

WEEK 3 Reading and writing non-fiction Instruction texts

Day II	Day 12	Day 13	Day 14	Day 15
Think and link	Instruction detectives	Grammar: imperative verbs	Improving instructions 2 🖥	Write 2
Grammar: adverbs of time 🖥	Evaluating instructions I 🖥	What's missing?	Write I 🖥	Write 3
Zoom in on features of instructions 🖥	Improving instructions I 🖥	Planning improvements 🖥		Evaluate and edit
Class log 🖥	Personal log	Class log – sequencing 🖥		Proofread

🖥: shows that a file should be printed out from the Software.

Overview of the Unit

In Weeks 1 and 2 of this Unit children study a playscript, *A Tune of Lies* by Lou Kuenzler. In the reading week, the focus is on developing children's enjoyment of plays, exploring key themes. In the writing week, the children will become more familiar with the conventions of the script form, leading up to writing their own episodes.

The Non-fiction week continues the link of music with a focus on instruction texts about making musical instruments. For more information about the Non-fiction week and the Non-fiction writing evaluation criteria, see p.62.

Where appropriate, the children will be encouraged to develop an awareness of audience and purpose in relation to the fiction and non-fiction texts they are reading and writing.

Teacher modelling is provided in the teaching notes, Software and the Pupils' Book, supporting the children's writing at every stage in the Fiction and Non-fiction weeks.

The Homework Book provides a homework activity related to the content of this Unit for each of the three weeks.

Fiction

Reading

Children will:

- connect and explore the central themes and ideas of friendship and lying in *A Tune of Lies* by making connections with other texts and their own experience
- recognise and understand the features of a playscript
- explore how characters change and develop throughout the play.

Writing

Key writing purpose to be shared with the children:

To write a new ending to the play, including some new ideas for action, stage directions and dialogue.

Writing evaluation to be shared with the children

My new ending:

- shows what the characters are thinking and feeling through dialogue and stage directions
- is set out as a playscript
- sounds convincing because the dialogue is based on what I know about the characters in the play.

Grammar:

- includes the suffix -ing for stage directions which are verbs, e.g. *laughing, whispering*.

See the Planning section of the Software ('Timetables' tab) for a printable version of the Writing purpose and evaluation.

Fiction: Playscripts
A Tune of Lies by Lou Kuenzler

READING FICTION

Resources
PB Pupils' Book pp.16–25
A Anthology pp.20–34
CD CD on Interactive whiteboard Unit 2
GB Grammar Bank on CD
HB Homework Book pp.8–10

DAY 1

Curriculum link:
listening to and discussing a wide range of fiction, identifying themes

The story store (CD)

Purpose: for children to focus on other stories that introduce themes to be explored in the main study text

- Use **CD (file 1.1)** to show the covers of two story books: *It Was You, Blue Kangaroo!* by Emma Chichester Clark and *The Tunnel* by Anthony Browne.
- Ask the children to read each title and look at the cover pictures and then to TTYP (Turn to your partner) to share what they think each story might be about. Collect feedback, showing how much you value their ideas.
- Click to the next two slides and read the summary of *It Was You, Blue Kangaroo!* TOL (Think out loud) about what the main themes are. Take your time and ask children to help you: '*Lily was doing things she shouldn't and she let Blue Kangaroo take the blame. She didn't want to take the blame. I think she was probably jealous of her little brother.*'
- Click to the next slide and read the summary of *The Tunnel*. Ask the children to TTYP and talk about the main ideas. For example, explore how the sister has to face something she is really scared of in order to help her brother. Support them using questions and by referring back to *The Tunnel*.
- Show the final slide. Draw attention to the title of the play *A Tune of Lies* and the illustration. Ask them to TTYP and talk about what they think the story will be about.

discussing words and phrases that capture the reader's interest and imagination

Word power 1

Purpose: for children to learn the meaning of specific vocabulary used in the playscript

> elated   astounded   perplexed   dejected

- Display **CD (file 1.2)** to show these words and their definitions. Look at the words with the children and then use MT/YT (My turn/your turn) as you read the sentences to them, putting special emphasis on the relevant words.
- Print these words and definitions from **CD (file 1.3)** to display on your Playscripts wall. Let the children hear you using these words in your conversation and teaching throughout the day, e.g. '*I'm astounded that you've all managed to finish so quickly!*'

discussing and recording ideas; write for a range of real purposes

Personal log

Purpose: for children to keep a personal log for recording and reflecting on their exploration of stories

- Tell the children that just like the children in the stories you have sometimes found it hard to face up to something you are scared of, or to tell the truth.
- Tell them that you are going to record some instances of when you have had similar problems, perhaps feeling jealous and not finding telling the truth easy. (For example, use a story from your childhood about being jealous about someone else being better than you at something, which made you do something unkind or silly and then not want to own up to it.)

- Write down your ideas. Then say: '*In the stories Lily and Rose were helped or thought of ways to solve their problems and own up to the mistakes they had made or to face their fears.*' Ask the children to TTYP to help you work out what you could do to solve your problem with being jealous and not telling the truth right away. Take feedback and write down one or two of their solutions.
- Ask the children to TTYP to share a time when they had problems with jealousy and telling the truth and talk about how it made them feel.
- Take feedback, emphasising the way the children feel and where possible enriching their vocabulary, e.g. '*when your friend got more sweets than you at a party you felt* angry, *you felt it wasn't fair, it made you see red, you were* jealous'. Or '*when you kicked the ball over the wall you felt* embarrassed. *You were* hot and bothered. *It made you feel* anxious'. You may wish to scribe a couple of the sentences on the board.
- Now ask the children to write their own sentences in their Personal log. Remind them to say their sentences aloud to their partner before writing them down.
- Tell the children that as they helped you to think of ways to solve your problem, you and the class are going to help them think of ways to solve their problems too. Take some examples and write down some suggested solutions. Once you have a big enough bank of possible solutions, tell the children to TTYP and together discuss possible ways of solving their particular problem. Ask the children to write the possible solutions in their Personal log.

Curriculum link:
discussion;
develop, agree
on, and evaluate
rules for effective
discussion

Big Question

Purpose: for children to develop their skills of argument and discussion through a mini enquiry session based on a philosophical question relating to the work of the day

- Display today's Big Question on **CD (file 1.4):**

  Is it ever acceptable to lie?

- Ask the children to TTYP to talk about this question. Collect feedback and scribe some responses on the board or flipchart.
- Click 'Prompts' to show some statements that may help to encourage discussion.

DAY 2

Playscript language

Purpose: for children to become familiar with words associated with playscripts

> *character   setting   dialogue   stage directions   scene*

- Display **CD (file 2.1)** to show the words associated with playscripts (the words are spread over two slides). Explain that these words are useful when learning and talking about playscripts.
- Use MT/YT to read the first word and its explanation aloud. Continue with all five words.
- Now ask the children to look at the first activity on p.16 of their Pupils' Book. Tell them to TTYP to read the words and use them in a sentence. Walk around the class as they do this and choose two examples to feed back to the whole class.
- You may wish to print these words from **CD (file 2.2)** to display on your Playscripts wall.

Curriculum link:
predicting

Read a playscript 1 – clues (CD)

Purpose: for children to be motivated to read the play

- Explain to the children that you have found some clues about a play and you need their help to find out more. Convey your own eagerness and enthusiasm and draw them into your excitement. Perhaps tell them they are 'playscript detectives'. Explain that you will use these clues and the ideas from the Story store to work out more about the play.
- Display **CD (file 2.3)**. Explain that every time you click, you will see a clue. (Note that there are two clues on each slide.) After each clue appears, ask the children to TTYP and talk about what it shows and how it might relate to the play.

predicting,
identifying
how language,
structure, and
presentation
contribute to
meaning

Read a playscript 2 – evidence (CD)

Purpose: for children to hear more about the play and make predictions

- Tell the children that more evidence has come to light about the play. Say that you are really excited about what the evidence might be. Display **CD (file 2.4)** to show the diary extract. Point out that it is from someone's diary, i.e. what they have written about their day. Read it aloud. Ask them to TTYP to make a prediction about the play.
- Open **CD (file 2.5)** and click 'Audio' to listen to the diary entry. Tell the children to listen particularly carefully to the end of the diary extract, which wasn't on the previous slide. Ask them to TTYP to discuss the question at the end and then take feedback.

checking that the
text makes sense,
asking questions,
drawing inferences

Read a playscript 3 (CD) (A) (PB)

Purpose: for children to hear and enjoy the full version of the play for the first time

- Tell the children that they are now going to hear the whole play for the first time. TOL about which parts you can't wait to hear about. Ask them to TTYP to share what they are looking forward to in the play.
- Play the audio file on **CD (file 2.6)** to hear the play being performed. The children can follow the text on pp.20–30 of their Anthology.
- At the end of the play, ask the children to look at the second activity on p.16 in their Pupils' Book. Guide them as they TTYP to discuss the questions and feed back to the class.

participate in
discussions taking
turns to listen to
what others say;
record ideas

Class log

Purpose: for children to share the process of keeping a class reading, writing and thinking log to record responses to texts and activities in a variety of forms

- Ask the children to TTYP and talk about their first impressions of the play. Popcorn (see Introduction, p.17) feedback.
- Give each partnership four sticky notes; one for each character. Say you are going to collect their initial thoughts about each of the characters. Write the name of each character on a separate page of the Class log.
- Choose one character and ask the children to TTYP and discuss their initial thoughts about them. Take feedback and then ask the children to write their thoughts about that character on the sticky note as a short sentence. Ask the children to stick their note onto the character's page.
- Review some of the children's ideas as you get them. Repeat the process for the three remaining characters.

Big Question

Purpose: for children to develop their skills of argument and discussion through a mini enquiry session based on a philosophical question relating to the work of the day

- Display today's Big Question on **CD (file 2.7)**:

  Is exaggerating the same as lying?

- Follow the process as explained on Day 1.

Curriculum link:
discussion;
develop, agree
on, and evaluate
rules for effective
discussion

DAY 3

Word power 2

discussing words
and phrases
that capture the
reader's interest
and imagination

Purpose: for children to learn the meaning of specific vocabulary used in the play

> *impressed*   *jealous*   *excited*   *pride*   *a shame*   *embarrassed*

- Tell the children that there were some words in the play they heard yesterday that the writer of the play had chosen because they were powerful. Display the words on **CD (file 3.1)**. With the children, look at the words listed on the left of the screen. Use MT/YT to say each word.
- Point out that down the right of the screen there are definitions for the words. Explain that they need to help you match each definition to the correct word. Use MY/YT to read each definition.
- Focus on the first word in the list and ask the children to TTYP to decide which is the right definition for this word. Take feedback, then drag and drop the correct definition alongside the first word. Continue with the other words and definitions.
- Click to reveal the next screen and explain that the children are going to work with you to sort the words under the headings *Positive* and *Negative feelings*. Choose a word and use TTYP to encourage the children to decide where it should be placed. Take feedback and place the word under an appropriate heading. Note that some words should provoke discussion, e.g. *pride* has both positive and negative connotations. Continue the process with each word, placing it under an appropriate heading.
- You may wish to print these words and their definitions from **CD (file 3.2)** to display on your Playscripts wall. If possible, use these words in your conversation and teaching during the day and praise the children if they use any of them.

Re-read a playscript 3

checking that the
text makes sense,
asking questions,
drawing inferences

Purpose: for children to gain a deeper understanding of the play and to see the text for the first time

- Let the children follow their own copy of the text in the Anthology pp.20–30 as they listen again to the play on the audio file **CD (file 2.6)**.
- After listening, organise the pairs of children into groups of four and explain that they are going to act out the script. Tell one pair that they are going to be Lucy and Fib and tell the other pair that they are going to be Sam and Amy. Say that all four in the group will take turns to read the cast list, scene descriptions and stage directions.
- Explain that you will be watching as you move around the class and hoping to hear and see some strong emotions where appropriate. Encourage the children to show their character's personality and feelings.
- Give feedback to the whole class, commenting on good examples of the readings for individual characters.

Quiz the character 🅿🅱

Purpose: for children to consider the reasons behind a character's actions

• Tell the children to imagine that they are Lucy and that you are an Agony Aunt (explain this term if necessary). Referring to your own copy of the Pupils' Book p.17, use the questions to develop the children's understanding of Lucy's motivations and feelings (but don't show these questions to the children yet). Ask the first three questions, and ask the children to TTYP in role as Lucy after each question to share what they think Lucy would say in response. Take feedback and then ask further questions until you have teased out as much information as possible. Ensure children listen to and respond to each other.

• Now ask the children to act in role as Agony Aunt and Lucy using all of the questions in the Pupils' Book p.17 as guidance. Move around helping children as they conduct the interview.

• Take feedback and ask the children what advice they would give Lucy. Use the feedback to write some advice to Lucy, as a class.

Curriculum link: inferring characters' feelings, thoughts and motives

Class log

Purpose: for children to share the process of keeping a class reading, writing and thinking log to record responses to texts and activities in a variety of forms

• Give each pair of children two sticky notes. Tell them to TTYP to choose and discuss one character from the play. Ask them to think of two words to describe how that character felt at two different points in the play, e.g. when Lucy tells the first fib and when she is found out and tells the truth.

• Write the name of each of the four characters in the playscript on a separate page of the Class log. Ask the children to write the feelings of their chosen character on their sticky notes and to stick them in the Class log. Review what the children have written and discuss their findings.

discussion; develop, agree on, and evaluate rules for effective discussion

Big Question ⓒⒹ

Purpose: for children to develop their skills of argument and discussion through a mini enquiry session based on a philosophical question relating to the work of the day

• Display today's Big Question on **CD (file 3.3)**:

  Is it always bad to let your emotions go out of control?

• Follow the process as explained on Day 1.

(DAY 4)

Not just . . . 🅿🅱

Purpose: for children to learn the meaning of vocabulary used in the play and to use synonymous language to give shades of meaning

• Tell the children that Lucy's fibs got out of control. Explain that when she said she was *really musical* that was a fib but when she said she was a *virtuoso* it was 'Not just *a fib, it was an … enormous lie.*'

• Use more examples of Lucy's lies and MT/YT as you use these phrases to explore Lucy's fibs: '*It was not just a fib, it was a … terrible invention/horrible pretence/ awful untruth.*'

• Ask the children to turn to p.18 of the Pupils' Book to look at the Not just… activity. Model using the Word bank to choose better words for the first example: *Lucy said she was* not just *a good harp player, she was…*

• Ask the children to TTYP and to take turns to choose words from the Word bank for the Not just … statements with their partner. Take feedback using MT/YT to share the children's ideas.

Explore stage directions (CD) [A] [PB]

Purpose: for children to understand how stage directions are used and what they tell us about the characters

- Display **CD (file 4.1).** Explain that it shows all the stage directions used in Scene 4 of the playscript. Use MT/YT to read the directions.
- Ask the children to TTYP and to talk about what they think is happening in the play from the stage directions alone. (If they need prompting, remind them of when Sam and Amy come to Lucy's house when they haven't seen her for a while. Also remind them of why Lucy may be avoiding them. Children who need more support might benefit from reading through the complete scene in their Anthology.)
- Highlight the first stage direction with your whiteboard tools and explain how this stage direction does three things:
  - it sets the scene (so we know where the characters are)
  - it tells us what the characters are doing (so what actions they have to take)
  - it also gives us clues as to how the characters are feeling (which in turn gives us ideas about how they might say their words).
- Ask the children to TTYP and discuss how they would act out that stage direction. Take feedback, encouraging the children to make the link between the stage direction and how the characters might act, e.g. *Sam and Amy ringing the bell with confidence, Lucy looking anxious and worried, Fib looking thoughtful and devious.*
- Repeat for the other directions, helping the children see how the stage directions help the actor know how to move and speak.
- Ask the children to get into their groups of four and act out Scene 4 on pp.27–29 of the Anthology. Remind them to think carefully about the information the stage directions give the characters about how to move, speak and show their emotions.
- Now ask the children to look at the activity on p.19 of their Pupils' Book. Guide them as they TTYP to discuss the questions and write their findings in their Personal log.

Grow a setting (CD)

Purpose: for children to understand the importance of setting to a play

- Put the children in role, with Partner 1s as Lucy and Partner 2s as Amy or Sam. Tell them to imagine they are in Scene 4 of the play (on Lucy's doorstep). Display **CD (file 4.2)** and point out the list of questions. Ask the children to TTYP in role to answer each question.
- Take feedback and make notes to help you remember the children's ideas. Make sure you make separate notes for Lucy, Amy and Sam.
- TOL as you build up some sentences using the children's responses. Use TTYP to encourage the children to help you improve the sentences. Use MT/YT as you expand each sentence together. For example, Lucy might say, '*I am standing clutching the door so that Sam and Amy cannot see my dreadful lie.*' Compose separate notes orally from Lucy's and then Sam and Amy's point of view.

Personal log

Curriculum link: drafting and re-reading to check their meaning is clear

Purpose: for children to keep a personal log for recording and reflecting on their exploration of stories

- Ask the children to use the ideas from the Explore stage directions activity and the Grow a setting activity to write three sentences about Lucy as she stands behind the door. Encourage them to describe what she is seeing, thinking and feeling.
- Tell them to TTYP and share the sentences with their partner before they write them down in their Personal log.

Big Question (CD)

Purpose: for children to develop their skills of argument and discussion through a mini enquiry session based on a philosophical question relating to the work of the day

- Display today's Big Question on **CD (file 4.3):**

  Why do some people show off?

- Follow the process as explained on Day 1.

DAY 5

Word power 3 (CD)

Purpose: for children to learn the meaning of vocabulary used in the playscript and increase their knowledge of synonyms

brilliant   inventive   disturb

- Display **CD (file 5.1)** to show some of the multi-syllabic words that are in the script. Click to the next screen to display these words and their definitions. Look at the words with the children and then use MT/YT to read the definitions.
- Remind them that the writer could have chosen different words that mean the same thing. Click to the next screen to show some sentences and synonyms.
- Use MT/YT to say the first sentence, substituting a synonymous word for the Power word. Repeat with the other sentence. Navigate to the final screen and repeat the process.
- You may wish to print these words and definitions from printable **CD (file 5.2)** to display on your Playscripts wall for this Unit. Let the children hear you using these words in your conversation and teaching throughout the day and praise them if they use one of the words.

Most powerful and most important? (CD)

Purpose: for children to explore the importance of individuals and events in the script

- Tell the children that all the characters are important in the playscript, but they might think that some are more powerful than others. Display **CD (file 5.3)** to show one section from Scene 2 of *A Tune of Lies,* over two slides. Ask the children to read it chorally with appropriate intonation and expression.
- Click on 'TOL' to show think bubbles and use them and/or your own ideas to discuss who seems to be the most powerful character in this part of the play; make sure you use discursive language (explain that this is language which puts forward and compares different points of view), e.g. *on one hand it could be … but on the other hand …*
- Draw the children into the TOL and then ask them to TTYP to discuss who they think is the most powerful and why (in Scene 2). Take feedback and make sure the children can support their ideas.
- Ask the children to turn to pp.27–29 of their Anthology. Explain that you now want them to TTYP to read Scene 4 of the play and then discuss who is most powerful in this scene. Make sure they understand that there is not one right answer to this activity, but lots of opinions are valid if they can be explained. Take feedback and give particular praise when the children use discursive language in the way that you modelled.
- Now display **CD file (5.4).** Ask them to TTYP to read the statements about what the most important moment is in the whole play.
- Tell them to discuss which statement they agree with the least and which one they agree with most and why. Collect feedback and lead a short, whole class discussion based on their responses.

Feelings map

Purpose: for children to explore how characters' emotions change throughout the play

- Before the lesson, print a copy of **CD (file 5.6)** for each pair of children.
- Display the map of the play on **CD (file 5.5).** Remind the children how Lucy's emotions changed during Scene 4 from worry and anxiety to relief.
- Model Lucy's emotional journey on the map. TOL as you use the words in the feelings box to help you describe Lucy's feelings through the play. Use your whiteboard tools to scribe what she is feeling on the map.
- Give each pair of children a copy of the map and the feelings words from **CD (file 5.6)**. Now ask the children to choose either Amy or Sam and TTYP to describe what they are feeling at the different places on the map. Take feedback, ensuring the children are tracing the emotions of their character through the different scenes.
- Ask the children to write the feelings of their character on their copy of the map. Note: encourage them to use alternative feeling words if they wish to. Those given are just for guidance.

> **Curriculum link:**
> building a varied and rich vocabulary

Class log

Purpose: for children to share the process of keeping a class reading, writing and thinking log to record responses to texts and activities in a variety of forms

- Tell the children to TTYP to choose three words that best sum up how their character feels at the end of the play, using the ideas in the Feelings map activity. Ask them to note their ideas down, ready to feed back to the class. Take feedback, and write the favourites in the Class log.

> discussion; develop, agree on, and evaluate rules for effective discussion

Big Question

Purpose: for children to develop their skills of argument and discussion through a mini enquiry session based on a philosophical question relating to the work of the day

- Display today's Big Question on **CD (file 5.7):**

  Which is better: a truth that can hurt you or a lie that makes you feel happy?

- Follow the process as explained on Day 1.

WRITING FICTION

What if not...?

Purpose: for children to understand how small changes can have big consequences in narratives

> drawing inferences, participate in discussion about books

- Remind the children of their previous What if not...? discussions. Show a picture of Fib on **CD (file 6.1)** and ask 'What if not Fib crushed? What if Lucy had been crushed?' TOL some ideas to get the children started: 'If Lucy could not crush Fib and Fib crushed her instead, she would start telling even bigger and bigger lies ... She would never go to the "Have-a-Go Orchestra" event, and so wouldn't get to know Amy better ... Also as she started telling even bigger lies her friends might start not believing her.'
- Ask the children to TTYP and discuss their own ideas about the What if not ...? Take feedback. Then ask the children to TTYP and discuss the other questions in the activity on p.20 of their Pupils' Book. Collect feedback and develop answers.

Voices

Purpose: for children to develop their awareness of the narrator's and characters' voices

- Before the lesson, print a copy of **CD (file 6.3)** for each pair of children.
- Display the text on **CD (file 6.2)** and explain that it is part of the playscript, written as a story. Read the text together using MT/YT, stopping just before the first piece of dialogue. Click on 'Highlights' to highlight the dialogue in the text (not all the dialogue from the playscript has been included). Ask the children to TTYP to say who is speaking and how they are saying the words. Take feedback and experiment with different characters' voices.
- Say that Partner 1 is going to be the narrator and Partner 2 is going to be the characters. Remind them that the text which is not highlighted is the narrator's voice, and the highlighted parts are the voices of the different characters.
- Give each set of partners a copy of **CD (file 6.3)** and ask them to work together to highlight all the dialogue. They should use a different colour for each character.
- When the children have highlighted the dialogue, they should practise reading aloud once through, using appropriate voices and expression based on what they know about the characters.
- Then ask them to TTYP and discuss which characters' voices could be changed or improved.
- Swap partners and ask them to read through again.
- Then ask partners to TTYP to discuss the question: *Why doesn't this play need a narrator?*

Step into the script

Purpose: for children to improvise dialogue in an imaginary context

- Ask the children to look at the Step into the script activity on p.21 of their Pupils' Book. Explain that they are going to take turns to play Lucy and Fib in an additional part of Scene 4 where Lucy is struggling to stop Fib.
- Ask them to look at the script for the new scene. Point out that there are gaps in the dialogue after Lucy's name. Explain that you want the children to improvise Lucy's responses to Fib as if they were in the script.
- Now ask the children to TTYP to read the scene aloud in their Pupils' Book first of all, without adding their own responses. When they have read through the scene, ask them to go through it again, but this time with Partner 2 improvising the missing parts of the script. Note that this is an oral activity, so no writing is required at this stage. Choose two or three confident sets of partners to share their improvisations.
- Display **CD (file 6.4)** and scribe some of their improvised dialogue in the appropriate boxes. Don't make it look easy; TOL as you repeat what they have said to make sure it makes sense. Break their dialogue down into smaller chunks to show how it helps you to 'hold' the words in your head as you write them down.

Personal log

Purpose: for children to keep a personal log for recording and reflecting on their exploration of stories and scripts

- Print out and give each child a copy of the comic strip on **CD (file 6.5)**. Explain that it shows the part of the play that they have just improvised. Point out that the dialogue is in speech bubbles, although Lucy's are empty.
- Explain that you now want them to write the full dialogue for this scene, filling in Lucy's speech bubbles. Tell the children to TTYP to recall the dialogue they improvised, but encourage them to edit and make changes if they want to. Ask them to stick their comic strip into their Personal log.

Curriculum link: composing and rehearsing dialogue orally; discussing and recording ideas

Curriculum link:
discussion;
develop, agree
on, and evaluate
rules for effective
discussion

Big Question CD

*Purpose: for children to develop their skills of argument and discussion through a mini
enquiry session based on a philosophical question relating to the work of the day*

- Display today's Big Question on **CD (file 6.6):**

  Should you change who you are to keep a friend?

- Follow the process as explained on Day 1.

DAY 7

Build a scene CD

Purpose: for children to participate in the creation of an expanded scene of the play

- Say that you have had an idea to alter Scene 4. Explain that you are going to
  expand and tweak the scene so that Lucy and the Fib have to fight it out a bit
  longer. Display **CD (file 7.1)** to show some lines from the end of Scene 4.
- Explain that you thought about what Lucy and Fib might do next from this point in
  the script. Click on 'Notes'. Read the notes to the children.
- Tell the children to Popcorn words that could describe how Amy and Sam will feel
  when they hear Lucy having a conversation with an invisible person. Scribe some
  of their words and ideas on the board or a flipchart. Ask the children to write
  these words and ideas as notes in their Personal log for use later on.

plan writing by
discussing writing
that is similar

Build a script 1 CD

*Purpose: for children to see a script grow through three stages of development that will
provide a model and stimulus for their own writing*

- Explain that you will now use your notes (from the Build a scene activity) and your
  ideas about Lucy's struggle with Fib (from the Step into the script activity on Day
  6) to write what Lucy and Fib might say next. Display your notes on **CD (file 7.2)**.
  Explain that you are going to use the notes to create a script. Click on 'TOL' to
  show the think bubbles on each slide and read them through with the children.
- Tell the children that you are going to go back through the notes and think bubbles,
  to find words that you can use as dialogue for the actors playing Lucy and Fib. Click
  'Highlights' to reveal these.
- Explain that you would like the children to help you to write the next part of the
  new scene. Display **CD (file 7.3)** and explain that you've used your ideas to start
  writing a script for the new part of the episode.

composing
and rehearsing
sentences orally;
creating settings,
characters, plot

Write a script 1 CD

Purpose: for children to develop the first stage of a script

- Keeping **CD (file 7.3)** on display, remind the children that Sam and Amy are shut
  out and they are listening to Lucy talking to an 'invisible' person. Refer to the
  notes that the children made about Amy and Sam's reaction to this. Click 'Reveal'
  to show your version:

  Amy Who is she talking to?

  Sam I don't know, but it sounds like she's in trouble.

- Ask the children to TTYP and say what they think Amy and Sam will say to each
  other when they hear Lucy and Fib fighting. Take feedback and write down some
  of the children's ideas as dialogue.
- Tell the children to TTYP to choose (or improvise) and rehearse some additional
  dialogue for Amy and Sam. Tell them that this is to try out the new dialogue
  before they write it down. The new dialogue will need to be at least six more lines.

Remind them to think about whether Sam and Amy want to help Lucy. Will they agree or disagree? Maybe one will have to try to persuade the other one to their point of view.

- As the children improvise, remind them to think about using appropriate emphasis, and to vary their tone and volume in order to make the dialogue dramatic and interesting. Encourage them also to use powerful language to create more tension, e.g. making one of the characters say that they *dread* what might be happening behind the closed door.

- Now ask the children to write out the dialogue from their improvisation. Walk around, supporting and guiding as they write. Note examples to share with the whole class.

> **Curriculum link:**
> learning the grammar of word structure; composing and rehearsing sentences orally

Personal log

Purpose: for children to keep a personal log for recording and reflecting on their exploration of stories

- Tell the children they will need to write stage directions in their scripts. Remind them that stage directions are often verbs, telling the actors what to do as they say their lines. They are therefore written in the present continuous tense.

- Display the verbs on **CD (file 7.4).** Explain to the children that these are *root words* of words used in the playscript. Remind them that a root word is the smallest form of a word, but that you can add suffixes (endings) and prefixes (beginnings) to these words to make more words.

- Explain that you are going to add the suffix -ing to these root words. Click to the next screen to display the grid. Use MT/YT to say each root word and then each root word with the suffix -ing, making the new word. Draw the children's attention to what happens to the end of these root words when the suffix -ing is added:
  - *Chew* ends in a consonant, so the suffix -ing is simply added.
  - *Smile* ends with an 'e', but you can't have an 'e' before -ing, so the 'e' is dropped.
  - *Cry* ends in 'y', so you keep the 'y' and just add -ing.
  - *Get* has a short vowel followed by a consonant, so the consonant is doubled before adding -ing.

- Click to the next screen to display some stage directions with missing words. Read the first stage direction and TOL as you choose one of the words from the box. Drag and drop your chosen word to complete the stage direction.

- Read the next stage direction and ask the children to TTYP to decide which of the words is the right one. Take feedback and use drag and drop to insert the word. Repeat with the next two stage directions.

- Ask the children to look at the dialogue they have written in the activity above. Ask if they can improve it by using stage directions to give information about how the characters move or speak.

- Remind the children to write in script form, not as a narrative story. Walk around, supporting and guiding as they write. Note examples to share with the whole class.

> discussion; develop, agree on, and evaluate rules for effective discussion

Big Question

Purpose: for children to develop their skills of argument and discussion through a mini enquiry session based on a philosophical question relating to the work of the day

- Display today's Big Question on **CD (file 7.5):**

  What makes a good friend?*

- Follow the process as explained on Day 1.

  * *This Big Question will be revisited on Day 11 – the first day of the Non-fiction week.*

DAY 8

Curriculum link:
discussing writing
in order to learn
from its structure,
grammar and
vocabulary

Build a script 2

Purpose: for children to participate in the development of a new scene that will provide a model and stimulus for their own writing

- Print off the teacher's script for Fib from **CD (file 8.1)** before you start this activity. Tell the children that they are going to focus on creating the most powerful part of their new episode for the script, where Lucy will struggle to take control. They need to imagine themselves in Lucy's role and to try and think how she might respond.
- Read each of Fib's lines in turn and ask the children to TTYP and decide how they think Lucy would respond if the writer wanted Lucy to lose the argument against Fib and to give in to Fib in the end. Take feedback and decide how Lucy could respond.
- At the end of the activity ask the children to TTYP and reflect on the outcome. Did they make it obvious that Fib won? Take feedback.
- Give the children time to write notes in their Personal log about the way Lucy responded in the fight. Encourage them to note any good words or ideas collected from the activity that they might want to use later.
- Now repeat the whole activity, but this time ask the children to make Lucy win the argument. At the end of the activity, encourage the children to reflect on how it felt to be in Lucy's role.

composing
and rehearsing
sentences
(including
dialogue) orally;
drafting and
re-reading to make
sure their meaning
is clear

Write a script 2

Purpose: for children to develop the second stage of their script

- Remind the children that in the last activity they explored Fib and Lucy's big fight. Now they can act out the fight and see which words and ideas they think work best. Then they can write these down as dialogue. Note that the children can choose whether Fib or Lucy wins the argument.
- Tell them to use the prompts on p.22 of the Pupils' Book and their notes to help them act out the scene with Lucy and Fib. Make sure both children get a chance to try out their ideas with their partner.
- Encourage the children to add to their notes, jotting down more ideas for dialogue and stage directions. Remind them to TTYP to share their ideas and say their sentences before writing them in full in their Personal log. Make sure they know that they are allowed to cross out and edit as they think and write.
- Ask the children to TTYP to read each other's writing. Choose a few children to read out their dialogue. Remind them to use intonation to emphasise different words, and to vary their tone and volume to make their dialogue clear.

discussing and
recording ideas

Class log

Purpose: for children to share the process of keeping a class reading, writing and thinking log to record responses to texts and activities

- Tell the children that although you like the title *A Tune of Lies*, now that you have made the fight between Lucy and Fib more important, you have been thinking about using an alternative title.
- Write some possible new titles in the Class log, e.g. *Fib Forever, No More Lies, Lie to Me, Lucy Leaves the Lie, Forget the Fib!* TOL about the alliteration and play on words, plus the relevance of the titles to the new storyline. Use MT/YT to say each alternative title.
- Ask the children to TTYP to discuss which title they would choose as an alternative to *A Tune of Lies*. Tell them to Popcorn their choices and then have a vote, tallying up the votes for each alternative until you have a winner. Circle the winning title in the Class log.

Big Question

Purpose: for children to develop their skills of argument and discussion through a mini enquiry session based on a philosophical question relating to the work of the day

- Display today's Big Question on **CD (file 8.2):**

  Is it always difficult to stop doing something that we know is bad for us?

- Follow the process as explained on Day 1.

DAY 9

Build a script 3

Purpose: for children to participate in the final stage of writing of a script that will provide a stimulus and model for their own writing

- Before the lesson, print a copy of **CD (file 9.2)** for each pair of children.
- Tell the children that you have used some of your notes to write more of the scene where Amy and Sam decide to step in and help Lucy whilst Lucy continues to fight with Fib. Display **CD file (9.1)** to show how you have developed the dialogue into a scene. Give each pair of children a copy of the script from **CD (file 9.2)** and ask them to read your new episode together, using expression and intonation to show meaning.
- Point out the stage directions. Ask the children to TTYP and discuss how they would say the dialogue and move if they were giving a performance of the play.
- Click on the final slide of **CD (file 9.1)** to display the evaluation questions. Use the questions and TTYP to help the children to evaluate the new scene orally. Collect feedback and encourage further discussion and constructive criticism.

Write a script 3

Purpose: for children to write their scene

- Tell the children that they are now going to write their developed scene for the end of the play. Remind the children that at the start of your new idea for a developed scene, Lucy did not let Sam and Amy into the house when they came round to call. However, instead of leaving, Sam and Amy stayed outside the house and overheard Lucy arguing with Fib. Display **CD (file 9.3)**. This sets the scene for the part of the script.
- Tell the children that they will now be planning and developing their own extended ending for the play. Ask them to look at the Write a script 3 prompts on p.23 of their Pupils' Book. Explain that this has some notes about developing the script. Ask them to decide whether Lucy or Fib will win in their developed scene.
- Remind the children of the conventions of scripts and to share ideas and sentences with their partner before writing them down. As the children are writing, walk around, encouraging, supporting, and noting good examples to share at the end of the writing session.

DAY 10

Special effects

Purpose: for children to understand special effects and where they could use them

- Explain to the children that some stage directions are about how to create atmosphere during a performance of a play. These usually involve lighting and sound effects, and are known as *special effects*. Display **CD (file 10.1)** and explain that you are going to show the children some Top Tips for special effects in playscripts. Play the slide show of Top Tips with some examples based on *A Tune of Lies*. (The file will open to show a blacked-out slide but this will display correctly when the file is displayed in slide show mode.)

- Ask the children to read through their new scene and decide where they would add sound or lighting effects and why. You may want to model an example for them first, on the board. For example, the lighting could change, getting darker, as Lucy tells lies through the door, so the light could reduce down to just a spotlight on Amy, Sam and the door. Ask them to TTYP to share their ideas and then collect feedback from a few children to share with the whole class.

Evaluate and edit

Purpose: for children to evaluate their own and their partner's work against specific criteria and then discuss how they could improve their work

> **Curriculum link:** assessing the effectiveness of their own and others' writing

- Explain that you want the children to read their partner's script from their writing books. Display **CD (file 10.2)** to show the evaluation prompts and read them aloud using MT/YT.
- As a model, select an example of work where the writing has met the criteria, and share this with the other children, explaining why it works well.
- Tell the children to take turns to read their partner's writing in pairs and discuss together how well each piece of writing has met the criteria.
- Ask children to discuss at least two changes they could make to improve their work following the partner discussion.

Proofread

Purpose: for children to proofread their work and make changes to improve the accuracy of their grammar, punctuation and spelling

> proofread for spelling and punctuation errors

- Now ask the children to proofread their work. If you have noticed that several children need to improve on a particular aspect of spelling, grammar or punctuation, use this as a focus for the Proofread activity. Write an example which includes common errors from the children's writing and use this as a model.
- The children should always be checking for standard use of punctuation and correct spelling of common exception words.
- The following points would be relevant as the particular focus for this Unit:
  – checking the correct spelling of words with -ing endings.

Act a script

Purpose: for children to perform and evaluate their own and other children's scripts

> preparing playscripts to read aloud and perform showing understanding through intonation, tone, volume and action

- Ask the children to work in groups of four to practise and perform one of their scripts.
- When the children have had enough rehearsal time, gather the class to watch each other's performances.
- Model how to give feedback to the actors that is positive and helpful in improving the script/performance. Encourage the children to give feedback to each group.

Further activity

- Publish: ask the children to type up their playscripts, making any changes from the Evaluate and edit and Proofread activities.

Instruction texts

READING AND WRITING NON-FICTION

In the Non-fiction reading and writing week, the focus is on developing children's ability to follow and write instructions for making musical instruments.

See p.46 for the daily timetable for the Non-fiction week.

Non-fiction

Reading

Children will:

- consider why people need and use instructions
- notice how instructions are organised to make them easy to follow
- evaluate instructions against a set of criteria.

Writing

Key purpose to be shared with the children:

To write clear instructions about how to make a bottle band.

Writing evaluation to be shared with the children

My instructions:

- lay out information clearly (e.g. *with subheadings, pictures, list of equipment*) so the reader can follow the instructions easily
- use precise language so the reader knows exactly what to do.

Grammar:

- includes imperative verbs, to make it clear that I am instructing the reader to do something
- uses adverbs of time, so the reader knows which order to do things in, e.g. *First, Then, Next.*

See the Planning section of the Software ('Timetables' tab) for a printable version of the Writing purpose and evaluation.

Curriculum link:
reading for a range
of purposes

Think and link

Purpose: for children to become interested in instructions via a Big Question they have explored

- Display the Big Question from Day 7 on **CD (file 7.5):**

  What makes a good friend?

- Ask the children to TTYP to recall some of what they discussed before and take feedback. Write on a flipchart some of the ideas about what we need to do to be a good friend. Explain to the children that you could use these ideas to write some instructions about how to be a good friend. (If necessary, remind the children that instructions tell us what to do. They can be simple commands, such as 'Sit still!' or they can be a set of commands that teach us how to do or make something, e.g. *how to bake a cake.*)

- Display the **CD (file 11.1)** which shows a set of instructions for being a good friend. Share each instruction with the children using MT/YT. Ask the children to TTYP and talk about anything they could add to the instructions.

Year 3
Grammar
using adverbs to
express time

Grammar: adverbs of time

Purpose: for children to understand how adverbs of time are used to create instructions

- Tell the children that adverbs can show us how and when to do something and that they are very useful when we read or write instructions. Display the list of adverbs and sentences on **CD (file 11.2)** and share the adverbs with the children using MT/YT. Tell the children that these words are often at the beginning of sentences in instructions to help make the order clear to the reader.

- Share the sentences using MT/YT. Model choosing one of the words for the first sentence and drag and drop it into place.

- Now ask the children to TTYP to decide which word would be best for the next sentence and so on. (Note that some are interchangeable, e.g. *now, next* and *after that.*)

- You can print off the adverbs on **CD (file 11.3)** to display on the Instructions wall.

Homework Book p.10 provides further practice on adverbs.

Zoom in on features of instructions

Purpose: for children to learn about the key features and language used in instructions

- Display the first slide of **CD (file 11.4)** to show some of the key features of instructions: adverbs of time, imperative verbs (commands), adverbs of manner (that describe how to do something), pictures and captions, list of materials (what you will need), bullet points and numbers. These features and some examples can be printed from **CD (file 11.5)** for display on your Instructions wall.

- Remind the children of the instructions text work they did in Unit 4 of Year 2 and ask them to TTYP and talk about any of the words that they are familiar with. Take feedback.

- Click to the second slide of **CD (file 11.4)** to focus in more detail on adverbs of time. Point out the examples of adverbs of time used in the instructions in a recipe. Use MT/YT to say each whole sentence first, then just the adverbs of time (words and phrases in bold).

- Tell the children to TTYP and think of another example of an adverb of time. Take feedback. Click to the next slides and repeat the process for imperative verbs and adverbs of manner.

- Click to the next slide to show an example of a picture with a caption. Use MT/YT to say the word *caption* and then to read the whole caption aloud.

- Click to the next slide to display a list of materials. Point out that this is introduced with the phrase *You will need*. Explain that in a recipe this list of materials is often called the *ingredients*.
- Finally, click to the last slide which shows the recipe instructions displayed with both the use of bullets and numbers. Ask the children which they prefer, or which they think is the most useful way to display the instructions.
- Ask the children to TTYP to talk about any other ways they can think of to organise instructions. *(They could be shown as pictures with captions underneath, the instructions could be filmed, the instructions could be written very simply in a paragraph without any organisational features.)*

> **Curriculum link:** discussing writing in order to learn from its structure, grammar and vocabulary

Class log

Purpose: for children to share the process of keeping a class reading, writing and thinking log to record responses to texts and activities in a variety of forms

- Tell the children that you have three different types of instructions to show them. Display **CD (file 11.6).** Show them each set of instructions, one at a time.
- Ask them to look carefully at them and then to TTYP to tell their partner what the instructions are for. Take feedback. Ensure they understand that the instructions are all about the same thing – how to make chocolate rice pop cakes – but are all presented in different ways, with different amounts of text to explain the method.
- Ask the children to TTYP to decide which of the instructions they think are the easiest to understand and encourage them to say why. Take feedback. Print off all three sets of instructions and stick them in to the Class log.

DAY 12

Instruction detectives

Purpose: for children to become aware of the key features and language in instructions

- Remind the children of the work they did on Day 11, looking at the key features of instruction texts. Tell them that now they are going to be like detectives, and find these key features in another instruction text. Display **CD (file 12.1).** Explain that this shows part of an instruction text which is printed in full in their Anthology (do not ask the children to look at this yet). Point out the labels down the left hand side of the slide. Tell the children that these labels are some of the key features they have already seen in the activity on Day 11.
- Point to one label and use MT/YT to read it. Then ask the children to TTYP to find an example of this feature in the extract. Share their responses and use your whiteboard tools to draw a line from the feature to the correct place in the text.
- Go through all the labels in turn, following the same process, then navigate to the next slide and do the same again. Ask the children to turn to pp.31–34 of their Anthology where they can see the complete instruction text. Remind them of the key features of instruction texts (on the wall display) and ask them to identify more examples of these key features in their Anthology text.

> assessing the effectiveness of others' writing

Evaluating instructions 1

Purpose: for children to read and evaluate a set of instructions

- Before the lesson, print a copy of **CD (file 12.2)** for each pair of children.
- Tell the children they are going to read and evaluate some instructions for making a one-string guitar. They are going to be detectives and think of ways these instructions could be improved.

- Give each set of partners a copy of the instructions and the evaluation sheet from **CD (file 12.2)** and read the first criterion: 'Does the title tell you clearly what you are going to make/do?' Model reading and finding the example, e.g. *'There is a title and it tells you that you will make an instrument, but it doesn't say what you will be making'*. Then ask the children to TTYP and discuss: *'Are there any ways that the title can be improved?'* Take feedback.

- Read each of the criteria with the children making sure they understand exactly what they are looking for each time. Ask the children to TTYP to find examples of each criterion, and then TTYP to discuss how that aspect of the instructions could be improved. Encourage the children to offer alternative ideas for layout, e.g. *it would be better if the instructions were numbered; the pictures could be showing how to make the one-string guitar and they could be next to the relevant step of the instructions.*

- Once you have gone through the evaluation sheet orally with the children, ask them to fill it in with their partner, giving examples of how to improve the instructions. (Do not ask them to compare with the Anthology instruction text yet.)

- Take feedback from the class and write on a flipchart a list of changes and tweaks that could be made to the instructions, ready for the next activity.

Improving instructions 1

Purpose: for children to help to improve a set of instructions and evaluate their success

- Display the example of unclear instructions on **CD (file 12.2)**. Remind the children of the list of improvements that you have gathered up from the last activity on the flipchart.

- Tell the children the first improvement you are going to make is adding a clearer and more interesting title. Ask the children for suggestions.

- Next, tell the children that the reader really needs to know everything they need at the start of the instructions. Model finding the things needed and writing a clear list, with bullet points. Ask the children to help, using their notes from the previous activity.

- Next, model moving the instructions around into a clearer and more logical order, and numbering the steps consecutively. Continue editing and improving the instructions using your list of improvements on the flipchart. You can continue to use the Build a sentence technique (i.e. prompt and improve the children's ideas) and TTYP to compose new sentences. You can save and print off the instructions at any time.

- Now ask the children to work with their partner to annotate the instructions from their printout of **CD (file 12.2)**, to show how they would improve them.

- When the children have finished, these notes can be stuck into their Personal log.

- Now ask the children to compare their annotated instructions with the version in the Anthology, pp.31–34. Take feedback and discuss whether the Anthology instructions could be improved further, e.g. *by adding subheadings, making the title more interesting*. If you wish, they can try out the instructions by making the one-string guitar.

Non-fiction: Instruction texts

Curriculum link:
discussing and recording ideas

Personal log

Purpose: for children to keep a personal log for recording and reflecting on their exploration of instruction texts

- Ask the children to TTYP and discuss what title they would give the instructions for making a one-string guitar, if they were going to write their own. Remind them that it could be a question or start with *How to …* for example. Ask them to write their title above their instructions in their Personal log.

DAY 13

understand grammatical terms; increasing range of sentence structures

Grammar: imperative verbs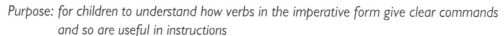

Purpose: for children to understand how verbs in the imperative form give clear commands and so are useful in instructions

- Display **CD (file 13.1)** which contains some of the text instructions for making the one-string guitar without the imperative verbs. Ask the children to TTYP to read the first instruction with their partner and discuss what is missing. Take feedback.
- Confirm that the verbs are missing and these verbs are essential to instructions because they tell us what to do. Click to the next screen to show one instruction with the same verb in different tenses that can be dragged and dropped into the sentence. Drag and drop the different verbs into the sentence and use MT/YT to share the different versions of the sentence with the children.
- Ask the children which of the verbs they would choose for their instructions and why. Take feedback. Repeat with the other sentences on the next three screens.
- Emphasise that the imperative verb is used in instructions to tell the reader what to do. It is sometimes called the *bossy* or *commanding* verb form for this reason.
- Click to the final screen to show the children some more imperative verbs. Model using one in an instruction, e.g. *'Point to the floor.'*
- Now ask the children to take turns to choose an imperative verb from the screen to use in a command or instruction to their partner. Tell them to continue until they have used all the verbs. Move around listening to the children. Remember good examples and share them with the class.
- Ask the children to TTYP and remind their partner what an imperative verb is.

What's missing?

Purpose: for children to read and evaluate a set of instructions

- Display **CD (file 13.2)**. Ask the children to take turns to read the instructions for a bottle band with their partner.
- Point out the labels down the left hand side of the slide, which refer to key features of instruction texts. Read each label and ask the children to TTYP and discuss whether the feature is present in the text. Share their responses and use your whiteboard tools to draw lines from the labels to the correct places in the text. (Note that there will not be examples of all the key features in this text and many of them are deliberately very poor examples.)
- Once you have found all the possible key features, ask the children to TTYP and decide what they think is missing. Take feedback and write their ideas onto a flipchart.
- Display **CD (file 13.3).** Explain that you are going to look a bit closer at what is missing. On the first slide, click on the buttons ('Title', 'Introduction', etc.) to display the think bubbles and use these to help you explore what is lacking or inadequate in the text. Do the same with the remaining text and labels on the second slide.

Planning improvements

Purpose: for children to plan additional material to improve the instructions

- Before the lesson, print copies of **CD (file 13.5)** and **CD (file 13.6)** for each child.
- Tell the children that you are going to plan how to improve the instructions, building on ideas from the last activity. Display **CD (file 13.4)** which is a plan for improving the Bottle Band instructions. Click each of the features to show the think bubbles. Use the think bubbles and the children's ideas on the flipchart from the previous activity to model filling in the plan.
- Give each child a copy of the planner from **CD (file 13.5)** and of the Bottle Band instructions from **CD (file 13.6)**. Tell the children to use their planner to make notes as to where and how they would improve the instructions. Remind them that they are just writing notes and deciding which parts of the instructions they need to improve. They are not writing out new instructions yet!

Curriculum link: discussing and recording ideas

Class log – sequencing

Purpose: for children to share the process of keeping a class reading, writing and thinking log to record responses to texts and activities in a variety of forms

- Print off one copy of **CD (file 13.8)** before the lesson.
- Show the children the pictures on **CD (file 13.7).** Tell them that they are pictures to support their instructions. Ask them to TTYP and discuss which order the pictures should be in. Drag and drop them into the appropriate order.
- Once you have decided on the order, ask the children to TTYP to identify additional information the pictures give the reader. Ask the children to TTYP and discuss: '*Where would be the best place to put the pictures in the instructions?*'
- Stick the pictures, printed from **CD (file 13.8),** into the Class log in the correct order.

DAY 14

Improving instructions 2

Purpose: for children to read, evaluate and improve their plans for the instructions

- Before the lesson, print a copy of **CD (file 14.2)** for each pair of children.
- Display **CD (file 14.1).** Explain to the children that this grid shows your planning notes for how to improve the instructions for making the bottle band. Talk through your notes, ensuring children realise that they are just ideas and notes, NOT the actual written improvements at this stage.
- Give out copies of the printed **CD (file 14.2)**, which gives a checklist of key features for instruction texts. Use MT/YT to read through the checklist, then ask the children to TTYP to talk about which of these features are missing in your plan notes. Take feedback and note on a flipchart anything they have noticed is missing from your notes, such as ideas about using pictures or choosing exact language, e.g. *adverbs of time.*
- Ask the children to go back to their own plan that they drew up on the planner printout from **CD (file 13.5).** Tell them to give their plan to their partner and use the checklist on the printout to go through their partner's plan, pointing out anything they have missed or need to add.
- Tell the children to take back their own plans and to make any improvements they wish to, bearing in mind suggestions from their partner, and their own new ideas.

Curriculum link:
discussing writing
that is similar to
that which they
are planning to
write; composing
and rehearsing
sentences orally

Write 1 ⓒᴰ 🖨 🅿🅱

Purpose: for children to write a set of instructions independently

- Tell the children that today they are going to write their improved instructions, but first you are going to model writing some of the early parts. Use a printout of **CD (file 14.3)** to support you with this.
- Refer to your notes from the previous activity which you can display on screen from the **CD (file 14.1).** Model deciding on a title and then writing it down, and then do the same for the introduction. Involve the children in this process using the Build a sentence technique (see Introduction, p.12), TTYP and MT/YT.
- When you have modelled writing the title and the introduction, ask the children to write theirs. Ask them to look on pp.24–25 of the Pupils' Book for some Top Tips on writing the main core of their instructions.
- Now model writing some of the main core of instructions, using TOL to decide how you will use bullet points, pictures or numbers. Remind the children to leave space for Top Tips and captions.
- Ask the children to write their main instructions. Support them, using as much or as little modelling as the class requires. (Note that they may not have time to finish all their writing in this lesson, but extra time is allocated in the next lesson.)
- Before the end of the lesson, display an example of the finished instructions on **CD (file 14.4).** Point out that these may not be exactly the same as the children's instructions, but many different versions may be equally good. Navigate to the final slide to reveal the list of key features as a checklist. Ask the children to help you evaluate your instructions using the checklist questions.

DAY 15

Write 2

Purpose: for children to write a simple set of instructions independently

- You may need to allow time for the children to complete their written instructions from Day 14 for the first 15 minutes of this session.

read aloud their
own writing, to
a group; monitor
whether their
own writing makes
sense

Write 3

The children will need all the materials for the bottle band to be assembled in the classroom, before they can demonstrate making a bottle band using their own written instructions. Ask them to work in groups of six, and provide five bottles for each group if possible. Soak these and remove the labels before the lesson.

Purpose: for children to follow a set of instructions they have written and evaluate its success

If the children can be filmed following their own instructions, then have the film played back to them, they will be able to evaluate the effectiveness of their instructions. If this is not possible, the children can work in groups of three pairs, and evaluate the other pairs' demonstrations, as they watch.

- Make sure each pair of children has a full set of instructions that one of them wrote. Tell the children that they will be testing their instructions to see if they are easy to follow. (You will be helping them with providing the materials they need.) Remind the children to read each part of the instructions before they do it.
- Tell them that they should write notes on their instructions if they think of any tweaks or improvements that they need to make, as they make the bottle band.
- When you have set up the camera, or organised the children into groups, tell the children to start following their instructions. Move around the room supporting the children and suggesting any tweaks that the children might need to make to their instructions as they go through them.

Evaluate and edit **PB**

Purpose: for children to evaluate their own work

Curriculum link: assessing the effectiveness of their own and others' writing

- When the children have made their bottle band, ask them to look at the questions in the Pupils' Book on p.25. Ask them to follow the prompts as you read through them. Explain that you want them to use them to check how clear and useful their instructions were and how well their bottle band works.
- Ask the children to TTYP to share what they think about their bottle band instructions. They may notice other points from the video which are not in the evaluation prompts – encourage them to give suggestions about anything they noticed which is useful. (If they filmed their work, ask them to watch the video of them making the bottle band and to TTYP to share their thoughts.) Collect feedback and ask for a few suggestions for improvements to their instructions.

Proofread

proofread for spelling and punctuation errors

Purpose: for children to proofread their work and make changes to improve the accuracy of their grammar, punctuation and spelling

- Now ask the children to proofread their work. If you have noticed that several children need to improve on a particular aspect of spelling, grammar or punctuation, use this as a focus for the Proofread activity. Write an example which includes common errors from the children's writing and use this as a model.
- The children should always be checking for standard use of punctuation and correct spelling of common exception words.
- The following points would be relevant as the particular focus for this Unit:
  - checking spelling of high frequency adverbs of time (e.g. *First, Then, Next*)
  - checking correct spelling of verbs in the imperative form.

Fiction: Science fiction/Fantasy
Non-fiction: Discussion texts

Timetable

WEEK 1 **Reading fiction** *A Tale of Two Robots*

Day 1	Day 2	Day 3	Day 4	Day 5
The story store	Science fiction language 🖶	Word power 🖶	Points of view	What do I want to know?
Say it, show it	Read a story 1 – clues	Similes	Most powerful?	Quiz the character 1
Personal log 🖶	Read a story 2 – evidence	Re-read a story 3	Class log	Quiz the character 2 🖶
Big Question	Read a story 3	Grammar: determiners *a* and *an*	Big Question	Personal log
	Class log 🖶	Personal log		Big Question
	Big Question	Big Question		

WEEK 2 **Writing fiction** *A Tale of Two Robots*

Day 6	Day 7	Day 8	Day 9	Day 10
Story language 🖶	Build a story 1	Build a story 2	Build a story 3 🖶	Who says?
Grammar: conjunctions	Write a story 1 🖶	Write a story 2 🖶	Evaluate a story	Write a story 3
What if not . . . ?	Role-play and dialogue	Class log and Personal log	Dramatic reconstruction 1	Evaluate and edit
Build a sentence 🖶	Big Question	Big Question	Personal log	Proofread
Personal log 🖶				Dramatic reconstruction 2
Big Question				Class log

WEEK 3 **Reading and writing non-fiction** Discussion texts

Day 11	Day 12	Day 13	Day 14	Day 15
Think and link	Grammar: adverbs and adverbials 🖶	Hear it	Evaluate, edit and proofread	Deconstruction 3
Human scales	Deconstruction 1	Deconstruction 2	Fact or opinion?	Write 3
Discussion words 🖶	Write 1	Organise it	Personal log	
Class log	Personal log	Write 2 🖶		
		Class log		

🖶: shows that a file should be printed out from the Software.

Overview of the Unit

A Tale of Two Robots by Roy Apps is a humorous story that introduces a science fiction element into a familiar setting. Children will be encouraged to develop empathetic responses to characters and situations and an awareness of different points of view.

The linked Non-fiction week will develop the children's understanding of discussion texts, fact and opinion. For more information about the Non-fiction week and the Non-fiction writing evaluation criteria, see p.90.

Where appropriate, the children will be encouraged to develop an awareness of audience and purpose in relation to the fiction and non-fiction texts they are reading and writing.

Teacher modelling is provided in the teaching notes, Software and the Pupils' Book, supporting the children's writing at every stage in the Fiction and Non-fiction weeks.

The Homework Book provides a homework activity related to the content of this Unit for each of the three weeks.

Fiction

Reading

Children will:

- connect and explore the central themes and ideas in *A Tale of Two Robots* of invention and science, by making links with other texts and their own experience
- explore how Roy Apps develops plot
- devise questions for the main character to ask and answer in role.

Writing

Key writing purpose to be shared with the children:

To write a new episode for the story.

Writing evaluation to share with the children

My new episode:

- has a problem, reaction and resolution
- has dialogue that sounds convincing because it is based on what I know about the characters
- shows the characters' reactions to new situations.

Grammar:

- includes correct use of first person (*I, we*) for a short part of the episode written by a first-person narrator.

See the Planning section of the Software ('Timetables' tab) for a printable version of the Writing purpose and evaluation.

Fiction: Science fiction/Fantasy
A Tale of Two Robots by Roy Apps

READING FICTION

Resources

PB Pupils' Book pp.26–35

A Anthology pp.35–51

CD CD on Interactive whiteboard Unit 3

GB Grammar Bank on CD

HB Homework Book pp.11–13

DAY 1

Curriculum link:
listening to and discussing a wide range of fiction, identifying themes

The story store (CD)

Purpose: for children to meet themes to be explored in the main study text

- Use **CD (file 1.1)** to show the front cover of a children's version of Mary Shelley's *Frankenstein*. (Note that the text of this particular version is not suitable for Year 3 students, but the cover is a good stimulus for discussion.)

- Ask the children to read the title and look at the illustration and then TTYP (Turn to your partner) to share what they already know about the story or what they think it might be about.

- Collect feedback and encourage the children to share how they know about it already or to justify their suggestions about the story. Show how much you value their ideas and experiences of the story.

- Go to the next slide to show the beginning of a Frankenstein storyboard. Click 'TOL' (Think out loud) to show the think bubbles as you describe what is happening in the pictures. Use these and TTYP to draw out the main themes of the story as you navigate through this and the following slides, e.g. *creating new life, creator's responsibility, loneliness, consequences of our actions.*

- Say that you have another story to show them. Display **CD (file 1.2)** to show the illustrated front cover of *The Trouble with Sisters and Robots*.

- Ask the children to read the title and look at the illustration and then TTYP to share what they think it might be about. Collect feedback and encourage the children to justify their suggestions about the story.

- Click to the next slide to show the blurb about the story and read it aloud to the children. Ask them to TTYP and say if it reminds them of any other stories they know, e.g. *King Midas, who found everything he touched turned to gold.*

- Ask them to TTYP to say how they think the *Frankenstein* story and *The Trouble with Sisters and Robots* could be linked. What ideas are similar in them?

Say it, show it

Purpose: for children to communicate their emotions using drama

- Ask the children to stand up. Tell them that they are inventors. Use MT/YT (My turn/Your turn) and TTYP to say '*I am an inventor!*' Explain that they have just finished creating a creature and it has just come to life. Ask them to Popcorn (see Introduction, p.17) words (adjectives) that describe how they might feel at that exact moment, e.g. *excited, scared, nervous, thrilled, proud, terrified, astonished.*

- Say that you are going to call out a 'feeling' word (one of the adjectives mentioned above) and you want them to create a freeze frame of that moment and feeling. Repeat with a few more contrasting but appropriate words. Now tell them that they are the new creature. Use MT/YT and TTYP to say '*I am a new creature!*' Explain that they have just come to life.

- Ask them to Popcorn words (adjectives) that describe how they might feel at that exact moment, e.g. *puzzled, surprised, anxious, stiff or creaky, shocked, frightened, annoyed, unsure.* Say that you are going to call out a 'feeling' word and you want them to create a freeze frame of that moment and feeling. Repeat with a few more contrasting but appropriate words.

Personal log

Curriculum link:
opportunities to
write for a range
of real purposes
and audiences

Purpose: for children to keep a personal log for recording and reflecting on their exploration of stories

- Tell the children that they are going to create their own creature or robot and make up a very short (oral) story about it. Display **CD (file 1.3)**. Tell the children to TTYP and tell their partners which parts they would use to make a new robot, and what their new robot would look like. (If you wish, you could print this for children to look at with their partners.)
- Now ask them to TTYP to invent a mini story about their creature or robot. Allow thinking and sharing time.
- Choose two or three partners to show their invention and to share their mini stories with the whole class. Select one of the oral stories and say that you are going to write a short, simple piece of blurb about it, e.g. *He wanted a new friend, but when he made one, he got more than he bargained for! Meet Master Muddle ...* Write your blurb on a board or flipchart and use MT/YT to read it aloud.
- Remind the children that a blurb never reveals the ending of a story. It should make the reader want to find out what happens. Ask them to TTYP to create a short piece of blurb for their own mini stories and to write it in their Personal log.

Big Question

discussion; develop,
agree on, and
evaluate rules for
effective discussion

Purpose: for children to develop their skills of argument and discussion through a mini enquiry session based on a philosophical question relating to the work of the day

- Display today's Big Question on **CD (file 1.4)**:

  Where do ideas come from?

- Ask the children to TTYP to talk about this question. Collect feedback and scribe some responses on the board or flipchart.
- Click 'Prompts' to show some statements that may help to encourage discussion.

DAY 2

Science fiction language

Purpose: for children to learn the meaning of specific vocabulary

explaining the
meaning of words
in context

inventor   laboratory   equipment   experiment   robot

- Tell the children that there were some words they heard during the Story store activity yesterday that are useful and special because they gave us clues that the stories are science fiction. Explain that science fiction means made-up stories (fiction) about scientific things that may happen in the future.
- Display these words and their definitions on **CD (file 2.1)**. Look at the words with the children and then use MT/YT as you read the definitions to them.
- You may wish to print these words and definitions from printable **CD (file 2.2)** to display on your Story wall for this Unit and or to paste into the Class log.

Read a story 1 – clues

Purpose: for children to be motivated to read the new story. To make connections between the new story, those in the Story store and any other stories they might know

- Display **CD (file 2.3)** to show a picture of the Story laboratory. Tell the children that you have been told there are some clues about a new story in the Story laboratory and you need their help to find out more. Convey your own eagerness and enthusiasm and draw them into your excitement.

- Say that they are like 'story scientists', experimenting with ideas as to what the story might be about. Explain that there are three clues about the new story in this laboratory and you have to find them. Ask the children for suggestions where to look (where to click) in the laboratory.
- The clues will be revealed when you click on the steaming test tube, the bubbling bottle and the top drawer. (Note that you will have to click back to the story laboratory picture to find each of the clues.) Each clue shows a scene from the story and a think bubble.
- Use the 'TOL' bubble and your own ideas to introduce the clue, then ask the children to TTYP to talk about how it might relate to the new story.
- Repeat until you have found all three clues. Make sure you do not reveal the title, any surprises or the ending of the final story at this stage.

Read a story 2 – evidence (CD)

Curriculum link:
predicting,
identifying how
language, structure,
and presentation
contribute to
meaning

Purpose: for children to become more familiar with the story so far before they hear the full version and to make predictions about the final story

- Tell the children that more clues have come to light about the story. Display **CD (file 2.4)** to show a letter. Say that you are really excited about what it might be about. Click on the audio button to hear the contents read out by a narrator.
- Ask the children to TTYP to make a prediction about the story.
- Click the audio button again to hear the letter again. Ask the children to imagine that they have bumped into Callum in the town and they want to warn him that inventions don't always turn out as planned.
- Explain that you want them to TTYP to decide what they would say to him. Now tell them to take turns saying their warning to Callum, i.e. Partner 1 says it to Partner 2 and vice versa. Choose two or three to share what they would say to Callum with the whole class.

Read a story 3 (A) (teacher only) (PB)

*checking that the
text makes sense,
asking questions,
drawing inferences*

Purpose: for children to hear and enjoy the full version of the story for the first time

- Tell the children that they are now going to hear the whole story for the very first time. TOL about which parts you can't wait to hear about. Ask the children to TTYP to share what they are looking forward to in the story.
- Say that you need to switch on your Storyteller voice! Make it a special moment as if you are getting ready for a performance. Then read the full story from the Anthology pp.35–45 aloud, using expression and intonation to convey meaning.
- At the end of the story, ask the children to look at the Read a story 3 activity on p.26 of their Pupils' Book. Guide them as they TTYP to discuss the questions and feed back to the class.

Class log (CD) 📄

*discussing and
recording ideas*

Purpose: for children to share the process of keeping a class reading, writing and thinking log to record responses to texts and activities in a variety of forms

- Tell the children that today is the day to start a new section in their Class log called Science fiction. On the title page for this new section write *Science fiction* and the title of the story: *A Tale of Two Robots*.

- Explain that you want their help in choosing an illustration for the title page. Remind them that a book cover or title page should be appropriate to the story and encourage people to want to read it.
- Display **CD (file 2.5)** and ask the students to decide which of the three pictures they think is the most appropriate for a title page for the story *A Tale of Two Robots*.
- Ask for feedback and reasons for choices and then take a vote for the most popular cover.
- Before the next lesson, print the chosen illustration from printable **CD (file 2.6)** and paste it onto the title page of this section of the Class log. Remind the children that they can offer things to be pasted or attached to the Class log at any time, e.g. pictures of Frankenstein's creature, robots, relevant poems.

Curriculum link: discussion; develop, agree on, and evaluate rules for effective discussion

Big Question (CD)

Purpose: for children to develop their skills of argument and discussion through a mini enquiry session based on a philosophical question relating to the work of the day

- Display today's Big Question on **CD (file 2.7)**:

  Would it be a good thing if robots did all our work for us?

- Follow the process as explained on Day 1.

DAY 3

discussing words and phrases that capture the reader's interest and imagination

Word power (CD)

Purpose: for children to increase their knowledge of and application of rarer vocabulary and synonyms

> absent-mindedly   fumed   tentatively   brusquely

- Tell the children that there were some words in the story they heard yesterday that the writer of the story had chosen because they were powerful. Display **CD (file 3.1)** to show the first power word. Use MT/YT to say the word.
- Click on 'Reveal' to display the synonyms and the use of the original word in an example sentence. Ask the children to repeat the sentence using MT/YT giving dramatic emphasis and actions as you say it.
- Repeat the process for the second, third and fourth words.
- Now ask the children to look at the Word power activity on p.27 of their Pupils' Book and to TTYP to complete the activity.
- Let the children hear you use the words in your teaching and conversation throughout the day in an exaggerated or ironic fashion: *'Oh dear, I am behaving* absent-mindedly *this morning!'* Encourage them to use the words at home with friends and family so that they become embedded in the children's own spoken (and eventually, written) vocabulary.
- Remind them that these words are on the Story wall for this Unit and are there for us all to use. Praise them if they use one of the words.
- Print the Power words and their synonyms from **CD (file 3.2)** and display them on your Story wall.

opportunities to discuss language, including vocabulary; discussing words and phrases that capture the reader's interest and imagination

Similes (CD)

Purpose: for children to become familiar with special phrases particular to the story and consolidate their understanding of similes

> ...like a thunderbolt   ...like a firework display gone crazy   ...like a TV chat show set

- Tell the children that you are going to show them some special phrases from the story. Explain that these are special because they are similes.
- Ask them to TTYP to remind each other what a simile is. Collect answers and examples and clarify if necessary. (Emphasise that a simile creates a picture in the reader's mind to compare with what is happening in the text. It uses the words *like* or *as* in the comparison.)
- Now display **CD (file 3.3)** and focus on the first simile from the story: 'Panic struck Callum **like a thunderbolt.**' Use MT/YT to read the phrase aloud. TOL about why you think the writer chose this simile.
- Now focus on the second simile and repeat MT/YT and a TOL about the writer's choice: '. . . sparks started to fly off the robot's hands and legs, **like a firework display gone crazy.**' Repeat the process for the third simile: '. . . it shone **like a TV chat show set.**'
- Now ask the children to TTYP to choose their favourite simile in the story. Make sure they can explain to their partner what they like about it and why it helps the reader. Choose some partners to feed back.

Re-read a story 3 🅐

Curriculum link: checking that the text makes sense, asking questions, drawing inferences

Purpose: for children to gain a deeper understanding of the story and to see the text for the first time

- Ask the children to read aloud with their partners the story on Anthology pp.35–45. They should read alternate sections each, and ensure they use expression and intonation to convey meaning and impact to their partner. Explain that you will be listening in and looking out for particularly good reading.
- For some groups, you may wish to read aloud to the children first as they follow the text in their own copy so that they can Jump in (see Introduction p.13).

Grammar: determiners *a* and *an* ⓒⒹ 🅿🅑 🅗🅑

Year 3 Grammar use of the determiners *a* and *an*

Purpose: for children to develop awareness of the appropriate use of the determiners a and an

- Tell the children that that they are going to zoom in on the word *a* because although it is very common, it is special. Display **CD (file 3.4)** to show a sentence from *A Tale of Two Robots*. Use MT/YT to say it aloud.
- Ask the children to TTYP to talk about whether the noun *tip* begins with a vowel or a consonant. Tell them to Popcorn their answer. Click on 'Reveal' to show the initial consonant in the word and on the Complex Speed Sounds chart.
- Tell them that words that begin with a vowel after are tricky to pronounce smoothly. Navigate to the next slide to show two examples and use MT/YT to say them, exaggerating the clumsiness of the vowels together.
- Explain the reason that *a* is special. To make the pronunciation easier and smoother when it comes before a word that begins with a vowel, it is changed to *an*.
- Click on 'Reveal' to show the changes and 'TOL' to show a think bubble. Use MT/YT to say the examples to make sure they hear and feel the difference as well as seeing it on the slide. Read the think bubble to help them to understand why it is altered.
- Now ask them to look at Grammar: determiners *a* and *an* on p.27 of their Pupils' Book. Tell them to TTYP and take turns to read the sentences aloud and to complete the activity. Tell them to write their sentences in their Personal log.

Homework Book p.11 provides further practice on similes and determiners.

Curriculum link: building a varied and rich vocabulary and an increasing range of sentence structures

Personal log

Purpose: for children to keep a personal log for recording and reflecting on their exploration of stories

- Tell the children that you want them to create some similes of their own. Explain that you have chosen a section of the story *A Tale of Two Robots* where they could add a simile.
- Explain that you have looked at the beginning of the story where Callum's mum is really cross because he hasn't tidied up his bedroom. Write this sentence on a board or flipchart and explain that you have added the part that is underlined: *"Well, I'm not going to tell you again," his mum fumed <u>like a. . .</u>* Use MT/YT to say the sentence. Now ask the children to TTYP to think of a great simile to complete the sentence. Tell the children that their simile could start with an *a* or an *an*.
- Collect examples from a few sets of partners and write them down, e.g. *"Well, I'm not going to tell you again," his mum fumed* like a boiler about to burst. / *Well, I'm not going to tell you again," his mum fumed* like a rocket launching into space. / *"Well, I'm not going to tell you again," his mum fumed* like a smoking bonfire.
- If you wish to repeat the process with another sentence or two, use the ones shown below, explaining the context of the extract: *By the time dawn rose over the horizon, he had finished building his room cleaning robot. It lay on his bed* like a . . . Examples could include: *By the time dawn rose over the horizon, he had finished building his room cleaning robot. It lay on his bed* like a lifeless puppet. / *By the time dawn rose over the horizon, he had finished building his room cleaning robot. It lay on his bed* like a giant metal doll.
- TOL as you choose your favourite example, giving a reason for your choice. Write it in the Class log. Ask the children to choose their favourite simile from the board or use their own and to write the whole sentence in their Personal log, reminding them to check whether they should use *a* or *an* in their similes.

discussion; develop, agree on, and evaluate rules for effective discussion

Big Question ⓒⒹ

Purpose: for children to develop their skills of argument and discussion through a mini enquiry session based on a philosophical question relating to the work of the day

- Display today's Big Question on **CD (file 3.5):**

  Should children be made to do chores at home?

- Follow the process as explained on Day 1.

DAY 4

Points of view ⓒⒹ 🄰 (teacher only)

Purpose: for children to be able to identify different characters' points of view

- Tell the children that just like us, characters in stories can have their own point of view about other characters and events that happen. Display **CD (file 4.1)** to show first person statements and some characters. Use MT/YT to say the first statement and then ask the children to TTYP to say which character is the most likely to have this point of view.
- Collect feedback and encourage the children to support their answers based on their knowledge of the story and their empathy with characters. Use your own Anthology and TOL as you model finding evidence in the text to support their ideas.
- Drag the statement into the speech bubble for the correct character. (Callum's mum is most likely to say 'Children should clear up their own mess!') Repeat the process using the other statements.

- Now ask the children to TTYP to decide which character they want to be (one each or both can be the same character) and to think of another statement that their character is most likely to say, e.g. *Callum's Mum might say, 'I wish Callum would stop arguing and just do as he is told!' Shannon might say, 'Callum had no idea that I am an inventor as well.'*
- Choose sets of partners to feed back and scribe their answers on the board or a flipchart in large speech bubbles. Write the character's name underneath. Reflect on how they made their decisions and give reasons.

Most powerful? ⓒⒹ 🆎

Purpose: for children to explore and develop their own opinion about the importance of individuals and events in the story

- Tell the children that all the characters are important in the story, but that some characters seem to be more important than others – they have more power than others. Display **CD (file 4.2)** to show one section of *A Tale of Two Robots*. Ask the children to read it aloud chorally with intonation that shows their understanding of the characters.
- Click 'TOL' to show think bubbles and use them and/or your own ideas to discuss who seems to be the most powerful character in this part of the story; make sure you use discursive language, *on one hand ... on the other hand ... it could be ... but ....*
- Draw the children into the TOL and then ask them to TTYP to discuss who they think is the most powerful and why. Take feedback and make sure the children can support their ideas.
- Now ask them to look at the Most powerful? activity on pp.28–29 of their Pupils' Book. Explain that you want them to TTYP to read another section of the story and then discuss *who* is most powerful.
- Point out that they are also asked to discuss which moment of the story is most important and to explain why. If necessary, explain that it could be the most important moment because it changes the way the story develops, or it could be the most exciting moment in the story. Make sure they understand that this is a *your opinion* not a *one right answer* activity. Take feedback and give particular praise when children use discursive language in the way you modelled.

Class log ⓒⒹ

building a rich and varied vocabulary

Purpose: for children to share the process of keeping a class reading, writing and thinking log to record responses to texts and activities in a variety of forms

- Display **CD (file 4.3)** to show the children the illustration of Callum's bedroom/laboratory and his angry mum. Use MT/YT to describe the picture, e.g. say you think the room is *Not just a mess ... it is a chaotic catastrophe. / Mum is not just cross ... she is terrifyingly furious! / The room is not just a bedroom ... it's a laboratory – a mad dream factory!*
- Ask the children to TTYP and think of their own Not just ... for the bedroom, Mum and the laboratory. Take feedback.
- Scribe some of the best ideas into the Class log. If the children wish to add their own Not just ... to the class collection, ask them to write it on a sticky note and put it in the Class log.

Curriculum link: discussion; develop, agree on, and evaluate rules for effective discussion

Big Question

Purpose: for children to develop their skills of argument and discussion through a mini enquiry session based on a philosophical question relating to the work of the day

- Display today's Big Question on **CD (file 4.4):**

  Is it good to disagree with someone? *

- Follow the process as explained on Day 1.

  * This Big Question will be revisited on Day 11 – the first day of the Non-fiction week.

DAY 5

What do I want to know?

Purpose: for children to use their imagination to compose questions to ask a character

- Remind the children that there are lots of things that we don't know about Callum in the story *A Tale of Two Robots*.
- Tell the children to imagine that Callum is coming to visit the class, giving them a chance to ask him some questions. Explain that they will need to think carefully about how he behaves in the story and what happens in the story to help them to make up interesting questions.
- Explain that you have thought of some headings to help them. Write these headings on the board or a flipchart: *Home and family   School and friends   Inventing*
- Now ask the children to choose one of the headings and to TTYP to think of something they would like to know about Callum. Choose a set of partners to feed back. First ask which heading they have chosen and then what they would like to know. Use TOL to model either expanding or narrowing down their idea as necessary and re-wording into the form of a question if required, e.g.

  Partners: *We want to know about his inventing.*

  Teacher: *Well, you could ask Callum what he loves so much about inventing things and what else he has invented. So your question could be: 'What do you love so much about inventing things and what else have you invented?'*

  Or you may simply have to model re-wording a straightforward question by changing the verb and pronoun, e.g.

  Partners: *Was he scared when the robot came alive?*

  Teacher: *That's a great question about Callum's feelings! So your question would be: 'Were you scared when the robot came alive?'*

- Write each question down on the flipchart under its heading and use MT/YT to say the question aloud. Repeat the process until you have at least two questions per heading.
- Check you have a good range of questions about feelings, facts, opinions and imaginings. If not, involve the children in adding some more questions.

Quiz the character 1

Purpose: for children to show their engagement with and imaginative response to a character from the story through role-play

- Make sure you can see the list of questions composed in the last activity, written on the flipchart. Tell the children that *they* are going to be in role as Callum and *you* are going to interview them. Explain that each time you ask a question they will have time to TTYP to think of their answer as Callum. Ask them to TTYP to say (proudly): *'I am Callum and I am an inventor!'*

- Begin with a factual question but remind them that the answer will be from their own imagination in the role of Callum, e.g. we don't have much information about his family so if the question asks *Have you got any brothers or sisters?* they will have to make up an answer. Model how to extend a basic answer, e.g. *Yes, I've got a sister.* to sound more like an answer the Callum we know would give, e.g. *Well, I have got a sister but I'd rather have a robot!*
- Ask the children to TTYP to answer *Have you got any brothers or sisters?* in the role of Callum. Make sure they know that they can have a different answer to their partner. Choose two or three partners to feedback.
- Repeat with other questions, encouraging the children to use what they know about Callum to make inferences about how he might feel or behave.
- Draw some large speech bubbles on the board or a flipchart and scribe a few of their answers in the bubbles. Ask the children to TTYP to share what they now know about Callum.

Quiz the character 2

Purpose: for children to record their ideas in an appropriate form

- Note that you will need to print off **CD (file 5.1)**, one for each child, and one copy of **CD (file 5.2)** before the start of the lesson.
- Give each child a copy of **CD (file 5.1)**. Remind them how you wrote some of their answers in speech bubbles.
- Tell the children to use the questions on the flipchart and the answers they discussed with their partners to write Callum's answers in the empty speech bubbles.
- Remind the children that they are using the first person pronoun in role (speaking as 'I' and 'me') as Callum and to try to echo Callum's attitude and voice as you modelled in Quiz the character 1.
- Tell them to say their answers to their partners before writing them down. You may wish to ask them to paste the speech bubbles sheet into their writing books.
- Choose and photocopy a few speech bubbles to paste in the Class log. You may wish to copy more to display on the wall for this Unit. There is an option to print a large 'talking head' of Callum for a wall display on **CD (file 5.2)**.

> **Curriculum link:** discussing and recording ideas

Personal log

Purpose: for children to keep a personal log for recording and reflecting on their exploration of stories

- Ask the children to think of one question they would like to ask Shannon and one question they would ask Nita, the girl robot. Tell them to write their questions down in their Personal log and then to TTYP to answer each other's questions in role. Choose two or three sets of partners to share their questions and answers.

> discussion; develop, agree on, and evaluate rules for effective discussion

Big Question

Purpose: for children to develop their skills of argument and discussion through a mini enquiry session based on a philosophical question relating to the work of the day

- Display today's Big Question on **CD (file 5.3)**:

  Are machines as important as humans?

- Follow the process as explained on Day 1.

WRITING FICTION

DAY 6

Curriculum link: using dictionaries to check the meaning of words

Story language

Purpose: for children to develop understanding of specific vocabulary used to talk about stories

character   dialogue   narrative   narrator

- Tell the children that there are some words in the dictionary that are useful to know when they are talking about or writing stories. Display **CD (file 6.1)** to show the story language words. Use MT/YT to read each word. You may wish to print them out from **CD (file 6.2)** to display on your Story wall for this unit.
- Click to the next slide to display the front cover of the *Oxford Junior Dictionary*. Click to the third slide to show the entry for the word *character* on p.37. Read the word and its first definition using MT/YT. Click 'Definition' to reveal the next word and its definition (*dialogue*).
- Click to the next slide again to show the entry for the word *narrator*. Read the word and its definition using MT/YT. Then click 'Definition' again to reveal the final word (*narrative*) and its definition. Explain that you will be using these words during the next few days and will be asking the children to recall what they mean!

Year 3 Grammar expressing time and cause using conjunctions

Grammar: conjunctions **HB**

Purpose: for children to develop an understanding of subordinating conjunctions to express cause or time

- Remind the children that a conjunction links words or groups of words together in a sentence.
- Tell the children that when we discuss what has happened and why in stories we are likely to use particular types of conjunctions, to help to explain when things happen (time), or why things happen (cause), e.g. *before, after, while, because, when, so.*
- Use MT/YT to say the sentence below with slight emphasis on the conjunction shown in bold: '*Callum goes to Shannon's house **after** school.*'
- Write the sentence on the board or flipchart and ask the children to TTYP to decide which word is the conjunction. Ask them to give their answers chorally. Clarify that **after** is the conjunction. Underline **after** and explain that it is a linking word that helps us to understand when something happens – it is conjunction expressing time.
- Repeat the process using the following sentences:
  - *Callum's mum gets angry **because** his room is a mess.* (why/cause)
  - *Callum enjoys milkshakes **while** Robert cleans his bedroom!* (when/time)
  - *Ms Shelley introduces Robert **before** she begins the lesson.* (when/time)
  - *Shannon wants to help Robert **so** she introduces him to Nita.* (why/cause)
  - *Robert is very pleased **when** he meets Nita.* (why/cause)
- Now ask the children to TTYP to make up a sentence using any of the conjunctions. Choose two or three to share their sentences. Scribe their examples on the board or flipchart, clarifying and correcting where necessary.
- Tell them that they are very likely to hear or use some of these conjunctions during the next activity as they discuss What if not...? questions.

Homework Book p.12 provides further practice on compound sentences and conjunctions.

Curriculum link:
asking questions
and predicting

What if not . . . ?

Purpose: for children to understand how stories can be changed and developed

- Ask the children to look at the What if not. . . ? activity on p.30 of their Pupils' Book.
- TOL about the first What if not. . . ? question with the children, '*What if not a success? What if Callum's robot invention had gone wrong?*' modelling how you think the story would be different if Callum's robot invention had gone wrong. Use your own ideas and/or use this TOL to help you:

  Well, if the invention went wrong and the robot didn't come alive, then I suppose Callum's mum would have tidied his room and wrecked his laboratory! Perhaps Callum would even have given up being an inventor and taken up a new interest . . . On the other hand, what if the robot did come alive, but it was like the creature Dr Frankenstein made? It could be a monstrous robot that Callum would really regret inventing . . .

- Now use your own TOL to guide the children to TTYP and discuss the next What if not . . . ? question. Emphasise the importance of their own ideas and opinions rather than a 'right' answer. Take feedback, develop their responses and scribe a few key points or ideas on a flipchart or large piece of paper.
- Repeat for the final What if not . . . ? question.

discussing writing
similar to that
which they are
planning to write

Build a sentence ⓒ 🖶

Purpose: for children to participate in shared writing as a model for their own writing

- Tell the children that they are going to look at a sentence written by the author of *A Tale of Two Robots,* from the very end of the story. Display **CD (file 6.3)** to show the sentence: 'In fact, the more untidy Callum and Shannon left their rooms, the happier Robert and Nita seemed to be – it gave them more to talk about, after all.'
- Ask the children to read it out chorally with you. Remind them that one of their What if not . . .? questions was '*What if not . . . happy? What if Robert and Nita were* fed up *cleaning bedrooms all day, every day?*' Ask the children to TTYP and mime looking really fed-up and unhappy. Use MT/YT to say: '*Nita and Robert were fed up.*'
- Tell the children that this would make a good opening sentence for a new episode for *A Tale of Two Robots.* Write the new sentence on the board or a flipchart: *Nita and Robert were fed up.* Use the TOL script on printable **CD (file 6.4)** to develop the sentence orally.
- When you have developed your sentence, ask the children to read the whole Build a sentence chorally with you, using great expression and intonation: '*Nita and Robert were* not just *fed up, they were bored out of their metal minds! They were sick and tired of cleaning those filthy, disgusting bedrooms. *They needed a change and a day out was just the thing. . .*' (Note that you may have a slightly different last line.)
- Explain that you really like the idea of Nita and Robert going out by themselves and it would make a good starting point for a new episode to add to the story.

Personal log

Curriculum link: composing and rehearsing sentences orally; increasing range of sentence structures

Purpose: for children to keep a personal log for recording and reflecting on their exploration of stories

- Before the lesson, print a copy of **CD (file 6.5)** for each pair of children.
- Tell the children that they were really helpful when you were composing your sentences and now you want to help them to write their own. Distribute copies of the printed **CD (file 6.5)**. (Note that this printout could be adapted for differentiation for different ability groups, if you wish.) Ask them to look at Section A first. Guide them through the instructions and prompts and explain how they can compose their own sentence as a beginning for a new episode for the story *A Tale of Two Robots*.
- Ask the children, either individually or working as partners to compose the first version of their own sentence orally. Remind them to TTYP to share what they want to say before they write in their Personal log.
- Now ask the children to look at Section B. Explain that they are going to use the prompts to develop, edit and improve their writing. Read through the instructions and ideas with the children to check their understanding. Tell them to TTYP to try out their improvement orally first. Then encourage crossings out, changing punctuation and adding adjectives or using synonyms in the way you modelled during Build a sentence. Make sure they understand that this is writing in action, not a neat, finished piece of writing.

Big Question

discussion; develop, agree on, and evaluate rules for effective discussion

Purpose: for children to develop their skills of argument and discussion through a mini enquiry session based on a philosophical question relating to the work of the day

- Display today's Big Question on **CD (file 6.6)**:

  Are we like characters in a story?

- Follow the process as explained on Day 1.

Build a story 1

plan writing by discussing writing that is similar

Purpose: for children to see a story grow through three stages of development as a model and stimulus for their own writing

- Tell the children that you have thought of some questions to help you plan the next part of your new episode for *A Tale of Two Robots*. Display **CD (file 7.1)** to show the questions.
- Explain that the first two questions were easy for you to answer as you planned the story, as they were linked to the What if not. . . ? activity and the writing in Build a sentence. Click to the next slide to show the answers to the first two questions.
- Say that you had trouble thinking of ideas to answer some of the other questions and then you remembered the Story laboratory. Remind the children that they found clues about *A Tale of Two Robots* in the Story laboratory last week.
- Tell them that because you were experimenting with ideas for a new episode, you had another look in the Story laboratory to get some ideas. Click on to the next slide to show the Story laboratory. Click on the steaming test tube, the bubbling bottle and the top drawer to show three new scenes and thought bubbles.
- Use each 'TOL' bubble to talk about how you might use each idea for the new episode. Tell the children that you can now show them the answers you came up with based on the items in the Story laboratory. Click to the next slide to show the questions and answers.

- Say that you can now show them the first version of your new episode. Click to the last couple of slides to show an outline of the first version of your new episode. Read it aloud to the children.
- Ask the children to TTYP to talk about whether they think Robert and Nita go straight home or pop into the rubbish tip and recycling centre first. Collect feedback and encourage them to explain their predictions.
- Explain that this is just the bare bones of a story and it will be developed further later on and then they will find out more about the ending!

Curriculum link: composing and rehearsing sentences orally; creating settings, characters, plot

Write a story 1

Purpose: for children to plan the first stage of their story

- Note that you will need to print out copies of **CD (file 7.3)** before the start of this day's lesson. This Word file can be adapted for differentiation if required.
- Tell the children that they are going to plan and write their own first version of the robots' day out. Explain that if the Story laboratory had given you other ideas, your new episode would have looked a bit different.
- Display **CD (file 7.2)** to show the Write a story 1 grid and notes. Use the notes to explain what you could change to develop the story further. (The changes to the text are highlighted.)
- Remind them that this is the bare bones of a new episode and they are now going to experiment using the Story laboratory to write their own bare bones of a new episode.
- Give out copies of the printable **CD (file 7.3).** Talk the children through the process of using the headings and the prompts from the Story laboratory to plan their own new episode.
- Remind them to TTYP to share ideas. Choose two or three to share with the whole class. Explain (model if necessary) how to write their plan using the headings in the boxes to organise their ideas.
- Ask them to TTYP to share their new story plan and compare choices they each made and why. Choose two or three to read out their plan.

preparing playscripts to perform

Role-play and dialogue ▲

Purpose: for children to empathise with characters through drama and develop ideas for dialogue, to use later in their writing

- Ask the children to look at p.36 of their Anthology and to TTYP to find a piece of dialogue. Choose two or three sets of partners to share the dialogue they have found and ask them to say how they knew it was dialogue. Clarify where necessary.
- You may wish to write one of their examples on the board or flipchart to use to talk through inverted commas and the conventions of writing dialogue.
- Tell the children that it would be good to have some dialogue to add to their new story sentences. Say that they are going to create a mini role-play to help them.
- Display the **CD (file 7.4)**. Guide the children through the scenario and prompts.
- Give them time to plan a very short role-play and then ask them to perform it, with half of the class performing at a time. Ensure children select a pair from the other half of the class to watch when it is their turn to observe.
- Walk round noting good dialogue to scribe on the board or flipchart as a model for writing dialogue again, ready for them to use in their new episodes later in the week.
- Now ask the children to write a short piece of dialogue between Robert and Nita.

<table>
<tr><td>

Curriculum link:
discussion; develop, agree on, and evaluate rules for effective discussion

</td></tr>
</table>

Big Question

Purpose: for children to develop their skills of argument and discussion through a mini enquiry session based on a philosophical question relating to the work of the day

- Display today's Big Question on **CD (file 7.5):**

  Is it wrong to be bored?

- Follow the process as explained on Day 1.

DAY 8

> plan writing by discussing writing that is similar, recording ideas

Build a story 2

Purpose: for children to see a story grow through three stages of development as a model and stimulus for their own writing

- Tell the children they are now going to see another version of your new episode with a lot more detail added. Explain that to develop your episode, you had to decide: what to keep, what to change, and what new information, dialogue, action or descriptions to add.
- Display **CD (file 8.1)** to show Build a story 2. Go through all four slides, reading the text aloud to or with the children.
- Then, look at each slide separately, clicking on 'Highlights' to show what has been added to each section and showing the author notes in the think bubbles. Use these to draw the children into a TOL to identify additional information, adjectives and detail.
- Ask them to TTYP to discuss the best thing about the new version. Choose two or three to share what they think.

> composing and rehearsing sentences orally; creating settings, characters, plot

Write a story 2

Purpose: for children to plan the second stage of their story

- Note that you will need to print copies of **CD (file 8.3)** before the activity begins, unless you wish the children to word process their stories.
- Tell the children to look at the first version of their own new episode and to read it through to remind themselves of what they have written. Display **CD (file 8.2)** which shows some prompts to help the children decide what they want to keep, change or create.
- Tell them to experiment, crossing out and inserting words and sharing ideas with their partners.
- When they are happy with their revised story, give each child a copy of printable **CD (file 8.3)**.
- Explain that you want them to copy their Build a sentence writing, and their dialogue from Days 6 and 7 into the top boxes of the sheet.
- Now tell them to copy their revised story into the appropriate boxes.

> discussing and recording ideas

Class log and Personal log

Purpose: for children to share the process of keeping a class reading, writing and thinking log to record responses to texts and activities in a variety of forms

- Tell the children you have been thinking that if their own new episode was a chapter in *A Tale of Two Robots,* it would need a title or heading. Clarify what a chapter is using books from your bookshelf.
- Ask the children to TTYP to think of a couple of appropriate chapter titles, and note them down in their Personal log.
- Choose two or three to share their chapter titles and then ask them to choose some to write in the Class log. Ask them to write their favourite chapter title from the class feedback in their Personal log.

Curriculum link:
discussion; develop, agree on, and evaluate rules for effective discussion

Big Question

Purpose: for children to develop their skills of argument and discussion through a mini enquiry session based on a philosophical question relating to the work of the day

- Display today's Big Question on **CD (file 8.4):**

  Is disappointment always a bad thing?

- Follow the process as explained on Day 1.

DAY 9

understand the skills and processes that are essential for writing

Build a story 3

Purpose: for children to see a story grow through three stages of development as a model and stimulus for their own writing

- Note that you will need to print out copies of **CD (file 9.2)** before this lesson begins.
- Explain to the children that you emailed your latest story version to a writer friend and asked for advice on how to improve it. Say she has emailed back with some suggestions. Display **CD (file 9.1)** to show the email and read it aloud to the children.
- Tell them that this helped you to write a third version of the new episode and you can now share it with them. Give out copies of the printed **CD (file 9.2)** which shows the whole story – version 3.
- Read it aloud to the children with enthusiasm and appropriate intonation.

assessing the effectiveness of others' writing

Evaluate a story

Purpose: for children to evaluate the modelled writing

- Ask the children to take turns reading a section each of your new episode.
- When they have read the whole new episode, display **CD (file 9.3)**. Read through the first question and ask them to TTYP to answer it. Choose two or three to feed back. TOL about their ideas and evaluations. Repeat the process for each question.

preparing playscripts to perform, showing understanding through intonation, tone and action

Dramatic reconstruction 1

Purpose: for children to explore narrative point of view through oral storytelling from the point of view of one character

- Tell the children that they are going to listen to two short role-plays of Robert and Nita telling Callum and Shannon about their day out based on your new episode.
- Display the first slide on **CD (file 9.4)** which shows Robert telling Callum about the trip to the beach, from his point of view. Click the audio button to listen to the recording.
- Click to the next slide to see Nita telling Shannon about the same trip to the beach from her point of view. Click the audio button to listen to the recording.
- Click to the third slide to see questions about these two role-plays. Ask the children to TTYP to talk about their answers to the questions on display.
- Now tell the children to look at the Dramatic reconstruction 1 activity on p.31 of their Pupils' Book and explain how they can use the prompts to plan their own role-plays.
- Note, praise and record good examples of points of view shown through what they say in role as well as good, co-operative partner work.
- You may need set aside time on Day 10 to allow all the children to perform their role-plays.

Personal log (CD)

Purpose: for children to keep a personal log for recording and reflecting on their exploration of stories

- Tell the children they are going to listen to the two role-plays once more. Play the audio on **CD (file 9.4)** again.
- Ask the children to decide whose point of view they agree with most and then to TTYP to share their thoughts and the reasons for their choice.
- Now ask them to write a couple of sentences explaining whose point of view they agreed with most of all and why. They should write it in their Personal log under the heading *What do I think?*

Who says? (CD)

Purpose: for children to develop awareness of narrators in stories

- Remind the children that the role-plays they listened to and performed gave us a character's personal point of view as they explained or *narrated* what happened on the day out.
- Explain that when a writer creates a story, she or he has to decide who is going to explain or *narrate* what is happening, where it is happening and who is involved.
- Explain that the *narrator* in your new episode and the new episode they have written isn't a *character* in the story but a separate *narrator* who just tells us who is who and what happens without taking sides or showing us a particular *point of view.*
- Display **CD (file 10.1)** to show an extract from your new episode of the story. Click on 'Highlights' to highlight the *narrative.* Tell the children that they will read the narrator's words and you will read the characters' *dialogue.* Remind children that dialogue/direct speech can be recognised by its layout and punctuation with inverted commas.
- The children should read the highlighted parts of the text chorally.
- Explain that some stories have one of the characters as the narrator and they tell the story from their own point of view. Say that you decided you would like Robert the robot to narrate the story and you have had a go at changing the narrator. Click to the next slide to show the same extract written from Robert's point of view. Ask the children to join in with you to read the extract aloud.
- Click 'Highlights' to show how you have changed the personal pronouns to make it a first person narrative (i.e. Robert telling the story himself).

Write a story 3 (CD)

Purpose: for children to experiment with narrative in their own writing

- Ask the children to TTYP to re-read their own new episode written on Day 8, from printable **CD (file 8.3).**
- Tell them to choose one short section of their own story to change into a first person narrative in the way you modelled. Remind them to think about how they had to use the pronouns *I* and *we* instead of *he, she,* and *they* in their dramatic reconstruction. Ask them to TTYP to share their ideas about which part of their story they want to change and what they want to write.
- Choose two or three to share ideas with the whole class. Re-phrase and clarify where necessary and scribe a few examples on the board or a flipchart.

- Remind them to say their first person narrative to their partner before writing it down in their Personal log. It is important for children to feel confident about experimenting with narrative rather than focusing on 'getting it right' first time.

Evaluate and edit

Purpose: for children to evaluate their own and their partner's work against specific criteria and then discuss how they could improve their work

Curriculum link: assessing the effectiveness of their own and others' writing

- Display **CD (file 10.2)** to show the evaluation prompts and read them together using MT/YT.
- As a model, select an example of work where the writing has met the criteria, and share this with the other children, explaining why it works well.
- Tell the children to take turns to read their partner's writing in pairs and discuss together how well each piece of writing has met the criteria.
- Ask children to discuss at least two changes they could make to improve their work.

Proofread

Purpose: for children to proofread their work and make changes to improve the accuracy of their grammar, punctuation and spelling

proofread for spelling and punctuation errors

- Now ask children to proofread their work. If you have noticed that several children need to improve on a particular aspect of spelling, grammar or punctuation, use this as a focus for the Proofread activity. Write an example which includes common errors from the children's writing and use this as a model.
- The children should always be checking for standard use of punctuation and correct spelling of common exception words.
- The following points would be relevant as the particular focus for this Unit:
  - using third person narrative or first person narrative consistently, as appropriate
  - checking their punctuation of direct speech.

Dramatic reconstruction 2

Purpose: for children to use drama to reconstruct mind pictures

justifying inferences with evidence; predicting what might happen from details stated and implied

- Remind the children of your new episode about the visit to the zoo, when Robert is thrown out of the chimps' enclosure. Say that you thought it would be interesting to have the zoo keeper's point of view of the same incident.
- Ask the children to TTYP to discuss how they think the zoo keeper might describe what happened. To encourage inferential thinking and empathetic responses, explain that they need to think about the different reasons *why* the zoo keeper was angry with Robert, e.g. *he felt responsible for Robert's safety, he didn't want the chimps to be frightened, he was worried that he hadn't seen what was happening in time to stop it, he thought Robert might be trying to set the chimps free.*
- Choose two or three sets of partners to feed back and encourage them to give reasons for their answers. Tell the children that Partner 1 is Robert in the chimp's enclosure and Partner 2 is the zoo keeper at the moment he spots Robert and shouts at him.
- Ask them to TTYP and take turns to say, in role, what they were thinking and feeling at that moment. Choose two or three to share their ideas. Explain that you want them to create a freeze frame of that moment at the zoo.

- Allow time for them to plan and practise. Ask them to freeze their frames on the count of three.
- You may wish to extend the activity through *thought tapping*. Tap a child on the shoulder and ask them to say what they are feeling or thinking (in their role). Repeat with a few other children.

Curriculum link:
discussing and
recording ideas

Class log

Purpose: for children to share the process of keeping a class reading, writing and thinking log to record responses to texts and activities in a variety of forms

- Tell the children that the story *A Tale of Two Robots* was written by the author Roy Apps, who has written many books for children.
- Explain that he has his own website (www.royapps.co.uk) that has answers to the Top 10 questions that children have asked him about his life as a writer and his books.
- Ask the children to TTYP to think of at least one question that they would like to ask Roy Apps, if they could.
- Take feedback, paraphrase and scribe their questions in the Class log under the heading *Questions for Mr Apps*. You may wish to show the website and look at the questions that other children have asked and to see if their own questions are there.

Further activity

- Ask the children to type up their new episode, making any changes from the Evaluate and edit and Proofread activities. They could also design a front cover and write a blurb for their episode.

Discussion texts

READING AND WRITING NON-FICTION

In the Non-fiction reading and writing week, the focus is on understanding the structure and purpose of a text that gives a balanced argument on a topic, i.e. a discussion text. Children will explore discussion texts that about how long break times should be and whether books or computer games are more worthwhile. They will also participate in a class debate about whether dogs or cats make better pets.

See p.70 for the daily timetable for the Non-fiction week.

Non-fiction

Reading

Children will:

- consider what makes a discussion balanced
- look at the language we use to structure a balanced and discursive argument
- role-play a debate in order to engage fully with both points of view.

Writing

Key writing purposes to be shared with the children:

To write a balanced discussion text about whether break times are too short.

My discussion text:

- is balanced (it includes statements that show I have thought about both sides of the argument)
- shares information with the reader in clear sentences that make sense
- shows clearly what is a fact and what is an opinion.

Grammar:

- includes adverbs and adverbials to show that I am considering both sides of the argument, e.g. *Some people think that, However, On the other hand.*

See the Planning section of the Software ('Timetables' tab) for a printable version of the Writing purpose and evaluation.

(DAY 11)

Curriculum link:
learn the
conventions of
different types
of writing

Think and link

Purpose: for children to become interested in discussion and argument texts via one of the Big Questions they have explored

- Remind the children that all of the Big Questions that you have looked at together have helped you to share opinions about something.
- Display the Big Question from Day 4 on **CD (file 4.4):**

  Is it good to disagree with someone?

- Ask the children to TTYP to recall some of the *opinions* they shared and take feedback. Give special emphasis to the words in italics (in these teaching notes) whenever you say them throughout this first non-fiction day.
- Point out to the children that if we only heard from people who thought it is good to *disagree* with someone, we would only hear one *side of the argument* or set of *opinions*.
- Display **CD (file 11.1)**. Explain that it shows a set of balance scales. Click on 'No' to reveal the statements which support the negative response to the question. Watch the scales tip and TOL to explain that this is not a *balanced* argument at this point.
- Then click on 'Yes' to reveal the statements that support the positive response to the question. Watch the scales tip the other way and TOL to explain that now the scales are balanced – there are equal positive and negative responses to the question, so we have a *balanced argument*.
- Explain that when we have a text that shows a balance of arguments (both sides of the argument), we call it a *discussion text*.

Human scales

Purpose: for children to develop awareness of different points of view and balance in arguments, and to practise using vocabulary associated with discussion texts

- Clear a space for children to move about in the classroom or take them into a hall or studio. Ask them to stand up. Tell the children that you have chosen one side or corner of the room as the *agree* corner and the opposite one as the *disagree* corner and they are going to be like human *balance* scales. (If necessary, label the two corners.)
- Explain that you are going to make a *statement* and when you say '*go*' they should walk to the *agree* or *disagree* corner. If they are not sure or undecided, they should remain in the middle.
- Tell them to think carefully about each statement you read before making up their mind. Ensure you allow enough time for this.
- Once they are in their places after each statement, comment on the number and balance of *agrees* and *disagrees* and ask them to turn to the person next to them to ask them why they chose to agree or disagree.
- Choose two or three children from each area to share one reason for their choice with the whole group and tell the children that they can move to the opposite corner if they change their own *point of view*.
- Use the first statement and then the others or make up some of your own, e.g. '*There must be life on other planets.*' (Use this statement as you will re-use it on Day 12.) '*Dogs make better pets than cats. School holidays are too short. Robots are more intelligent than humans. Children should have to work for their pocket money. Pop stars should not get more pay than firefighters. Chips should be banned from school lunches.*'

Discussion words

Purpose: for children to become familiar with some words associated with discussion texts

> *statement   balanced   point of view   conclusion*

- Tell the children that they have already been using some special words and phrases that are useful when talking about or writing about discussion texts. Explain that there are other special words that are useful for this too.
- Display **CD (file 11.2)** to show some of these words. Use MT/YT to read them with the children. Click 'Reveal' to show a definition for each term. Use MT/YT to read them with the children. These words and definitions can be printed from **CD (file 11.3)** for display on your Discussion text wall.
- Now ask the children to look at the Discussion words activity on pp.32–33 of their Pupils' Book. Ask them to TTYP to complete the first part of the activity, then explain the second part of the activity and ask them to complete it together.
- Choose two or three partners to share their answers. Clarify where necessary.

Curriculum link:
learn the conventions of different types of writing

Class log

Purpose: for children to share the process of keeping a class reading, writing and thinking log to record responses to texts and activities in a variety of forms

- Tell the children that you are going to start a new section in the Class log, called *Discussion texts*. Write the heading at the top of a new right-hand page.
- Ask them to TTYP to think of a statement that people could agree or disagree with, e.g. *pizza is better than pasta*.
- Take feedback and use MT/YT to say their statements. Some children will ask a question rather than make a statement so make sure you model turning questions into statements, e.g. Do you think pizza is better than pasta? '*That is a good question, so our statement would be* pizza is better than pasta.'
- Scribe some of their statements in the Class log.
- Now ask the children to Popcorn any special discussion words that they have been learning, and scribe their answers in large writing in the Class log.
- You may wish to draw or paste a picture of some balance scales on the same page, to remind children of the need to balance viewpoints in a discussion text.

DAY 12

Grammar: adverbs and adverbials

Purpose: for children to become familiar with some words and phrases associated with discussion texts

Year 3 Grammar adverbs

- Explain to the children that discussion texts usually contain useful words and phrases that help the writer to organise and connect different points of view and make them clear to the reader.
- Display **CD (file 12.1)** to show some examples of these words and phrases. Use MT/YT to say them.
- Remind the children that one of the statements they heard when they played Human scales (Day 11) was *There must be life on other planets*. Click to the next slide to show a piece of text based on that statement. Click 'Highlights' to highlight the discussion words and phrases that are used to structure the argument.
- Tell the children that you are going to read the text aloud and they should follow it and read aloud all the highlighted phrases.
- Explain that you want the children to look out for these discussion phrases as they explore more discussion texts during the week. Remind them also to listen out for them when they are watching TV news or discussion programmes.

- You may wish to print these and other useful discussion phrases from printable **CD (file 12.2)** to display on your Discussion wall.

Deconstruction 1 ▲ (CD)

Curriculum link:
discussing writing
similar to that
which they are
planning to write;
using simple
organisational
devices such as
headings and
subheadings

Purpose: for children to develop awareness of the structure of written discussions

- Tell the children to look at the 'Nose in a Book or Eyes on the Game?' text on pp.46–47 of their Anthology. Explain that it is a discussion text that looks at both sides of an argument.
- Now ask the children to TTYP and take turns to read a paragraph of the text each.
- On the board or a flipchart, write two headings: *Books rule OK!* and *Computer games rule OK!*
- Display **CD (file 12.3)** which shows a small section of the text on the first slide. Ask the children to TTYP to identify the same section in their Anthology.
- Explain that Partner 1 is to read the section to Partner 2. Then they should TTYP to say in their own words what the point of view is in that section of the text.
- Choose two to feed back and then ask the class to give a choral response to the question *'which heading should I put it under?'*.
- Scribe under the appropriate heading, e.g. *you can find information from the Internet and most jobs need computer skills* under the heading 'Computer games rule OK!' Some sections may have more than one argument for or against.
- Click to the next slide to show a different section of the text and repeat the process. Go through all six sections of text to complete the activity.

Write 1 ▲

composing
and rehearsing
sentences orally;
creating settings,
characters, plot

Purpose: for children to act in role to explore two sides of an argument, to prepare for writing a structured argument

- Tell the children that they are going to turn the points of view in the Anthology text into a role-play of an argument about books versus computer games. Organise groups of four by joining together two pairs. One pair will argue that books are best and one pair will argue that computer games are best.
- Remind them that they have the points on the flipchart or board to help them to create their role-play but you would like them to think of their own arguments as well and to use their own words.
- Tell the children to TTYP to take turns to read the arguments on the flipchart or board and/or re-read the text on pp.46–47 of their Anthology.
- Allow enough time for the children to create one more argument each and to plan and practise their role-plays as friends arguing about it in the local park. Remind them to take turns in giving 'their' point of view.
- Walk around as they work, noting examples of good arguments on both sides. Give feedback based on what you have seen and heard during the performances.

Personal log

discussing and
recording ideas;
composing
and rehearsing
sentences orally;
increasing range
of sentence
structures

Purpose: for children to keep a personal log for recording and reflecting on their exploration of discussion texts

- Ask the children to TTYP to share what their own opinion is on which is best – a book or a computer game. Emphasise that they don't have to take the same viewpoint at they expressed during the role-play. Choose two or three to feed back and encourage them to give their reasons.

- Now ask them to write the statement: *Books are better than computer games*, in their Personal log. Tell them to TTYP to say to their partner *I agree with this statement because . . .* (adding one reason why they agree) **or** *I disagree with this statement because . . .* (adding one reason why they disagree). Explain that once they have said their whole sentence to their partner, they can write it in their Personal log.
- Ask the whole class to do 'thumbs up or down' to show whether they have agreed or disagreed with the statement: *Books are better than computer games*. Comment on the balance in the class between the two points of view.

DAY 13

Hear it

Purpose: for children to experience discussions and arguments in informal, spoken form

- Tell the children that they are going to look at how different points of view can be expressed in spoken form. Explain that when we are just discussing or arguing about something with our friends, we use informal, everyday language.
- Display **CD (file 13.1)**. Explain that the four small pictures are the storyboard for a scene which takes place at a school, where four friends are arguing. Tell the children that they are going to listen to the argument. Click on each image to hear the relevant audio file.
- Ask the children to TTYP to say what they think the main argument is about. Choose two to feed back.
- Now ask them to TTYP to recall one argument they heard for or against having a longer break. Choose two or three to feed back and paraphrase to clarify answers. You may wish to play the audio files again to allow them to become more familiar with the different arguments.
- Ask the children to look at the 'How Long Should Break Be?' text on pp.48–51 of their Anthology to see the full transcript of the discussion.
- Say that Partner 1 will be both Sally and Joe and Partner 2 will be both Matt and Eve. Set the scene for them again and ask them to read their parts aloud. Remind them to think about using tone, volume and intonation to convey meaning and impact.

Deconstruction 2

Purpose: for children to develop their ability to identify different points of view

Curriculum link: discussing writing similar to that which they are planning to write; using non-fiction, know what information they need to look for before they begin

- Tell the children that they are going to help you to explore the transcript to identify the main statement which triggers the discussion and then to see how balanced the following argument is.
- Ask them to look at the 'How Long Should Break Be?' text pp.48–51 of their Anthology and to TTYP to find the part of the text that gives the statement they end up discussing or arguing about. You may wish to give them some help by telling them it is Matt who makes the statement.
- Collect feedback and make sure they have identified the statement 'Break times are way too short' (spoken by Matt on p.49). Now ask them to TTYP to look at the text to decide who thinks that break times are too short and who thinks they should stay as they are. Collect feedback.
- Point out that Sally tries to convince the others by making up two outrageous 'facts' that are unlikely to be true. Ask them to TTYP to find Sally's 'facts'. (She claims that running tires out your brain, and that schools with longer breaks get worse test results.)
- Explain that in discussions it is important to stick to proven facts to support your point of view. Made-up facts do not count!

Organise it (CD)

Purpose: for children to see how to organise a discussion text as a model for their own writing

- Remind the children that if we wanted to write the main points of the argument as a discussion text, we would need to make them clearer and organise them to make a more balanced argument.
- Display **CD (file 13.2).** Point out the statement that 'School break times should be longer' at the top of the screen. Explain that under that statement are some points or arguments that Sally, Matt, Joe and Eve made in the Anthology text. There is also a conclusion that sums up the arguments and makes suggestions: 'There should be more time, with indoor activities and buddy patrols.'
- Tell the children that all of the statements are in the wrong order! Use MT/YT to read out the statements in the panels. Ask them to TTYP to say how they sound different from the words used by the children in the Anthology. Encourage them to express their own ideas and to pick up that they are not in the language they would use when chatting to their friends; it is more formal because it is being written down for others to read.
- Point out the ticks and crosses on the right hand side of the screen. Say that ticks show arguments that agree with the statement and the crosses show the arguments that disagree with the statement. Tell the children they are going to help you sort the statements into the right order (putting them against a tick or a cross, as appropriate).
- Pick any argument, agreeing or disagreeing with the statement from the bank and ask the children to tell you which part of the grid you should drag and drop it into: either a row with a tick or a row with a cross. TOL: *'Does this support the view that school break times should be longer?'*
- Repeat with all the sentences.
- Now go to the next screen where the points of view are already in place on the grid. (Note that the order may differ slightly from the order in which you placed them on the previous screen, but some variation is fine.) Point out the gaps in the text. Explain that you need to choose suitable phrases to fill these gaps. When you click on the gaps, a choice of phrases appears. Remind the children that these phrases link the arguments to help us to see that we have different sides of a discussion.
- TOL as you model choosing a discursive phrase to drag and drop into the gaps in the sentences.
- When you have filled all the gaps, ask the children to read the whole 'text' chorally with you putting great emphasis on the discursive phrase.
- Ask them to TTYP to say why Sally's made up 'facts' were not included. Choose two to feed back.

Write 2

Purpose: for children to write their own discussion text based on some example points of view

- Note that differentiated printable files need to be printed before the lesson starts.
- Explain to the children that they are now going to write their own discussion text showing different sides of the argument about school break times being too short.
- Give each child a copy of either **CD (file 13.3 a, b** or **c).** These are differentiated, with **13.3a** giving the most support and **13.3c** giving the least support. Hold up an enlarged copy of the printed **file 13.3b.** Explain to the children how to use the prompts and boxes to create their sentences and organise their writing.
- Explain that they can use any of the points that Matt, Sally, Eve and Joe made in the Anthology text but they can also make up their own. Remind them to say their sentences to their partner before they write them down.

Curriculum link: composing and rehearsing sentences orally; creating settings, characters, plot

- Walk around as they work giving support, praise and noting things to clarify with the whole class. You may need to allocate the first part of Day 14 to allow the children to complete their writing.

Curriculum link: discussing and recording ideas

Class log

Purpose: for children to share the process of keeping a class reading, writing and thinking log to record responses to texts and activities in a variety of forms

- Tell the children that reading, role-playing and writing about the points of view of Sally, Joe, Matt and Eve will have helped them to decide what their own point of view is on whether break-times should be longer in the school day.
- Ask them to TTYP to share their point of view for or against longer breaks, with a supporting argument.
- Use MT/YT to say the statement '*Our class had a vote for or against school break-times being made longer.*' Scribe the statement in the Class log and then add *For* and *Against* headings.
- Take a class vote and record the result. Now choose two children who voted *for* longer breaks to share their reasons. Scribe their reasons in the Class log. Repeat the process to record a couple of reasons *against* longer breaks.

DAY 14

assessing the effectiveness of their own and others' writing

Evaluate, edit and proofread ⓒⒹ

Purpose: for children to develop their ability to evaluate writing and to make changes to improve their own writing

- If necessary, allow time for the children to complete their writing from Day 13.
- When they have finished, display **CD (file 14.1)** to show an example of a child's writing. Make sure the children know that this is from a child in a different school who completed a similar activity to the one they have just finished.
- Read the piece of writing aloud exactly as it is written. Then explain that you are going to look at some questions that will help you to evaluate the writing. Click on 'Questions' to show the first question: *Do all the sentences make sense?*
- Read out the question and ask the children to TTYP to use it to evaluate the writing. Take feedback and then use TOL to sum up the comments, e.g. '*The first point of view is really clear but the next one is a bit muddled up. The writer needs to say it aloud to hear which bits don't make sense.* TTYP *to decide how you would write the same point of view.*'
- Click on 'Questions' to show the second question: *Is it a balanced discussion?* After the children have discussed this, use TOL to sum up the comments, e.g. '*It is a balanced discussion – there are two sentences agreeing with the statement and two sentences disagreeing with the statement.*'
- Click on 'Questions' again to show the third question: *Has the writer used language appropriate for discussion?* Look carefully at the discursive language, such as *On the other hand,* conjunctions and adverbs such as *However* and ask the children to TTYP to talk about how these signposts help the reader. Take feedback, drawing out how they link the different arguments in the text together.
- Click on 'Questions' again to show the last question: *Is the spelling and punctuation correct?* After reading it, ask the children to TTYP to talk about any spelling or punctuation errors. Ensure they spot the incorrect spelling of *because, their* and *naughty.* Prompt the children to check the use of capital letters and full stops.
- Now ask the children to read their own writing and evaluate it using the same questions. Tell them to TTYP to share their self-evaluations and discuss at least two changes they would make to their work to improve it. Choose two or three partners to share their feedback with the whole class.

Fact or opinion? ⓒⒹ

Note that you will need to prepare pieces of A5 card and felt pens for each child before the lesson begins.

Purpose: for children to develop their ability to identify facts and opinions and an awareness of how they can support an opinion

- Give each child a piece of card and a thick felt pen. Ask them to write the word *Fact* on one side of the card and *Opinion* on the other side.
- Ask them to TTYP to explain what a fact is. Choose two or three sets of partners to share their definitions and (using their words if possible) create a composite sentence that gives a simple explanation, e.g. *a fact is something that we know is true*. Scribe the sentence on the board or flipchart and say that you will add it to the Class log later on.
- Repeat the process for Opinion, e.g. *an opinion is what we think of something but others might think differently*.
- Remind the children of the Human scales activity they took part in on Day 11, and ask them to TTYP to decide whether they were giving facts or opinions in response to the statements.
- Ask them to Popcorn their answers. Clarify if necessary, that they moved to the *agree* or *disagree* corners based on their own opinions.
- Say that you are going to make some more statements and this time instead of agreeing or disagreeing, they should decide if each one contains a fact or an opinion. Ask them to hold up the Fact or Opinion side of their card.
  Use these statements or make up your own, but ensure a mix of facts and opinions:
  - *'Snakes do not have legs. Snakes are scary.'*
  - *'Winter is the most exciting time of the year. Winter follows autumn in the year.'*
  - *'This classroom has chairs in it. The tables and chairs in this classroom are comfortable.'*
  - *'Dogs make better pets than cats. Dogs and cats are kept as pets.'*
- When the children hold their cards up, check their understanding and clarify where necessary.
- Now tell them that facts and opinions are a bit harder to find when they are 'hidden' in a piece of writing. Display the **CD (file 14.2)**. Ask the children to spot the fact and opinion in each sentence. Allow time for them to TTYP and talk about each sentence, then check their understanding by asking them to use their Fact and Opinion cards again. Use the 'Highlights' button to reveal first the facts and then the opinions on the slide.
- Now click to the next slide and read the paragraph aloud. Ask the children to TTYP to spot the facts.
- Collect responses and click 'Highlights' to reveal the facts. Discuss how they identified the trickier ones to spot in the text. (Draw out that facts can be proven but opinions are personal and can vary.)
- Ask children to TTYP and remind each other of the definition of a fact and an opinion.

> **Curriculum link:**
> discussing and recording ideas

Personal log

Purpose: for children to keep a personal log for recording and reflecting on their exploration of discussion texts

- Tell the children that tomorrow is a special day because they are going to have a big debate or discussion about a topic that people usually feel quite strongly about.

- Explain that one way of recording different points of view about the topic is on a mind map.
- On a large piece of paper create the centre piece of a mind map. In the central panel write the question: *Best pets: dogs or cats?* Draw one branch on either side of the panel, one labelled *Dogs* the other *Cats*. You will be adding to both sides, so allow plenty of space for writing arguments.
- TOL about the question to start off the discussion and ask the children to TTYP to think of a reason why a dog makes a good pet.
- Collect feedback. Add a branch with an appropriate symbol (e.g. thumbs up or a plus sign), label it *Dogs* and scribe one or two answers.
- Repeat the process for why a cat makes a good pet. Repeat a couple of times for each animal. Use one colour for all the positives relating to both dogs and cats.
- Now ask the children to TTYP to think about reasons *not* to have a dog as a pet. Use a new branch with an appropriate symbol (e.g. thumbs down or a minus sign) to record negatives for dogs. Repeat the process for cats. Remember to use a different colour for the negatives relating to both dogs and cats.
- Explain that this will be useful to help them to decide their own point of view for tomorrow's debate.
- Display and retain the mind map as you will need to use it again on Day 15.
- Ask the children to decide which side they would take at the moment. Do they think a cat or a dog would make the best pet? Say that they should TTYP to tell their partner what they think at the moment and to give one reason why. Once they have said it to their partner, they should write their choice and a reason why in their Personal log.

DAY 15

Deconstruction 3 PB

Purpose: for children to use facts and opinions to form their own point of a view about a topic

Curriculum link:
discussing writing similar to that which they are planning to write; using non-fiction, know what information they need to look for before they begin

- Point to the mind map you created and displayed on Day 14. Remind the children that today they are going to debate which animal makes the best pet, a cat or a dog.
- Ask them to look at the Deconstruction 3 activity on pp.34–35 of their Pupils' Book. Explain that they can see two leaflets that give information about the good and bad sides of keeping cats and dogs as pets.
- Tell them to TTYP to take turns reading leaflet A. Choose two to feed back whether there were any reasons for choosing a dog or not choosing a dog to add to the Class log mind map. Add any positives or negatives to the mind map about keeping a dog that they identify. Ask them to TTYP to take turns to read leaflet B and repeat the process for cats as pets.
- Now tell the children to look at the point of view they wrote in their Personal log on Day 14. Ask them to TTYP to share whether they have changed their mind after finding out so much more about cats and dogs as pets or whether they still think the same way and why.
- Ask them to add one more reason to why they agree with their original choice or to write a reason for a new choice if they have changed their point of view.

creating settings, characters, plot; monitor whether their writing makes sense

Write 3 CD

Purpose: for children to participate in a whole class debate and vote

- The children will be taking part in a whole class debate as if they are participating in a live TV studio debate. Make sure you arrange the room appropriately for effective discussion. You may wish to arrange for this part of the lesson to be filmed so that children can watch it back and comment on it at a later date.

- Give each child a piece of card and a thick felt pen. Ask them to write *Agree* in large letters on one side and *Disagree* on the other side.
- Tell the children that they are going to take part in a mock children's TV programme called *Telly Talkers!* Explain that the 'programme' is a children's live studio debate show, which is going to discuss whether cats or dogs make the best pets.
- Ask for two volunteers to 'open' the debate: one to say why they think dogs make the best pets, and one to say why they think cats make the best pets. If necessary, allow them a short time to prepare their short, opening statements.
- You, the teacher, will be in the role of the TV presenter during the debate. Display **CD (file 15.1)** to show the introduction to *Telly Talkers!* (starting the slide show will automatically animate the first slide).
- Click to the next slide, then taking on the role of the presenter, you (the teacher) read out the words: 'Tonight's debate is all about. . . You decide!' Click to the next slide to share the rules of the debate with the children, still talking in the role of the presenter.
- Conduct the debate, encouraging every child to contribute something. At the end of the debate, vote on the key question and record the result.

Fiction: Poetic language and word play
Non-fiction: Explanations

Timetable

WEEK 1   Reading poetry   *Water-cycle*

Day 1	Day 2	Day 3	Day 4	Day 5
The poetry store (Tongue twisters, Riddles, Nonsense poems)	Poetic features 1 📄	Read a poem 3	Poetic features 2	Performing the poem 📄
Personal log	Read a poem 1	Word power 📄	Re-read a poem 3	Personal log
Big Question	Read a poem 2	Special phrases	Listen to a poem	Big Question
	Class log	Re-read a poem 3	Actions for a poem	
	Big Question	Personal log	Class log 📄	
		Big Question	Big Question	

WEEK 2   Writing poetry   *Water-cycle*

Day 6	Day 7	Day 8	Day 9	Day 10
Word shower	Build a poem 1	Build a poem 2	Build a poem 3	Shape
Build an image 1	Write a poem 1	Write a poem 2 📄	Evaluate	Share, evaluate and edit
Build an image 2	Class log	Personal log	Write a poem 3	Proofread
Personal log: strange combinations	Big Question	Big Question	Class log 📄	Publish 📄
Big Question				

WEEK 3   Reading and writing non-fiction   Explanations

Day 11	Day 12	Day 13	Day 14	Day 15
Think and link	Deconstruction 1	Deconstruction 2 📄	Deconstruction 3 📄	Write an explanation text
Introduction to explanation texts	In your own words	Write 2	Write 3 📄	Evaluate and edit
Pictures into words	Zoom in on features of explanations	Presentations	Class log	Proofread
Grammar: prefixes	Write 1 📄	Personal log		Words into pictures
Class log	Class and Personal log – similes			Personal log

📄: shows that a file should be printed out from the Software.

Overview of the Unit

Using a number of short tongue twisters, riddles, nonsense poems and a longer performance poem, this Unit encourages children to explore the impact of word play and unusual imagery. It also gives them opportunity to learn a poem and enjoy the experience of performing it in a dramatic way.

The Non-fiction week is linked to the scientific subject of the water-cycle and will develop the children's understanding of the language features of explanation texts in written and spoken forms. For more information about the Non-fiction week and the Non-fiction writing evaluation criteria, see p.122.

Where appropriate, the children will be encouraged to develop an awareness of audience and purpose in relation to the fiction and non-fiction texts they are reading and writing.

Teacher modelling is provided in the teaching notes, Software and the Pupils' Book, supporting the children's writing at every stage in the Fiction and Non-fiction weeks.

The Homework Book provides a homework activity related to the content of this Unit for each of the three weeks.

Fiction

Reading

Children will:

- explore and discuss key features of different types of poems
- recognise and discuss poetic techniques such as alliteration in 'Water-cycle'
- explore a poem and perform it.

Writing

Key writing purpose to be shared with the children:

To write a water-cycle poem, and participate in a class poetry performance.

Writing evaluation to be shared with the children

My poem:

- uses at least two of the special poetic techniques we have studied, e.g. *rhyme, rhythm, alliteration, repetition, onomatopoeia*
- uses some unusual combinations of two words to build interesting descriptions of water
- is presented in an interesting shape that helps the reader imagine what I am describing.

Grammar:

- uses punctuation and line breaks to show how my poem should be read.

See the Planning section of the Software ('Timetables' tab) for a printable version of the Writing purpose and evaluation.

Fiction: Poetic language and word play
Water-cycle by Andrew Fusek Peters

READING POETRY

DAY 1

Curriculum link:
listening to and
discussing a wide
range of poetry;
recognising some
different forms of
poetry

The poetry store

*Purpose: for children to be immersed in
word play and different types
of poetry, and revise what they
already know about poems*

Resources
PB Pupils' Book pp.36–45
A Anthology pp.52–55
CD CD on Interactive whiteboard Unit 4
GB Grammar Bank on CD
HB Homework Book pp.14–16

- Tell the children that a long lost dungeon has been discovered, known to have belonged to a wicked king, called King No-laugh who believed that playing with words was wrong. It is said that he ordered that all poems that played with words must be locked away in his dingy dungeon! Explain that through the power of the computer, they can help you to unlock this poetry store and read some of the poems.
- Display **CD (file 1.1)** to show the 'magic' rhyme to take you down to the dungeon. Use MT/YT (My turn/your turn) to say the rhyme. Click on the door to unlock it and reveal shelves of poetry books. Read some of the titles of the books and say that you would like to look at the book entitled 'Tongue twisters' first of all.

Tongue twisters

*Purpose: for children to explore and have fun with tongue twisters, and explore alliteration
and performance elements*

- Ask the children to TTYP (Turn to your partner) to share what they think the phrase *tongue twister* might mean. Collect feedback, and praise their ideas even if they are not technically correct – the phrase may conjure up interesting images for some children and that is what this Unit is about!
- Now explain that tongue twisters have lots of words that begin with the same sound and they trick the tongue to twist the sounds and words around to make lines or sentences sound funny. Remind the children that using words close together with the same beginning sounds is called *alliteration*. Use MT/YT to say the word (there will be an opportunity to print out important poetry words for the Poetry wall, later on).
- Click to the next slide of **CD (file 1.1)** and explain that it shows a page inside the 'Tongue twisters' book (displaying the tongue twister 'Fat frogs flying past fast.'). Read the tongue twister aloud at a normal pace. Say it again at a fast pace. Use MT/YT to read it again at a normal and then a fast pace. Ask the children to Popcorn (see Introduction, p.17) the sound that is repeated at the beginning of lots of the words.
- Ask the children to TTYP to share what happened when they tried to read it quickly. Ask a couple of partners to share their explanations with the group.
- Click to the next slide to show another tongue twister (Betty Botter). Ask the children to read it first at a normal pace and then much faster.
- Now ask them to count how many words in the tongue twister begin with the sound 'b'. Click on 'Highlights' to highlight the alliteration and check if they were right.
- Ask the children for a choral response to the question '*What word describes this poetic device?*' (alliteration) Choose two to answer. Clarify if necessary.
- Read the tongue twister aloud, with exaggerated emphasis on the alliterative sounds. Ask the children to read it chorally in the same way. Ask them to TTYP to think of other words that start with the same sound 'b'. Collect words orally and substitute some of their examples for tongue twister words to see what happens, e.g. Does it still make sense? Is it harder or easier to say? Why? Is it funnier or not as funny? Why?

- Explain that most alliteration uses consonants – point to the consonant sound boxes on your class Read Write Inc. Complex Speed Sounds chart (you can find this in the 'Planning' section of the CD) and ask the children to identify the right sound box for the alliteration in the tongue twister.
- Say that different tongue twisters might use different vowel sounds close together like this: *pop a pip in a pan, put a pen in a pot*
  Use MT/YT to say it aloud and then *you* say just the vowel sounds (not letter names), e.g. *o a i i a a u a e i a o!*
- Now explain that sometimes all of the vowels are the same but the consonants are different: *pop hot chop slops on top*
  You may wish to explain that this is called *assonance* and add it to the Poetry wall for this Unit.
  Use MT/YT to say it aloud and then *you* say just the consonant sounds, e.g. *p p h t ch p s l p s n t p!*
- Point to the Poetry store tongue twister on **CD file (1.1)** ('Betty Botter') and click on 'Highlights' again to highlight all the short vowel sounds. Ask the children to TTYP to identify whether they are:
  - all the same
  - different
  - different but one vowel used more than others
- Ask which tongue twister is harder to say quickly: **pop a pip in a pan, put a pen in a pot** (repeated consonant sounds) *or* **pop hot chop slops on top** (repeated vowel sounds)? Why?
- Write **pop hot chop slops on top** clearly on the board or a flipchart. Ask the children to stand up and split them into three small groups. Explain that they are going to chant this tongue twister four times each but each group will begin (and therefore end) at a different time and this is called a *round*.
- Group one begins and repeats four times. Start group two off when the group one get to the word **on**. Start group three off when group two get to the word **on**. Have fun conducting them as in an orchestra. Encourage them to keep a normal, regular rhythm. Then you might want to repeat the activity, a little faster. You might want to record the children's tongue twister rounds to play back to them later to allow them to hear the full effect.
- Draw attention to the echoing effects of the round. Move the children into different groups to experience being group one instead of two, etc. or try the activity with **pop a pip in a pan, put a pen in a pot** if you wish (starting the next group when the previous one reaches **pan**). Ask the children which one sounded the most effective as a round.
- Ask children to TTYP and remind each other of the things that make a poem a tongue twister.

Riddles ⓒⒹ

Purpose: for children to explore and have fun with riddles, and explore repetition and rhyme

- Display **CD (file 1.2)** to show the Poetry store bookshelf again. Say that you want to look at a riddle this time. Ask the children to TTYP to explain what a riddle is. Collect feedback and clarify if necessary, drawing out the important feature of mystery, a puzzle and clues using double meanings, hints, etc.
- Click on the 'Riddles' book. The book will open to show a riddle.
- Ask the children to read it aloud and to TTYP to decide what it is. Collect answers and ideas and guide the children to share which clues were hardest to work out and which ones gave the game away. The answer is a newspaper.

- Click to the next slide to show Clare Bevan's poem 'What Am I?'. Read the whole poem aloud, pointing to the relevant graphics as you read.
- Ask the children to Popcorn what they think the answer to the riddle poem is (a poem). Select one or two partners – you could include those who have not got the correct solution – to explain how they arrived at their answer.
- Ask the children to TTYP to see if they can spot any patterns they heard or saw in the riddle poem, e.g. *repetition, rhymes, strong rhythm*. If necessary, remind the children that rhymes are words that have the same end sounds, e.g. *bell* and *well*. Remind them that the rhythm of a poem is the pattern of beats in each line.
- Take feedback. Click on 'Highlights' to show first the repetition and then the rhymes. Lead the children in a choral reading of the poem, giving special emphasis to the strong, regular rhythm.
- Ask children to TTYP and remind each other of the things that make a poem a riddle.

Nonsense poems (CD)

Purpose: for children to explore and have fun with nonsense poems, and explore features such as made-up words and bizarre images

- Display **CD (file 1.3)** to show the Poetry store bookshelf again. Say that you want to look at nonsense poems this time. Ask the children to TTYP to talk about what the word *nonsense* means. Collect feedback and clarify if necessary. Explain that nonsense poems are very funny and silly as they don't make sense and that is why they are call *nonsense* poems!
- Click on the 'Nonsense Poems' book. The book will come off the shelf and open at a page to show Gina Douthwaite's poem 'Night Mer'. Read the poem aloud and then ask the children to read it chorally. Click on 'TOL' (Think out loud) to show the think bubbles and use them to talk about the word play and the absurd statements. Ask children to TTYP and remind each other of the things that make a poem a nonsense poem.

Personal log

Purpose: for children to keep a personal log for recording and reflecting on their exploration of word play and poems

- Tell the children the first sound in your own first name and use MT/YT to say the sound. Point the sound on your Read Write Inc. Complex Speed Sounds chart if you have one in the room (it can also be found in the 'Planning' section of the CD).
- Tell the children to TTYP to think of any three words beginning with that sound. Collect a few words and write them on the board. Play around with the words and your name to make a mini tongue twister. Make sure the children know that it doesn't have to make sense – remind them about nonsense poems and the importance of the *sound* of the words.
- Now tell the children to say the first sound in their own first name and to TTYP to tell their partner and then to write their name in their Personal log.
- Set a timer for one or two minutes and explain that you want them to jot down as many words beginning with the same sound as their own first name as possible before the timer goes off.
- Ask the children to TTYP to share their words and then give them some time to make a mini-tongue twister of their own. Tell them to use MT/YT with their partners to practise saying each other's tongue twisters.
- Choose a couple of partners to share with the whole group. Ask them what was hard about the activity and what was most fun and why.

- Check that they understand that they have used alliteration. Write the word on the board and ask them to write it in their Personal log underneath their tongue twisters.

Curriculum link: discussion; develop, agree on, and evaluate rules for effective discussion

Big Question

Purpose: for children to develop their skills of argument and discussion through a mini enquiry session based on a philosophical question relating to the work of the day

- Display today's Big Question on **CD (file 1.4):**

  Is laughing always a good thing?

- Ask the children to TTYP to talk about this question. Collect feedback and scribe some responses on the board or flipchart.
- Click 'Prompts' to show some statements that may help to encourage discussion.

DAY 2

Poetic features 1

Purpose: for children to develop confidence in using vocabulary to talk about poetry

> repetition   alliteration   rhythm   rhyme   nonsense   imagery

- Display **CD (file 2.1)** to show some of the words they have been using to describe different kinds of language play. Use MT/YT to say the words and their meanings.
  repetition – saying, writing or doing the same thing more than once
  alliteration – words close to each other with the same first letter sound
  rhythm – repeated beat pattern
  rhyme – a similar sound in the ending of words
  nonsense – rubbish, silliness, twaddle, gobbledygook
  imagery – using words to create a picture in the reader's mind
- You can print large versions of these words and definitions from **CD (file 2.2)** to display on your Poetry wall. Note that the word *imagery* will be used later on in the unit.

predicting, identifying how language, structure and presentation contribute to meaning

Read a poem 1

Purpose: for children to be introduced to themes to be explored in the main poem via a short riddle

- Explain to the children that tomorrow they will be looking at a special poem from the king's dungeon and today they are going to examine some clues to help them to work out what the poem will be about.
- Tell the children to turn to the Read a poem 1 activity on p.36 of their Pupils' Book.
  I thunder, / I creep, / I spit, / I seep.
  I trickle, / I gush. / I'm slow, / I rush.
  I'm in a cloud, / I'm in the sea.
  I'm trapped! / I'm free ...
- Ask them to read the short riddle aloud with you, chorally and then to TTYP to say what they think it is describing. Use Popcorn to hear what they think the answer to *What is it?* might be. (The answer is water.)
- Now ask them to TTYP to re-read the riddle and to use the questions to talk about it. Collect responses and develop their ideas, drawing attention to rhyme, rhythm and repetition.

Curriculum link:
predicting,
identifying how
language, structure
and presentation
contribute to
meaning

Read a poem 2 (CD) (PB)

*Purpose: for children to be introduced to themes to be explored in the main text/poem via a
short kenning*

- Display **CD (file 2.3)** to show the children another poem. Remind the children
  that this kind of poem is called a *kenning* and a kenning is another kind of riddle.
  *Stone rattler / Dam battler / Bubble foamer / Land roamer
  Song gurgler / Life burglar / Raft thriller / Sea filler.*
- Read the poem aloud and ask the children to TTYP to share what the kenning is
  describing. Collect ideas and ask for evidence to support their answers but don't
  reveal whether they are right or not yet. (The answer is a river.)
- Explain that you want Partner 1s to read lines 1, 3, 5 and 7 and Partner 2s to read
  lines 2, 4, 6, and 8. Draw attention to the strong rhythm of the poem (point to
  the word *rhythm* on your Poetry wall as you say it) and ask the children to make
  sure you can hear the rhythm when they read their lines.
- Ask them to TTYP to say whether their ideas about what the poem is describing
  have stayed the same or changed. Collect feedback and ask for reasons for their
  answers.
- Tell the children to turn to Read a poem 2 activity on p.37 of their Pupils' Book.
  Ask them to TTYP to read the kenning out together and then use the prompts
  to talk about it. Collect responses to the prompts and then explain that you are
  going to reveal what the poem is describing. Click on 'Reveal' on the slide to show
  the images which give the answer.
- Remind the children that some of the words in this kenning will pop up in the
  special poem tomorrow.

discussing and
recording ideas

Class log

*Purpose: for children to share the process of keeping a class reading, writing and thinking log
to record responses to texts and activities in a variety of forms*

- Remind the children of the nonsense poem 'Night Mer' and some of its made-up
  words and phrases: *dasty ream* – nasty dream, *duggled snown* – snuggled down,
  stunder thorm – thunder storm.
- Explain that the poet has switched the initial letters in each word to make a nonsense
  word and say that you are going to do the same thing with the poet's name.
- Tell them that the poet is called Gina Douthewaite but if the first letters are
  swapped over, she becomes Dina Gouthewaite! You might want to do the same
  thing with your own name.
- Ask the children to TTYP and do the same thing with their own names, e.g. Oliver
  Smith becomes Sliver Omith. (If you prefer not to use the children's names for this
  activity, look on your bookshelves for authors' names and/or book titles that you
  can use instead, e.g. Richael Mosen or Rittle Led Hiding Rood.)
- Collect some examples from the class orally and scribe some on the board.
- Show the children the new Class log for this unit. On the front cover, write:
  Class Log – Language Play! and then underneath write: *Llass Cog – Panguage Llay!*
  Ask the children to write their new nonsense names on very small sticky notes
  and to come out a few at a time to stick them in the Class log under the heading
  Our Class – Cur Olass.

Curriculum link:
discussion; develop, agree on, and evaluate rules for effective discussion

Big Question CD

Purpose: for children to develop their skills of argument and discussion through a mini enquiry session based on a philosophical question relating to the work of the day

- Display today's Big Question on **CD (file 2.4):**

  If we change our name, do we change who we are?

- Follow the process as explained on Day 1.

DAY 3

predicting, identifying how language, structure and presentation contribute to meaning; identifying themes

Read a poem 3 CD

Purpose: for children to hear and enjoy the main poem for the first time

- Display **CD (file 3.1)** to show the Poetry store bookshelves again in the king's dungeon. Tell the children that you have been told that there is a special poem here that was written by Britain's tallest poet!
- Focus on the 'Tall poets' book on the shelf then click to the next slide which shows the open book, revealing images from the Anthology, but no poem. The images usually accompany the poem 'Water-cycle' by Andrew Fusek Peters (he describes himself as Britain's tallest poet on his website). Do not tell the children what the poem is called at this stage!
- TOL in a wondering voice about the fact the poem is not shown on the page and whether the pictures are to do with the missing poem. Ask the children to TTYP to discuss what they think might have happened to the poem, encouraging them to use their imagination to speculate. Collect responses and build on their ideas.
- Now ask them to TTYP to look at the images and to share what the pictures make them think about or feel. Choose two or three sets of partners to share their thoughts and feelings and praise interesting, personal responses.
- Explain to the children that there is a secret message on this page. Click 'Reveal' and share the explanation: 'This poem escaped from the dungeon, leaving only its pictures and its voice behind!'
- Point out the 'Listen' button on the page. Tell the children they can now hear the special poem for the very first time. Click on 'Listen' to play the audio recording of the poem.
- Straight away, ask the children to TTYP to share three words that they remember from the poem. Take feedback and ask them to say why they think they remembered those particular words. Make sure they know that there is not a 'right' answer.
- Guide the children to talk about their chosen words and any theme that emerges and then ask them to TTYP to discuss what they think the poem might be describing. Collect responses and ideas – they are likely to pick up the water theme in some form – and then tell them that its title is 'Water-cycle'.
- Display **CD (file 3.2)** to show some of the images from the water-cycle and use the captions to give a brief explanation. Notice that they are arranged in a cyclical format, as an early link to the non-fiction focus on the water-cycle. Click on 'Audio' to hear the poem again and point to each image as it relates to the lines of the poem.

discussing words; building a varied and rich vocabulary

Word power CD

Purpose: for children to hear and use synonyms for vocabulary taken from the poems

> soak up   spit   weep   *longing*

- Display **CD (file 3.3)** to show words from the poem. Point to the words and explain that they are all from the poem they have just heard. Use MT/YT to say each word and synonyms.

- Now use MT/YT to read the sentences, giving special emphasis and dramatic actions as you say them. (You may wish to point out that spitting is not acceptable in public, although it is fine for when you are cleaning your teeth!)
- Use MT/YT to try out synonyms in the sentences given and use MT/YT to try it out, e.g. 'I was yearning *for a mobile phone of my own.*'
- Ask the children to TTYP to say which words they prefer.
- Make sure the children hear and repeat the words or their synonyms in your teaching and conversation throughout the day where appropriate. Encourage them to use the words at home with friends and family to ensure they become embedded in the children's own spoken (and eventually, written) vocabulary.
- Print the words, definitions and sentences from **CD (file 3.4)** and display them on your Poetry wall.

> **Curriculum link:** discussing words and phrases that capture the reader's interest and imagination

Special phrases (CD) (PB)

Purpose: for children to become more familiar with special phrases particular to the poem and to comment on the effect choices of words have on readers

> *Full of river-longing   Down, down, down underground, rushing round*
> *Cold cloud spit her out   Mountains weep and dream   A man-made hand stops her dead/With a dam*

- Remind the children that poets enjoy putting words together to create special phrases to paint pictures in our heads and we call this *imagery*. Explain that you have picked out some special phrases that create strong imagery in the poem 'Water-cycle'.
- Display the special phrases from the poem on **CD (file 3.5)**. Explain that you have chosen these because they have some important poetic features. Use MT/YT to read the phrases aloud.
- Click on 'TOL' to show the think bubbles linking to the first phrase and use these and/or your own ideas to draw attention to poetic features of the phrase that you like and the pictures it makes in your head.
- Use TTYP to encourage the children to share their own responses and ideas about the imagery conjured by the special phrases and their own experiences and observations.
- Click on 'TOL' again to show the think bubbles relating to the second special phrase. Repeat the process of adding your own thoughts about poetic features of the phrase and the picture it makes in your mind.
- Now ask the children to TTYP to look at the Special phrases activity on p.38 in their Pupils' Book. Tell them to follow the instructions to say the phrases and meanings and then to each choose their favourite special phrase and to explain to their partner what they like about it. Choose some partners to feed back.

> checking that the text makes sense to them

Re-read a poem 3 🅰

Purpose: for children to gain a deeper understanding of the poem and to see the text for the first time

- Let the children follow their own copy of the poem on Anthology pp.52–53 as you re-read the full version of the poem aloud with great enthusiasm. Put special emphasis on the powerful words you studied earlier and stop at the special phrases so that the children can Jump in. (See Introduction p.13 for further explanation.)
- Now ask the children to read their copy of the poem with their partners, alternate lines each. Remind them to read with great expression, in particular putting special emphasis on the powerful words and phrases that you have looked at. Explain that you will be listening in.

Curriculum link: building a varied and rich vocabulary; discussing and recording ideas

Personal log

Purpose: for children to keep a personal log for recording and reflecting on their exploration of word play and poems

- Write all or some of these words on the board or on a flipchart to make some new special phrases: *sleep stone sea spit deep dream dead cloud shout out* and explain that they are taken from the 'Water-cycle' poem and the riddle and kenning in their Pupils' Book.
- Model how you can play around with any of the words, creating unusual imagery, alliteration, nonsense phrases, rhymes to make *micro-poems*, e.g.
  deep sleep,
  stone dead
  dream cloud.
  or
  sea spit stone out,
  dream deep, dead shout.
- Now ask the children to write the same words in their Personal log and then to play around with the words, to make their own micro-poem. They can do this individually or with their partners.
- Stress the fact that experimenting with words and language is the important point here, not writing something that makes sense – remind them of what the poet does with language in the poem 'Night Mer'!
- When they have had time to experiment and write a line or two, ask them to TTYP to share and then choose a few children to read what they have written.
- Guide the children to pick out examples of alliteration, echoing sounds and rhymes, strange, interesting images and to talk about their choices.

discussion; develop, agree on, and evaluate rules for effective discussion

Big Question (CD)

Purpose: for children to develop their skills of argument and discussion through a mini enquiry session based on a philosophical question relating to the work of the day

- Display today's Big Question on **CD (file 3.6).**
  Is it easier to use words or pictures to explain or describe something? *
- Follow the process as explained on Day 1.
  ** This Big Question will be revisited on Day 11 – the first day of the Non-fiction week.*

DAY 4

Poetic features 2 (A) (CD) (PB)

Purpose: for children to focus on the effects of poetic devices

alliteration rhyme repetition

- Point to the poetry words on your Poetry wall as you remind the children that they have already looked at *alliteration* in tongue twisters and *rhyme* and *repetition* in riddles.
- Explain that you now want to see and hear the power of these poetry features at work in the poem 'Water-Cycle'.
- Ask the children to look at 'Water-cycle' on pp.52–53 of their Anthology and to read the whole poem chorally with you as you read aloud from your own copy.
- Display **CD (file 4.1)** to show a list of poetic features. Use MY/YT to read the words *alliteration, rhyme* and *repetition*.
- Say that you have picked out some parts of the poem that you really like that have these features. Click to the next slide to show the word *alliteration* and an example from the poem. Use MT/YT to say the words.

Fiction: Poetic language and word play

- Now click on 'TOL' to show a think bubble. Use this and your own ideas to explain your thoughts about the effect of the alliteration. Ask the children to TTYP to find another example of alliteration in the poem and to share ideas about how or why it works well.
- Choose two or three sets of partners to feed back. Make sure they know this is not a 'right answer only' activity. The point is to help them to engage with the sounds, feelings and imagery the poetic features create.
- Click to the next slide and repeat the process with the word *rhyme*. Clicking on 'TOL' again will give you a think bubble to use to talk about the effect of the *rhyme*. Ask the children to TTYP to find another example of rhyme in the poem and to share ideas about how or why it works well. Collect feedback as before.
- Now click to the next slide to repeat the whole process with the word *repetition*.
- Ask the children to look at the Poetic features 2 activity on p.39 of their Pupils' Book and explain that you want them to work with their partners to zoom in on the lines from the poem (A–C) and match them up with the statements in the think bubbles (1–3).
- During feedback, be willing to accept answers in addition to the obvious ones as long as the children can support their point of view. Check that their understanding of rhyme, repetition and alliteration is secure.

Curriculum link: checking that the text makes sense to them, discussing and asking questions to improve their understanding

Re-read a poem 3

Purpose: for children to deepen their understanding and enjoyment of the poem by increasing familiarity with the text

- Ask the children to look at 'Water-cycle' on pp.52–53 of their Anthology and to read the whole poem silently to themselves. Tell them to read it again and to stop and record in their Personal log:
  - favourite words and phrases
  - examples of alliteration, rhyme or repetition they really like
  - anything they think doesn't quite work.
- When they have had enough time to read the poem through twice and make their notes, ask the children to TTYP to share what they have noticed or asked.
- Take feedback and use their responses to guide the discussion and/or explanations for choices with the whole group. You may be able to link the feedback and discussion with the previous activity.

Listen to a poem

Purpose: for children to deepen their understanding and enjoyment of the poem through listening to an alternative reading with sound effects

- Tell the children that all poems should be read aloud as well as silently, but some are special 'performance' poems. Remind them that the poem 'Water cycle' has a subtitle *A rhythm poem for acting out or different voices*.
- Explain that they are going to listen to a recording of the poem with two different voices. They will hear it twice but the first time should be for pure pleasure and immersion in the poem.
- Play the audio on **CD (file 4.2)**. Straight away, ask the children to TTYP to say what they enjoyed most about it. Collect a few answers and try to use some key performance words in your responses, e.g. *voices, volume, rhythm, pace*. Ask the children how the two voices, and the sound effects, changed their experience of listening to the poem.

110

Actions for a poem (CD)

Purpose: for children to explore and understand the imagery of the poem further by making up actions for a performance

- Remind the children that the poem could be *for acting out* or for different voices. Tell them that you are going to practise making up some actions.
- Start with miming some clear everyday actions (e.g. *brushing your teeth, drinking a cup of tea*) and ask them to guess what you are doing.
- Tell the children that you are now going to mime an action that is mentioned in the poem. They need to find the line of the poem that mentions the action. Start with: *twist a tap* (line 16). Ask children to TTYP and discuss what they think your action could be and where it is mentioned in the poem (line 16, 'Someone twists a tap'). Then repeat for *weep* (line 6).
- Ask Partner 1s to choose an action from the poem to mime for their partner. If they need help for ideas, they can choose from: *falls asleep, falls, grows, stops, sings, shivers*. Ask Partner 2s to find the action in the poem. Then swap.
- Display part of the poem on **CD (file 4.3)**. The lines are: 'How she falls./Falls asleep, lies deep./Mountains weep and dream/And in the dreams she seems to grow.' Play the audio for these lines again and ask children to close their eyes and think about what pictures they see in their minds when they hear the lines. Ask children to open their eyes and TTYP to discuss with their partner what they saw, and to think about what actions they could use to show these lines.
- Tell the children that poetry language is special because it is often unusual and it can mean several things at the same time. For example, it says 'Mountains weep and dream' – but mountains don't usually have emotions or thoughts. Explore the idea that this could mean that water runs down the mountain as a river, but it *also* paints a picture of a mountain being alive and being able to cry and dream like a person. So when acting this poem out they could choose to show crying, or they could use their hand to mime a river rushing down a mountain, or they could show someone asleep and dreaming. Make sure they know there is not a 'right' action to show the meaning of each line or part of the poem!
- Ask the children look again at the lines on CD file and to decide together how they would act out them out. Walk around giving ideas where necessary. Choose some confident partners to share their actions with the class.

Class log

> **Curriculum link:** discussing words that capture the reader's interest and imagination

Purpose: for children to share the process of keeping a class reading, writing and thinking log to record responses to texts and activities in a variety of forms

onomatopoeia

- Before the lesson, print off one copy of the onomatopoeic words from printable **CD (file 4.4)** and cut them up.
- Explain that you have a lovely new poetry word to share. Write the word *onomatopoeia* on the board. Say the word rhythmically, exaggerating each syllable. Repeat the word in this way using MT/YT and TTYP for children to say it to their partners.
- Explain that it describes a type of word that sounds like the thing it is describing, e.g. *hiss, crash, thud, tinkle, crack*. Say that poets often use onomatopoeia to create sound effects in their poems.

- Give each set of partners two or three words, depending on the size of your group and ask them to TTYP to make sure they can say the words and they know what they mean. Collect feedback to clarify pronunciation and meaning where necessary.
- Say you are going to play Onomatopoeia popcorn. Explain that on the count of three, all Partner 1s must Popcorn (call out) their first onomatopoeic word.
- Repeat the process with all Partner 2s Popcorning their second onomatopoeic word.
- Play around and experiment with the words, e.g. Popcorn:
  - all the words beginning with the same sound.
  - all the words containing an 's' and/or a 'sh' sound.
  - compound nonsense words by asking each set of partners to add their two words together, e.g. *sizzle-clank*, *plop-whack*, *hiss-boing* and saying them twice, with a strong rhythm.
- Now ask the children to TTYP to choose their favourite onomatopoeic word and to bring it to you to paste in the Class log under the heading *Onomatopoeic words*.

Curriculum link: discussion; develop, agree on, and evaluate rules for effective discussion

Big Question

Purpose: for children to develop their skills of argument and discussion through a mini enquiry session based on a philosophical question relating to the work of the day

- Display today's Big Question on **CD (file 4.5):**

  Is it good to be silent sometimes?

- Follow the process as explained on Day 1.

DAY 5

preparing poems to read aloud and to perform, showing understanding through intonation, tone, volume and action

Performing the poem

Purpose: for children to explore a poem through performance

- Before the lesson, print out two or three copies each of **CD (files 5.1a, b, c and d)**.
- Remind the children of the performance of the activities they did yesterday, listening to 'Water-cycle' and thinking about voices and actions. Explain that you want them to plan and prepare their performance of part of the same poem.
- Create four groups of three sets of partners (adapt according to the size of your class, you may have to have uneven numbers in some groups). Give each group at least two copies of one section of the poem, prompts and plan box, from **CD (file 5.1a group 1, 5.1b group 2, 5.1c group 3 and 5.1d group 4)**.
- Tell the children that each group is going to plan and practise a performance of their section of the poem and that they must have a narrator who is going to read the lines while the others perform the actions.
- Explain that the prompts and the 'ideas for our performance' are there to help them. You may wish to model how to use them.
- Remind the children that they can use voice, exaggerated rhythm, sounds, actions, facial expressions, freeze frames and body language in their performance, to help the audience gain a deep understanding of the poem. Remind them to vary the pace and volume and to use pauses to create impact for their audience.
- Allow time for the groups to plan and then ask for groups to share just one of their ideas with the rest of the class. Then give them time to practise their performances. Walk around as they practise, giving instant feedback and encouragement. When they are ready, explain how the groups will perform in turn to create the whole poem. Give feedback to each group straight after this first performance.
- You might want to film or photograph the groups performing for a second time to play back to them at a later date or to display on the wall and/or in the Class log.

Curriculum link: discussing and recording words and phrases that capture the reader's interest and imagination

Personal log

Purpose: for children to keep a personal log for recording and reflecting on their exploration of word play and poems

Lines to keep forever

- Ask the children to look again at the poem 'Water-cycle' on pp.52–53 of their Anthology.
- Tell them to read the poem silently on their own and then to spend a couple of minutes choosing the line or lines they like the sound of best of all.
- Explain that by learning a favourite line from a poem, they can keep it forever. Say that they will probably be able to remember some favourite lines they learn now, when they are adults! Now ask them to use these ways to help them to learn the line they have chosen:
  - Write the line in their Personal log.
  - Draw a quick pencil picture to illustrate the line or certain words, e.g. a sobbing mountain.
  - Say the line aloud in different ways – softly, whispering, slowly, quickly, putting emphasis on certain words.

  Give the children a sticky note each to write their line on. Tell them to take it home and read it before they go to sleep as it is easier to remember things when they are relaxed.
- Tell them that over the next few days you will ask them to stop whatever they are doing and ask them to say their line to their partner.
- Encourage the children to learn more lines from the poem if they want to.

discussion; develop, agree on, and evaluate rules for effective discussion

Big Question (CD)

Purpose: for children to develop their skills of argument and discussion through a mini enquiry session based on a philosophical question relating to the work of the day

- Display today's Big Question on **CD (file 5.2)**:

  Is it always a good thing to work with others?
- Follow the process as explained on Day 1.

WRITING POETRY

Word shower (CD)

Purpose: for children to recognise sound patterns in words created by rhyme and onomatopoeia

- Remind the children that the kenning, the riddles and 'Water-cycle' poem they have been reading all created pictures in our heads (imagery) about water in different ways.
- Say that they are going have a shower with a difference now – a word shower!
- Display **CD (file 6.1)** to show the shower of words. Use MT/YT to say all the words and ask the children to TTYP to say what they notice about the words, i.e. they are all to do with water. Check children's understanding of the words, clarifying any they are uncertain of. Ask them to Popcorn any water words they recognise from poems they read last week.
- Ask the children to TTYP to find any rhyming words. Use drag and drop to put their suggestions in the 'rhyme bath'.

- Now say that you would like some onomatopoeic words. Use MT/YT to say the word 'onomatopoeia' and remind the children what it means. Look again in the Class log to remind children of their favourite onomatopoeic words. Display **CD (file 6.2).** Select one onomatopoeic word from the 'shower' to model what you want them to look for.
- Use TTYP to give the children a chance to decide which ones could be used to describe water sounds. Use drag and drop to put their suggestions in the 'onomatopoeia bath'. You may wish to explain that this is a 'right' or 'wrong' answer activity – but be generous if they can justify an odd choice!

Build an image 1 (CD)

Purpose: for children and teachers to share the process of building unusual imagery using rhyme and onomatopoeia

Curriculum link: discussing writing similar to that which they are planning to write

- Tell the children to find the special phrases/micro-poems they wrote in their Personal log (see Day 3 Personal log activity). Ask them to TTYP to share what they wrote.
- Write the micro-poems shown below (or your own if you kept them from Week 1) on the board or a flipchart to show how you experimented with the same words:
  deep sleep,
  stone dead
  dream cloud.
  and
  sea spit stone out,
  dream deep, dead shout.
  Remind them that the words were taken from the 'Water-cycle' poem and the riddle and kenning in their Pupils' Book. These words helped you to make pictures/imagery from the sounds 'inside' words and the sounds of different words together.

- Tell the children you want them to help you to create some unusual sounds and imagery for new micro-poems using the rhyming and onomatopoeic words from the Word shower.
- Display **CD (file 6.3)** to show a river of words and explain that when the words reach the waterfall, they will be tumbled and jumbled around to make new phrases and images.
- Now click on 'Waterfall' to make the words tumble and fall to make a new poem.
  Drizzle whoosh, sizzle seep,
  Splash splosh, splish weep.
  Hiss spit gush rain,
  Gurgle trickle, flush drain.
- TOL about the images created by the words and link your own experiences to the poem, e.g. *'This reminds me of when I was rushing across the school car park a storm and the rain was like little streams ...'* or *'Hiss spit gush rain makes a picture in my head of rain spurting from a broken gutter ...'* etc.
- Ask the children to TTYP to articulate what feelings, pictures and ideas the poem triggers, linked to their own experiences and observations.
- Take feedback and probe and build on responses. Emphasise that there are no right or wrong answers to these questions.

- Navigate to the next slide and click on 'Waterfall' to make another 'poem' and repeat the process.
  Plop
  Spit
  Hisssssss.
  Splosh, splash
  Whoosh!
  Sizzle, drizzle flush, gush
          Splish. . .
- Ask the children to TTYP to say which of the two poems they liked best and why. Take feedback and share your own favourite and reasons why you like it.

Build an image 2 (CD)

Purpose: for children and teachers to share the process of building imagery using compound words

- Tell the children that the title of the poem 'Water-cycle' is a compound word – two words that can be used separately to mean two different things, but when put together or combined, mean something else.
- Ask the children to close their eyes and take a 'snapshot' of the image in their heads when you say the word '*water*', e.g. a glass of water, a stream, the sea, a bath. Choose two or three to feed back straight away and compare images. Ask the children to TTYP to share what they pictured.
- Repeat with the word '*cycle*'. While most children will probably mention a bicycle, explain that there is another meaning of the word *cycle*: a series of events that repeat regularly.
- Display **CD (file 6.4)** and click 'Reveal' to show the words and pictures as individual words and then as a compound word. Clarify that they understand that *water-cycle* is different to *water* and *cycle*. Explain that there are lots of words that can be put together to make compound words. These compound words often mean something very different to the individual words.
- Click on the next slide and show the word *tap*. Say the word and ask the children to picture the word in their heads. Choose two or three to feed back straight away and compare images. Ask the children to TTYP to share what they pictured, then explain that, in this example, *tap* means a sound. Click 'Reveal' again to show the image of a hammer tapping a nail.
- Click on 'Reveal' again to show the next word *dancer*. Say the word and ask the children to picture the word in their heads. Choose two or three to feed back straight away and compare images. Ask the children to TTYP to share what they pictured.
- Click on 'Reveal' again to show the image of the dancer. Click on 'Reveal' again to show the compound word *tap dancer* and its picture. Clarify that they understand that *tap dancer* is different to *tap* and *dancer*.
- Click to the next slide and repeat the process to show the development of the compound word *crossbones*.

Personal log: strange combinations [PB]

Purpose: for children to keep a personal log for recording and reflecting on their exploration of word play and poems

- Tell the children to turn to the Strange combinations activity on p.40 of their Pupils' Book. Explain the activity and use the first nonsense compound word to model a TOL about possibilities and your enjoyment at the funny images it makes in your head.

- Ask the children to TTYP to share their own funny images using the other nonsense compound words. Choose two or three partners to share their TOL. Then ask them to complete the sorting out activity with their partners before writing the real compound words in their Personal log.

Curriculum link: discussion; develop, agree on, and evaluate rules for effective discussion

Big Question ⓒ🅓

Purpose: for children to develop their skills of argument and discussion through a mini enquiry session based on a philosophical question relating to the work of the day

- Display today's Big Question on **CD (file 6.5)**:

  Should we be able to make up and use our own words for things?

- Follow the process as explained on Day 1.

plan writing by discussing writing that is similar

Build a poem 1 ⓒ🅓

Purpose: for children to see the first stage of growing a poem

- Explain to the children that words don't always behave themselves and sometimes they trick us into thinking they mean different things, e.g. if we just *hear* the word *tale/tail* (a homophone), we might get a picture in our heads of a story or something a dog wags.
- Tell the children that some of the compound words they looked at yesterday could make us think of very strange and amusing images. Display **CD (file 7.1)** to show surreal pictures matched to the compound words *water-cycle*, *tap dancer* and *crossbones*.
- TOL as you briefly talk through the pictures and words. You may wish to make the link between the surreal pictures and the nonsense poem 'Night Mer' they heard last week by saying that these are *nonsense* pictures.
- Say that you love the idea of the bones that are really cross and you have made some funny phrases to describe them.
- Write these funny phrases on the board or flipchart:
  raging rattlers
  angry clatterers
  Use MT/YT to say the funny phrases.

- Say that you also have some funny phrases about the bicycle for riding on water. Write the following on the board or flipchart:
  water wheelers
  pedal ploppers
  Use MT/YT to say the phrases.
- TOL about your favourite bits and why you like them, e.g. '*I like the sound of the word* clatterers *because it makes me think of dry bones.*' Mention alliteration, rhyme or onomatopoeia where appropriate.
- Now ask the children to TTYP to talk about their favourite bits and why they like them. Collect feedback and again, mention alliteration, rhyme or onomatopoeia where appropriate.

composing and rehearsing orally; building a varied and rich vocabulary

Write a poem 1 🅿🅑

Purpose: for children to develop the first stage of their own poems

- Tell the children they are going to create their own funny phrases from some other compound words.
- Ask them to turn to the Write a poem 1 activity on pp.41–42 of their Pupils' Book. Explain the activity and model the first one on the board showing how you choose and use words from the word box and TOL as you experiment orally to

create a phrase (you could use different stems, e.g. '*It's a whizz-burner*' or '*fireworks are fizzing flamers*'). Model how you say it aloud to the class before you write it on the board. Make sure you include an example of alliteration and ask them to try to include some alliteration in one of their own phrases.

- Now give the children plenty of time to work individually to create their first phrase following your modelled process: planning it in their heads, saying it to themselves, saying it to their partners and then writing it down in their Personal log. Walk around as they work, supporting, clarifying and praising. Note interesting examples to share with the class.
- Ask the children to repeat the process for their second phrase. Repeat the sharing of interesting examples with the whole class, encouraging children to talk about the choices of words they put together and what effect they were trying to create.

Curriculum link: discussing and recording ideas

Class log

Purpose: for children to share the process of keeping a class reading, writing and thinking log to record responses to texts and activities in a variety of forms

- Give each set of partners a large sticky note. Ask them to TTYP to look at *their* phrases together and to choose one line that uses onomatopoeia and one that has alliteration. If any of the partners haven't got an example of one of these, ask them to choose what they think is the most powerful word they have used instead.
- Ask them to write the two lines on their sticky notes and take turns to stick them in the Class log. Read out a few and then arrange the sticky notes into clusters of threes or fours to show how they become nonsense poems. You may wish to repeat this to show different effects of juxtaposed images.

discussion; develop, agree on, and evaluate rules for effective discussion

Big Question (CD)

Purpose: for children to develop their skills of argument and discussion through a mini enquiry session based on a philosophical question relating to the work of the day

- Display today's Big Question on **CD (file 7.2)**:

  If we make something up, is it real?

- Follow the process as explained on Day 1.

(DAY 8)

discussing writing in order to learn from its structure and vocabulary

Build a poem 2 (CD)

Purpose: for children to see a second stage of growing a poem as a model for their own writing

- Display **CD (file 8.1)** to show your *cross bones* phrases from Build a poem 1. Tell the children that these are the seeds of a new poem that you are going to 'grow' by experimenting with the words, adding words and shaping them into the next stage. Use MT/YT to say the phrases/poem.
- Click on 'TOL' for the first two slides to show some notes. Read the notes aloud and share the thinking process with the children. Ensure the children understand that the notes explain how you are thinking about different ways to develop the poem.
- Click on the next slide to show the revised version of the poem. Use MT/YT to say the revised lines. Then click on 'TOL' to show more notes.
- Click on the next slides, repeating the process of using MT/YT to say the revised lines and revealing and reading out the notes to share the thinking process with the children.
- With the last slide, explain that the poem is still not finished, and so we can call it a *poem in progress* which means we can keep changing it and adding to it as we have more ideas.

Write a poem 2

Purpose: for children to use notes and prompts to grow their own poem

- Give each child a copy of the printable **CD (file 8.2)** and explain that they will be using section A first of all. Explain how you would like them to use the notes given to experiment with the poem in progress.
- Ask them to write another two or three lines and emphasise that this is a chance to try out ideas so crossings out and changed minds are good! Some children will prefer to do this kind of activity individually while others may want to work with a partner. The activity will work either way.
- When the children have completed their experiments, choose a few children to share their writing with the group. Scribe some of their contributions on the board to show the variety of ideas from the same source.
- Now tell the children to find their own phrases that they wrote in their Personal log yesterday. Tell them that they are going to begin to grow and develop their own poems by experimenting and adding to their own phrases.
- Ask them to look at section B of the sheet and read through the prompts in the notes again. You may want to explain and model how they could begin.
- Remind the children to think of their writing as a poem in progress and to be willing to try out lots of ideas, cross them out and try again.
- Tell them to remember to say their new phrases aloud to hear the effect of different words put together before they make up their minds what to keep and what to change.
- Give the children an opportunity to share what they have written with their partners and then ask for examples to read out to the class. In your feedback, draw attention to any alliteration, onomatopoeia, rhyme, repetition, etc. to reinforce their knowledge of poetic features as they begin to use them instinctively in their writing.

Personal log

Purpose: for children to keep a personal log for recording and reflecting on their exploration of word play and poems

- Remind the children that they now know lots of poetic features. Write these features on the board or a flipchart: *onomatopoeia, alliteration, rhythm, rhyme, repetition.* Ask the children to TTYP to talk about which feature they like best and why.
- Now ask them to Popcorn their answers. Tell the children to write down their favourite poetic feature in their Personal log and to write a sentence explaining in their own words, what it is and why they like it.
- Ask them to write a brief example from any poem, song, skipping song or nursery rhyme they know. Some children may need support for this part of the activity. Choose a few children to share their examples.

Big Question

Purpose: for children to develop their skills of argument and discussion through a mini enquiry session based on a philosophical question relating to the work of the day

- Display today's Big Question on **CD (file 8.3):**

  If we think something we have created is good and others say it isn't, should we change it?
- Follow the process as explained on Day 1.

DAY 9

Curriculum link:
understand
the skills and
processes that
are essential for
writing

Build a poem 3

Purpose: for children to see a third stage of growing a poem as a model for their own writing

- Tell the children you now want to experiment with growing the *water-cycle* funny phrases. Display **CD (file 9.1)** to show the phrases. Use MT/YT to say them.
- Click on 'Reveal' to show a notes page and an arrow linking the first few notes. Share the thinking and linking process with the children as you did before – keep it pacey and brief. Draw attention to the revised version of the poem. Use MT/YT to say the revised lines.
- Click again on 'Reveal' to show more notes and amends.
- Click to the next slide and repeat the process over the next screens using the arrows and notes to TOL about revisions and possibilities and using MT/YT to say the revised lines.
- Explain that the poem is still not finished, and remind them that we can call it a poem in progress which means we can keep changing it as we have more ideas.
- Explain that you have thought about adding the two poems together to make a longer poem. Display **CD (file 9.2)** to show the poem to the children.
- Ask the children to read the whole poem aloud chorally and TTYP to say what they like about the poem so far.
- Explain that you think there should be a longer line at the end of the first stanza to match the shape of the water-cycle stanza and you have one ready. Click 'Reveal' to add the extra line at the end of the first stanza.
- TOL about the effect of the words and the extra line and ask the children to read it aloud again chorally.
- Now ask them to TTYP to share whether the poem seems to be finished or still a poem in progress. Take feedback and accept any point of view, but ask for reasons to support their answers.
- Ask them to TTYP to think of a title for the poem and take feedback.

Evaluate

assessing the
effectiveness of
others' writing

Purpose: for children to develop a confident approach to critical analysis

- Tell the children to look at the Evaluate activity on p.43 of their Pupils' Book and ask them to use the prompts to evaluate the effectiveness of the poem and poetic features. Take feedback and then tell them that these sort of prompts will be useful when they are writing their own poems.

Write a poem 3

composing and
rehearsing orally;
drafting and
re-reading; read
aloud their own
writing

Purpose: for children to use notes, prompts and what they have seen modelled, to complete their own poem

- Tell the children that they are now ready to complete their own poems. Make sure that they have their Write a poem experiment sheets to look at and their own phrases (from Write a poem 1, Day 7) in their Personal log to refer to.
- Now ask them to look at the Write a poem 3 activity prompts on **CD (file 9.3)** and to use these plus ideas from your modelling, to complete their own poems.
- The children also have the final, developed poem you modelled with them, on p.43 of their Pupils' Book to refer to.
- Encourage children to rehearse their ideas with their partners before they begin to write. Remind them to be willing to make changes and play with the sounds and rhythm of words. Even though the children are being asked to complete a relatively small piece of writing, the emphasis is on confident language play and they should be given enough time to enjoy experimenting, reading work out to their partners and re-working ideas.

Fiction: Poetic language and word play

Curriculum link:
listening to a wide range of poetry; reading for a range of purposes

Class log

Purpose: for children to share the process of keeping a class reading, writing and thinking log to record responses to texts and activities in a variety of forms

- Note that before the lesson, you will need to print **one copy** of the poem from printable **CD (file 9.5)** for you to read out to the children later on in the session.
- Display **CD (file 9.4)** and ask the children to follow the poem 'Night Mer' again as you read it aloud to them. Show your relish for the crazy combinations of sounds that make up the nonsense words as you read.
- Remind them that the first letters and sounds in lots of the words have been switched to make nonsense words.
- Tell the children that you have the copy of your poem re-written in the style of 'Night Mer' and you would like to read it to them. Ask them to close their eyes as you read out from the copy of printable **CD (file 9.5)** so that they can savour the sounds.
- Now display **CD (file 9.6)** to show the re-worked poem and then when they have opened their eyes, they can read it out chorally with you. Make sure they know that it doesn't matter if they say the words slightly differently to you or their partner or get muddled up – stress the fact that it is the fun of nonsense words!
- Explain that you are going to paste a copy of the poem into the Class log. Tell them that when they get home, they could look and listen out for a short, everyday phrase (a maximum of three words) that they read or hear people say and have a go at switching the first letters round, e.g. *Time for bed!* could become *Fime bor ted!* and *Get down!* could become *Det gown!* Words that start with a vowel can be harder to switch!
- Ask them to write one or two phrases down and bring them to share and add to the Class log. You may want to warn the children that sometimes they may accidentally make a rude word but you don't want those in the Class log!

Note that children will need access to IT equipment in the next lesson.

Shape

Purpose: for children to experiment with writing lines from their poems in different shapes

- Tell the children that now they will think about how they could shape their poems. Remind them of the work you have done looking at shape poems, and ask them to TTYP and discuss with their partner how they could change the shape of the poem by ending or starting the lines in a different place. Scribe some examples of different shapes on the board or flipchart, e.g.

They are such water swooshers.

to

They are such…
water swooshers

or

They are such water
          swooshers!

TOL as you think about how changing the punctuation and line breaks would change a reading of the poem. Then model how they could change the size or spelling of special words for effect, e.g.

They are such water swooshers

or

They are such water swooooooooooshshshshers!

- Collect feedback of some changes they would like to make and scribe some examples to share with the class.

Curriculum link: assessing the effectiveness of their own writing

Share, evaluate and edit

Purpose: for children to share their own and other children's poems

- If necessary, give children some time to complete the poems they were working on in Write a poem 3 (Day 9).
- Now ask the children to read through their own poem, underlining their favourite words, or the line they think creates the best effect, such as repetition. Display **CD (file 10.1)** to remind them of what to look out for. Ask them to share their thoughts about where they have met the criteria with their partners.
- Collect feedback on these 'best bits' from partners and make sure that some of their favourite words or phrases are added to the Class log.

proofread for spelling and punctuation errors

Proofread

Purpose: for children to proofread their work and make changes to improve the accuracy of their grammar, punctuation and spelling

- Now ask the children to proofread their work. If you have noticed that several children need to improve on a particular aspect of spelling, grammar or punctuation, use this as a focus for the Proofread activity. Write an example which includes common errors from the children's writing and use this as a model.
- The children should always be checking for standard use of punctuation and correct spelling of common exception words.
- The following points would be relevant as the particular focus for this Unit:
  - checking and if appropriate, adding, different punctuation, e.g. exclamation marks or ellipses.

Publish

Purpose: for children to use IT to develop their presentation skills to publish their poems for a wider audience

- Tell the children that you want to publish your water-cycle and crossbones poems as a lovely, illustrated document. Explain that you have two examples of the poem in electronic form and you would like their opinion as to which one you should publish for others to read.
- Display **CD (file 10.2)** to show the first example. Ask the children to TTYP to say what they like most and what they like least about it.
- Now navigate to the next slide to show the second version and ask the children to TTYP to say what they like most and what they like least about it. Collect feedback from two or three sets of partners.
- Ask the children to make up their minds individually about which one you should keep and publish and put it to the vote. Print off the one they vote for from **CD (file 10.3)** and display it on your Poetry wall or paste into the Class log.
- Explain to the children that you want them to use their IT skills to create an electronic version of their own poems to publish in a booklet for the school library. If you have a school intranet, you could use this to allow staff and pupils to access the children's poems.

Explanations

READING AND WRITING NON-FICTION

In the Non-fiction reading and writing week, the focus is on investigating and understanding explanation texts, in particular focusing on water-cycles.

See p.100 for the daily timetable for the Non-fiction week.

Reading

Children will be taught to:

- explore the aspects of explanation texts that make them clear for the reader
- investigate different types of explanation texts.

Writing

Key writing purpose to be shared with the children:

To write two clear and useful explanations, then present them to the class.

Writing evaluation to be shared with the children

My explanations:

- describe a process using clear and useful diagrams, with labels and symbols
- use continuous prose to explain a process
- can be used as part of a presentation, so I can share my understanding of a process with my class.

Grammar:

- includes adverbs of time and conjunctions to help the reader understand the sequence in which things happen (*First, Then, Now*) and cause and effect (*so, therefore*).

See the Planning section of the Software ('Timetables' tab) for a printable version of the Writing purpose and evaluation.

DAY 11

Curriculum link:
reading for a range
of purposes; learn
the conventions of
different types of
writing

Think and link ⓒⒹ

Purpose: for children to become interested in explanation texts via one of the Big Questions
they have explored

- Display the Big Question from Day 3 on **CD (file 3.6):**

  Is it easier to use words or pictures to explain or describe something?

- Ask the children to TTYP to recall some of what they discussed before and take feedback.

- Remind them that when they were exploring the poem 'Water-cycle' by Andrew Fusek Peters, they read lots of words and looked at pictures that *described* parts of the water-cycle process. Say that these words and pictures created an impression of movement and energy and made the water seem almost human. (For example, the water *falls asleep*, is *full of river-longing*, she *weeps* and *sings*.)

- Tell the children that today you are going to look at another text about the same subject – the water-cycle – but instead of a poem full of description and images, it is going to be an *explanation* text. This explanation text will also have pictures, but instead of colourful, energetic imaginative pictures, they will be diagrams that give facts and information about the science of the water-cycle.

- Remind the children what an explanation text is. Emphasise that an explanation text is a non-fiction text. Say that when they read text that has a question in the title, such as *How does* … or *Why does* … or *What is* … or *Where does* … it usually means the following text is an *explanation* of how or why something happens, what something is or where something comes from. It *explains* something and so we call this an *explanation* text.

- Give special emphasis to the words *explain, explained, explanations, explaining* whenever you say them, throughout this first non-fiction day.

Introduction to explanation texts ⓒⒹ

Purpose: for children to revise their existing knowledge of the purpose and features of
explanation texts

- Display **CD (file 11.1)** to show some *where, how* and *why* questions and short explanations. Ask the children to read the questions and then you read the explanations.

- Click on 'Highlights' to highlight the parts of the questions that show they are inviting an explanation.

- Click to the next slide to show a *what* question and an answer which includes a simple diagram. Click on 'Highlights' to highlight *What is*, then ask the children to TTYP to share why they think a diagram was included in this answer. Take feedback and make sure the children understand the purpose of diagrams in explanation texts. (To make the information clear to the reader.)

Pictures into words ⓒⒹ 🄿🄱

Purpose: for children to develop their ability to interpret a diagram and give an oral
explanation

- Say that explanations can be spoken and listened to or written down and read. Diagrams help to make both spoken and written explanations clearer.

- Tell the children that one kind of explanation diagram is a *chain*, explaining how one thing can affect another.

- Display **CD (file 11.2)** showing a food chain. Tell the children that this is a food chain diagram and that you are going to explain the food chain in your own words using the diagram to help you.

- Explain the food chain, in everyday, informal language, hesitating and correcting yourself. Don't make it sound too easy.
- Now ask the children to TTYP to evaluate your explanation. Ask them to decide whether your explanation was clear and easy to understand. Take feedback and tease out whether they thought it:
  - was in a logical order
  - included useful adverbs of time such as *next* and *then*
  - helped to make sense of the diagram.
- Ask them to indicate with a 'thumbs up or down', whether they would have understood the explanation without seeing the diagram. Take feedback.
- Tell the children to look at the Pictures into words activity on pp.44–45 of their Pupils' Book. Explain that the first diagram (A) shows another cycle diagram, a bit like the water-cycle. Ask them to make the shape of the diagram with one hand, following the arrows. Point out that in cycle diagrams things start and finish at the same place, then go round again.
- Say that Partner 1 is to explain the first diagram to Partner 2. Tell Partner 2s that they might be asked to share their partner's explanation with the rest of the group so they must listen carefully.
- Choose a couple of Partner 2s to share the explanations and prompt them to discuss clarity, etc.
- Explain that the second diagram (B) is a different kind – it is a chain diagram rather than a cycle diagram. Encourage the children to make the shape of the diagram with one hand, following the arrows. Ask them to swap partner roles and repeat the interpretation and explanation process.
- Choose a couple of Partner 1s to share the explanation.
- Ask the children to TTYP to make up a title in the form of a question for each of the diagrams. Remind them to use *How ...? Why ...? What ...?* or *Where ...?* in the title.

Grammar: prefixes (CD) (PB) (HB)

<table>
<tr><td>

Curriculum link: Year 3 Grammar
formation of nouns using a range of prefixes

</td></tr>
</table>

Purpose: for children to develop awareness of the function of prefixes

- Tell the children that life-cycle diagrams usually have arrows going in a clockwise direction. Remind them what the word *clockwise* means.
- Explain that if something were moving in the *opposite* direction to the hands of a clock, we would say it is going in an *anticlockwise* direction.
- Say that anti- means against or opposite and it is a prefix. Display **CD (file 11.3)** to show a definition of the word *prefix*. Use MT/YT to read it aloud.
- Say that there are many more prefixes that help us to make new words from root words. Click on 'Next' to show the words and definitions grid. Tell the children that the definitions in the final column are in the wrong order. TOL about which definitions to use with which words. Drag and drop the correct definitions into the cells on the grid.
- Now click on 'Next' to show another grid. Ask the children to TTYP to say what they think the meaning of each prefix could be. Collect feedback, clarify and then and drag and drop the correct prefixes into the empty cells.
- Ask the children to look at the Grammar: prefixes activity on p.45 of their Pupils' Book. Guide them through the instructions and then ask them to TTYP to complete the activity.

Homework Book p.16 provides further practice on prefixes.

Curriculum link:
discussing writing
in order to learn
from its structure,
grammar and
vocabulary

Class log

Note that you will need to collect a few examples of different kinds of explanatory texts, including diagrams before this part of the lesson, e.g. a class evacuation diagram showing routes and exits in case of fire, a diagram showing positions on a netball court or sports field, a diagram of a domestic appliance, or an explanation of recycling from the council. Check that these example texts are explanations rather than instructions! If necessary, make photocopies of them, so they can be stuck in the Class log.

Purpose: for children to share the process of keeping a class reading, writing and thinking log to record responses to texts and activities in a variety of forms

- Tell the children that you have been collecting some examples of written explanations and diagrams from home and school to show them.
- Talk through how you know they are explanations and what they are for (perhaps remind them that these are for real audiences and purposes) and pass them round for partners to look at.
- Say that you are going to add an Explanations section to the Class log. Paste some of the examples you found into the Class log.

Deconstruction 1 🅰

Purpose: for children to develop experience of reading explanation texts

- Tell the children that they are going to see an explanation of the water-cycle given by Professor Tapp. Ask them to look at the 'Where does water come from?' text on pp.54–55 of the Anthology. Explain that it is a transcript of a children's TV science programme.
- Draw attention to the glossary and explain that a glossary explains unusual or difficult words. Use MY/YT to say the glossary words and their definitions and to practise the pronunciation of the words.
- Now ask the children to follow the text on the water-cycle diagram as you read it aloud. Remind them that they read an imaginative description of the same process in the poem 'Water-cycle'. (If necessary, ask the children to turn to the poem in the Anthology and read it to them to refresh their memories.) Ask them to TTYP to share which text explained the process most clearly – the poem or the non-fiction explanation? Stress it is a question of opinion rather than one with a right and wrong answer.
- Take feedback and tease out the reasons for their answers and link to the structure or language features of the different texts if appropriate, e.g. if a child says the non-fiction explanation is easier to understand, it might be the connecting adverbs or the scientific language that helps. If a child says the poem, it could be because of the powerful imagery that helps them to picture the process.
- Now ask them to TTYP and take turns to read sections of the explanation text aloud.
- Tell the children that explanation texts are usually written in the present tense. Write this sentence from the text on the board or flipchart: *The air cools down.* Draw attention to the verb in the present tense – *cools*.

In your own words 🅰

Purpose: for children to develop their ability to summarise parts of a text

- Ask the children to look again at the section of 'Where does water come from?' on p.55 of the Anthology. Use your own TOL to model picking out the most important points from a section and putting them in your own words.

DAY 12

reading for a
range of purposes;
checking that the
text makes sense
to them

- Explain that Partner 1 should read aloud the text panel starting *Warm winds . . .* to Partner 2. The book should then be turned over or covered up while Partner 2 uses his/her own words to summarise what has just been said.
- Ask them to repeat the process with Partner 2 re-reading aloud the text panel starting *The air cools . . .* and Partner 1 summarising.
- Repeat the process for the two remaining text panels.

> **Curriculum link:** discussing non-fiction; learn the conventions of different types of writing

Zoom in on features of explanations

Purpose: for children to become familiar with the language and features of explanation texts

- Tell the children that explanation texts have special language features that help us to understand how something happens or works. Display **CD (file 12.1)** to show a grid of some key language features of explanation texts. Read out the first one and remind the children that they have already seen an example of a sentence written in the present tense. Ask them to spot other examples of present tense verbs, e.g. *turns, joins, bursts*.
- Draw children's attention to the second entry in the grid and discuss why information needs to be clear and detailed, and why facts are important (e.g. so it is not confusing, and because it is real information that is being looked for, not imaginative ideas).
- Tell the children that to make spoken and written explanations easier to follow and understand, they are usually organised in a special way.
- Click to the next slide to show some key *structural* features of explanation texts. Read out the first one and ask the children to TTYP to find an example in their Anthology text. Take feedback and draw out the reasons why this might be an important feature.
- Repeat the process with the other structural features.

> discussing writing that is similar to that which they are planning to write; composing and rehearsing sentences orally

Write 1

Purpose: for children to develop their ability to interpret a diagram and to write a simple explanation

- Before the lesson starts, print out copies of **CD (file 12.2)** for every child. Give them out at the beginning of this activity.
- Tell the children to look at the diagram and to TTYP to say what kind of diagram it is (*a life cycle*). Take feedback. Now ask them to TTYP to interpret the diagram and explain what it is showing. Choose one or two partners to share their interpretations and explanations with the whole class. Make sure that they have understood the basic principle of the diagram, clarifying specific vocabulary where necessary.
- Explain that you would like them to TTYP and use the diagram and writing frame to create sentences to explain the life cycle. Model this for the children and then hide your example. Ask the children to rehearse their sentences before writing them in the frame provided.

> building a varied and rich vocabulary; discussing and recording ideas

Class and Personal log – similes

Purpose: for children to keep a personal log for recording and reflecting on their exploration of explanation texts

- Remind the children that a simile is when something is said to be like something else, e.g. *the iceberg is like a glass mountain*.

- Say that Professor Tapp used a simile in his explanation, i.e. 'Warm winds and the heat of the sun act like a giant hair dryer.' Write the simile in the Class log.
- Ask the children to TTYP to share why they think Professor Tapp used a simile in his explanation. Collect feedback, e.g. *it helps us to imagine the action he is explaining*.
- Now ask them to look at their Write 1 sheet.
- Explain that you would like them to TTYP to think of similes to describe a chrysalis hanging from a twig. For example, *like a bauble on a Christmas tree ... or like an earring hanging from an ear*.
- When they have said their similes aloud to each other, they should write them in their Personal log. Choose two or three partners to share their similes.
- You may wish them to paste their Write 1 sheets in their Personal log.

DAY 13

Deconstruction 2

Purpose: for children to be able to identify the intended audience of an explanation text and work out what key feature is missing

Curriculum link:
identifying how language, structure and presentation contribute to meaning

- Before the lesson, print a copy of **CD (file 13.2)** for each pair of children.
- Display the **CD (file 13.1)**. Tell them that 'How Your Loo Works' is another example of an explanation text and then ask them to follow the text as you read it aloud.
- Give each set of partners a copy of printable **CD (file 13.2)**. Ask them to TTYP to take turns to read each sentence aloud to each other.
- Tell them to look at the language of the text and TTYP to decide who the audience is meant to be: adults, teenagers, children, very young children? Collect feedback and ask them to explain why; what clues did they find to help them?
- Now ask the children to TTYP to identify something in the explanation that is not important or necessary for our understanding of how our loos work. Say that it needs to be something that is just there to make it more interesting or funny. Take feedback and ask the children to give reasons for their choices.
- Say that you have noticed that something is missing from this explanation text that you would have expected to see. Ask the children to TTYP to decide what is missing (a diagram).
- Ask them to Popcorn the answer and make sure they have noticed there is no diagram.

retrieve and record information from non-fiction

Write 2

Purpose: for children to work in a group to create an effective diagram to support a written explanation

- Organise the children into groups of four per table. There should be large sheets of paper, plain A4 paper, scissors, glue, etc. for the children to make large diagrams of a suitable size for presentation to other groups.
- Tell the children that they are going to work in small groups to create their own diagrams to go with the 'How Your Loo Works' text. They can each work on different parts of the explanation, then glue them all together at the end.
- Say that you have five Top Tips for creating good diagrams that will help them. Display **CD (file 13.3)**. Click on 'TOL' to show think bubbles, and use them to talk through the tips.
- When you have played it through once, ask the children to TTYP to recall at least two of the Top Tips. Choose partners to feed back.
- Explain that you will play the Top Tips again and they should watch carefully. Then display the summary of the tips on the CD file while they are creating their own diagrams.

- Remind the children to keep looking at the text in the printout, to check what they need to put in their diagrams. (If children need support, you could encourage them to think of a cycle diagram, focusing on the following stages: water flushing loo, pipes into a big sewer, treatment building for filtering and chemicals, water into reservoir or lake.)
- Give the groups enough time to complete the activity and walk round as they work, encouraging, supporting and praising good diagrams and good group discussions and co-operation. You may wish to take photographs of the groups working together and/or of the groups' presentations (see below) to add to the Class log or for display.

Curriculum link: read aloud their own writing, to a group or the whole class

Presentations

Purpose: for children to practise explaining a process clearly, using a visual aid

- Tell the children that when they have finished their diagrams, they can present and explain them to the rest of the class.
- Give them time to discuss which parts each person will be explaining, who will hold up the diagram, who will point to the relevant section, etc. Encourage them to make sure everyone has a role.
- You may wish to invite one group at a time to present to the rest of the class or have two or three presenting to two or three other groups simultaneously on a rotation basis.
- Give feedback to the whole class, talking through examples of clear, well-planned diagrams and presentations.

discussing and recording ideas; write for a range of real purposes

Personal log

Purpose: for children to keep a personal log for recording and reflecting on their exploration of explanation texts

- Ask the children to TTYP to discuss how they felt they contributed to the making of the diagram.
- Choose two to feed back. Now ask them to write a sentence or two in their Personal log about their contribution. Model how to do this under a heading: *How I helped to make the diagram.*
- Repeat the process with the heading: *How I helped in the presentation.*

DAY 14

Deconstruction 3

Purpose: for children to participate in shared writing of an explanation text

discussing writing in order to learn from its structure, grammar and vocabulary

- Ask the children to TTYP to share two or three things they know about the sea. Take feedback.
- Tell them that they are going to read some more *facts* and *information* about the sea from Professor Tapp. Display **CD (file 14.1)** and use MT/YT to read through Professor Tapp's statements, clicking on 'Reveal' to reveal them.
- Close the screen and ask the children to TTYP and recall any *facts* or *information* about the sea from what they have just read.
- Explain that you know it is a *fact* that the sea has waves because that *information* was given, but you now want an *explanation* to tell you how waves are made.
- Ask them to TTYP to share their own experiences of waves at the seaside or in a swimming pool where there is a wave machine. Choose two to feed back and draw out experiences of the strength and power of even small waves and encourage them to speculate about how waves are made.

- Say that Professor Tapp wrote a few notes that could help to explain, but they are not in the right order. Display **CD (file 14.2)**. Read the notes aloud to the children and then TOL about what order to put the notes in to make sense of them, e.g.
  Title: *How are waves made?*
  Opening sentence: *Have you got a lot of energy? Well, energy makes waves!*
  Main explanation:
  A lot of energy is created by the wind.
  As wind blows across the surface of the sea, it passes its energy to the water.
  The energy then turns the water into a wave.
  Stronger winds travel faster and blow longer. This makes more energy and larger waves!
  Closing sentence:
  So next time you see a wave, you know it is made from the wind's energy!
- Say that the notes can be used to make a good, clear explanation text and you are going to use the explanation grid they looked at before (on Day 12) to help you.
- Click to the next screen and draw attention to the explanation grid and use TOL and TTYP to decide which sentence you would use first of all. Drag and drop the sentence into the grid.
- Continue to use TOL, TTYP and feedback, trying out their suggestions using drag and drop for each sentence. Keep the most appropriate suggestions. The important thing is for them to think about the organisation of the text and to see the logic involved in the process.
- Continue the TOLs with the children, to complete the grid and ask them to follow the grid carefully as you read the whole 'text' aloud.
- You may wish to save and print the grid out before tomorrow (Day 15) and paste it into the Class log.

Write 3

Purpose: for children to create an explanation text

- Before the lesson, print a copy of **CD (file 14.4)** for each child.
- Explain that you now want the children to find out more about one of the other facts about the sea. Say you want to know why the sea is salty.
- Display the diagram on **CD (file 14.3).** Ask the children to look at the diagram showing how salt gets into the sea and to TTYP and talk about what they can work out from the diagram so far. Gather feedback from sets of partners to correct and clarify their understanding of the process.
- Point out that because the text is within a diagram, the arrows take the place of the adverbs of time. Click 'Reveal' to show how an adverb of time could be added. Click again to show them in a new position. Remind the children that because the process is a cycle, *First* could be put next to any part of the diagram.
- Give each child a copy of printable **CD (file 14.4)**, an empty explanation grid. Talk through the grid and model on the board or a flipchart how to use the diagram to create sentences that can be used to explain what makes the sea salty.
- Remind the children to say each sentence to their partner to check it makes sense before writing it down in their own grids.

Class log

Note that you will need a tray or large tub of water and some drinking straws.

Purpose: for children to share the process of keeping a class reading, writing and thinking log to record responses to texts and activities in a variety of forms

- Remind the children of the explanation about the wind's energy making waves in the sea. Say that you have thought of a way of showing how it works.

Curriculum link:
composing
and rehearsing
sentences orally;
drafting and
re-reading to
check meaning
is clear

write for a range
of real purposes
and audiences;
these should
underpin the
decisions about
form such as an
explanation

- Show the children a tray or tub of water. Say that this represents the sea. Explain that you are going to use a straw to blow air across the surface and this will represent the wind. Demonstrate how to create mini waves through wind-powered energy!
- Set out one tray of water and a few straws per table (e.g. one table per six children) and ask the children to take turns creating their own waves. Take photographs to paste into the Class log.

  Note that ICT access is desirable in the next lesson.

 DAY 15

Write an explanation text

Purpose: for children to re-write parts of an explanation text

- Allow time for the children to complete their grids from Day 14 if necessary.
- Ask them to TTYP to share what they have written and to check it makes sense.
- Explain that you want them to look at the opening sentence in the grid that was written for them. Use MT/YT to read it aloud.
- Say that you would like everyone to have a slightly different opening sentence. Write it out on the board or a flipchart and then model how you could change the wording, e.g.
  There are billions of tons of salt in the world's seas, so how does it get there?
  The world's seas are full of salt, but how does it get there?
  Have you ever wondered what makes the sea so salty? Read on!
- Use MT/YT to say the new sentences and then hide them. Ask the children to TTYP to share ideas for a different opening sentence. Collect feedback and scribe a couple of their ideas.
- Hide all the examples and ask them to cross out the old opening sentence in their grid. Ask them to create their own new opening sentence, say it to their partner and then write it in the grid underneath the old one.
- Now ask them to look at the closing sentence they were given on the grid and to TTYP to share ideas for a different sentence to end on. Collect feedback and then ask them to cross out the original sentence and to write their own underneath when they have said it to their partner.

Curriculum link: assessing the effectiveness of their own writing

Evaluate and edit (CD)

Purpose: for children to evaluate their own and others' work

- When the children have completed their writing, display the prompts on **CD (file 15.1)**. They should consider their group diagram and presentation, as well as the explanation they have written.
- Ask them to TTYP to follow the questions as you read through them. Explain that you want them to use the questions to check how clear their explanations are.
- Encourage them to share how well they think they did. Choose a few partners to feed back to the rest of the group.
- Now display 'What else could you do?' on **CD (file 15.2).** This gives some extra ideas of what the children could do to improve their explanations before they publish them. Ask them to follow the prompts and examples as you read through them.
- Ask them to TTYP to re-read their writing and discuss which ideas they will use.

Curriculum link:
proofread for
spelling and
punctuation errors

Proofread

Purpose: for children to proofread their work, and make changes to improve the accuracy of their grammar, punctuation and spelling

- Now ask the children to proofread their work. If you have noticed that several children need to improve on a particular aspect of spelling, grammar or punctuation, use this as a focus for the proofread activity. Write an example which includes common errors from the children's writing and use this as a model.
- The children should always be checking for standard use of punctuation and correct spelling of common exception words. The following points would be relevant as the particular focus for this Unit:
  - using present tense consistently
  - checking spelling of high-frequency adverbs of time.
- If you wish and have time, ask children to 'publish' their explanations by writing them up neatly or using ICT to word process them, taking in their Evaluate and edit and Proofread changes.

Words into pictures

Purpose: for children to use their own words to create a diagram

- As a final activity, remind the children that they have used the explanation in the form of a diagram to create an explanation in words. Tell them that they are going to reverse the process now and use just their own explanation – their own words – to create a diagram to show what makes the sea salty.
- Give each child a piece of paper and ask them to use their explanation text to draw and label a diagram. (This may have quite a few similarities to the diagram originally displayed on the CD file, but do not display it again. This is not a memory task, but a reworking through their own ideas.)

identifying how
language, structure
and presentation
can contribute to
meaning

Personal log

Purpose: for children to keep a personal log for recording and reflecting on their exploration of explanation texts

- Ask the children to TTYP to share their diagram with their partner. Choose a few to share with the whole class. Then ask the children to paste their diagrams in their Personal log.
- Ask children to TTYP and think about the different types of explanations they have looked at in this Unit, e.g. cycle diagrams, explanations in continuous prose, spoken explanations. Which did they find clearest and most interesting, as a way of finding out information about something? Take feedback, accepting any answer that is given with good justification.

Fiction: Mystery
Non-fiction: Non-chronological reports

Timetable

WEEK 1   Reading fiction   *Smash and Grab!*

Day 1	Day 2	Day 3	Day 4	Day 5
The story store	Read a story 2 – evidence	Grammar: adverbs and word families	Reading detective 1 📄	Reading detective 2
Think and link 📄	Word power 1 📄	Re-read a story 3	Re-telling the story	Reading detective 3
Class log 📄	Read a story 3	Similes 📄	Personal log 📄	What if not . . .?
Read a story 1 – clues	Class log	Personal log	Big Question	Personal log
Big Question	Big Question	Big Question		Big Question

WEEK 2   Writing fiction   *Smash and Grab!*

Day 6	Day 7	Day 8	Day 9	Day 10
What next? 📄	Build a story 1	Build a story 2	Build a story 3 📄	Write a story 3 (continued)
Build a character 📄	Write a story 1 📄	Write a story 2 📄	Write a story 3	Share a story
Personal log	Personal log	Solve the mystery		Evaluate and edit
Big Question	Big Question	Personal log		Proofread
		Big Question		

WEEK 3   Reading and writing non-fiction   Non-chronological reports

Day 11	Day 12	Day 13	Day 14	Day 15
Think and link	Key features of non-chronological reports	Grammar: sentences	Deconstruction 2 📄	Evaluate and edit
Introduction	Sentence starters	Deconstruction 1 📄	Write 1 📄	Proofread
Word power 📄	Class log 📄	Personal log	Write 2	Broadcast 📄
Read a non-chronological report		Class log 📄	Deconstruction 3	Make a broadcast
Class log 📄			Write 3	
			Personal log	

📄: shows that a file should be printed out from the Software.

Overview of the Unit

This Unit explores a mystery story: *Smash and Grab!* by John Dougherty. Children will explore how authors create mystery and suspense in their writing, and use similar techniques in their own writing.

In the Non-fiction week, the focus is on developing children's understanding of non-chronological reports. They will identify key features of this text type and, with support, write their own non-chronological report. For more information about the Non-fiction week and the Non-fiction writing evaluation criteria, see p.149.

Where appropriate, the children will be encouraged to develop an awareness of audience and purpose in relation to the fiction and non-fiction texts they are reading and writing.

Teacher modelling is provided in the teaching notes, Software and the Pupils' Book, supporting the children's writing at every stage in the Fiction and Non-fiction weeks.

The Homework Book provides a homework activity related to the content of this Unit for each of the three weeks.

Fiction

Reading

Children will:

- explore features of mystery stories by looking at *Smash and Grab!*
- explore how the author creates suspense by leaving clues
- examine how authors build suspense and interest by *showing* rather than *telling*.

Writing

Key writing purpose to be shared with the children:

To write a new mystery story.

Writing evaluation to be shared with the children

My mystery story:

- keeps up the suspense and mystery until the end
- *shows* how a character feels by giving clues, rather than *telling* the reader directly.

Grammar:

- includes speech which is set out and punctuated correctly
- uses carefully chosen adverbs, to create accurate images in the reader's mind.

See the Planning section of the Software ('Timetables' tab) for a printable version of the Writing purpose and evaluation.

Fiction: Mystery
Smash and Grab! by John Dougherty

READING FICTION

Resources
PB Pupils' Book pp.46–55
A Anthology pp.56–67
CD CD on Interactive whiteboard Unit 5
GB Grammar Bank on CD
HB Homework Book pp.17–19

DAY 1

The story store (CD)

Purpose: for children to explore other stories that introduce themes to be explored in the main study text

Curriculum link: listening to and discussing a wide range of fiction, identifying themes

- Note that this activity and the next one refers to two mystery stories: *The French Confection* by Anthony Horowitz and *Ruby Redfort: Look Into My Eyes* by Lauren Child. Summaries are supplied on CD files, but it might be helpful for teachers to familiarise themselves with the books beforehand, and to have copies available in the classroom.
- Ask the children to TTYP (Turn to your partner) and talk about any mystery stories they have read or seen (such as *Scooby-Doo*). Take feedback.
- Ask them to TTYP and talk about what they would expect to happen in a mystery story and what type of characters they would expect there to be. Take feedback.
- Display **CD (file 1.1)** and share the summaries of two mystery stories: *The French Confection* by Anthony Horowitz and *Ruby Redfort: Look Into My Eyes* by Lauren Child. Also look through the character lists for each story, checking understanding of any unfamiliar words.
- Ask the children to TTYP and discuss what makes these stories mysteries. Take feedback.

identifying conventions of different types of writing

Think and link (CD)

Purpose: for children to understand the main features of a mystery story

- Display **CD (file 1.2)** and explain to the children that you are going to look at some of the main features of a mystery story. Go through the slides together. TOL (Think out loud) to explain each of the features and link them to *The French Confection*. For example: '*Many of the characters are a mystery – we don't know if they are good or bad. Small clues give us hints that Erica Nice is indeed a baddie, but we are kept guessing to the end.*'
- Go through the slides again and ask the children to TTYP and discuss each feature, linking it to the other mystery story *Ruby Redfort: Look Into My Eyes*. Take feedback.
- Print off the key features of mystery stories from **CD (file 1.3)** and put them up on your Story wall display.

discussing and recording ideas; predicting

Class log (CD)

Purpose: for children to keep a log for recording and reflecting on their exploration of stories

- Print off the headings on **CD (file 1.4)** that describe the features of a mystery story. Stick them into your Class log, leaving plenty of space around them to add notes and examples.
- Ask the children to TTYP and discuss a mystery story that they have read or seen (such as *Scooby-Doo, The Sarah Jane Adventures, The Famous Five*). Take feedback and sum up some of the main ideas that the children have shared with the class.

- Open the Class log, look through each feature in turn and ask the children to TTYP and see if they can give an example of this feature from their story/programme. Take feedback and write some of their examples into the Class log.
- Repeat for all the headings and then review the information you have gathered. Use this opportunity to make some predictions about the mystery story that you are going to read tomorrow.
- Tell the children that the story title is *Smash and Grab!* Ask them to TTYP to make a prediction about what they think the story might be about. Take feedback. Write a few predictions in the Class log so that you can check them after reading the story tomorrow.

Curriculum link: predicting

Read a story 1 – clues ⓒ

Purpose: for children to be motivated to read the new story

- Explain to the children that you have had some clues about the story sent to you by a police officer called Sergeant Pemberton and he has asked for help in solving a tricky mystery. Convey your own eagerness and enthusiasm and draw the children into your excitement. Perhaps tell them they are 'story detectives'.
- Explain to the children that you will use these clues and the ideas from the Story store to help the sergeant solve his mystery.
- Display **CD (file 1.5)** to show the clues. After each clue appears, ask the children to TTYP and talk about what it means and how it might relate to the story. Note that when you click on the image on the first screen, an alarm sound effect will play.
- Make sure you do not reveal any surprises or the ending of the story at this stage!

discussion; develop, agree on, and evaluate rules for effective discussion

Big Question ⓒ

Purpose: for children to develop their skills of argument and discussion through a mini enquiry session based on a philosophical question relating to the work of the day

- Display today's Big Question on **CD (file 1.6)**:

  Does a person's behaviour always tell us about their intentions?
- Ask the children to TTYP to talk about this question. Collect feedback and scribe some responses on the board or flipchart.
- Click 'Prompts' to show some statements that may help to encourage discussion.

DAY 2

predicting, identifying how language, structure, and presentation contribute to meaning

Read a story 2 – evidence ⓒ

Purpose: for children to hear more about the new story, to make links with their own experiences and to make predictions before they hear the full version

- Remind the children of the clues that you explored yesterday, sent by Sergeant Pemberton. Tell them that Sergeant Pemberton has now found more evidence about the story. Say that you are really excited about what the evidence might be.
- Display **CD (file 2.1)** to show the evidence. Explain that it looks like a police report. Click on the audio button to hear what it says.
- Ask the children to TTYP to make a prediction about where the jewels might be hidden and who has stolen them. Take feedback.
- Say that some more evidence has been found. Click to the next slide to hear some more of the report. Then ask the children to TTYP to make a prediction about who stole the jewels. Take feedback.

Fiction: Mystery

Curriculum link:
discussing words and phrases that capture the reader's interest and imagination

Word power 1 (CD) (PB) (print)

Purpose: for children to become familiar with language in the story and to create a mental model of the language

> *encircled by its high stone wall   congestion and bustle   magnificent marble staircase*
> *The children, perplexed, hurried after Mrs McCreevy   ran breathlessly*

- Display **CD (file 2.2)** to show the phrases. Explain that these phrases are from the main story that the children will read later. Say that you want them to think about how these phrases create powerful images in the mind. Being familiar with these words and images will help the children to understand the story when they hear it for the first time.
- Focus on each phrase in turn. TOL as you describe what images/ideas the phrase brings to mind. For example: '*The magnificent marble staircase creates a picture in my mind of a huge sweeping staircase that curves around the edge of a vast room – the kind of staircase that Cinderella ran down as she left the ball.*'
- Now ask the children to look at the Word power I activity on p.46 of their Pupils' Book.
- You may wish to print these Power words from **CD (file 2.3)** to display on your Story wall. Let the children hear you using some of these in your conversation and teaching and praise them if they use one of them.

checking that the text makes sense, asking questions, drawing inferences

Read a story 3 (A) (teacher only) (PB)

Purpose: for children to hear and enjoy the full version of the story for the first time

- Tell the children that they are now going to hear the whole story for the very first time. TOL about which parts you can't wait to hear about.
- Ask the children to TTYP to share what they are looking forward to in the story.
- Say that you need to switch your Storyteller voice on! Make it a special moment as if you are getting ready for a performance.
- Now read aloud the full story from the Anthology on pp.56–62 with great enjoyment, enthusiasm and appropriate intonation to convey meaning and impact.
- At the end of the story, ask the children to look at the activity on p.47 of their Pupils' Book. Guide them as they TTYP to discuss the questions and feed back to the class. Ensure they have all understood who committed the crime and how.

discussing their understanding; identifying main ideas

Class log

Purpose: for children to share the process of keeping a class reading, writing and thinking log to record responses to texts and activities in a variety of forms

- Ask the children to TTYP and talk about the solution to the mystery. Did they guess the solution before the children in the story? Take feedback.
- Ask the children to TTYP and talk about the clues that helped them work out who stole the jewels. Take feedback and write the clues into the Class log (i.e. the agitated bees, the missing items of clothing, the woman with a sore spot on her throat).
- Tell the children that the author needs to keep the reader on their toes and so they sometimes lay a false trail so the reader thinks another character has committed the crime. We call these false clues *red herrings*.
- Ask the children to TTYP and talk about any time in the story when they thought another character had committed the crime. What clues made them think this? Take feedback and write these clues on another page under the heading *Red Herrings*. (For example, the fact that the man was red-faced and cross; and that the old woman was grumpy.)

Curriculum link: discussion; develop, agree on, and evaluate rules for effective discussion

Big Question (CD)

Purpose: for children to develop their skills of argument and discussion through a mini enquiry session based on a philosophical question relating to the work of the day

- Display today's Big Question on **CD (file 2.4):**

  Is keeping a secret as bad as telling a lie?

- Follow the process as explained on Day 1.

DAY 3

Year 3 Grammar adverbs; word families based on common words; perfect tense

Grammar: adverbs and word families (CD) PB HB

Purpose: for children to understand how adverbs tell us more detail about a verb and to use adverbs in sentences. To develop their awareness and understanding of word families

- Display **CD file (3.1)**. Share the first sentence with the children using MT/YT (My turn/your turn). Ask the children to TTYP to decide what the verb (doing word) is. Take feedback.

- Click 'Verb' to reveal the verb (*buzzed*) and make sure the children understand who or what is doing the verb – in this case it is the bees. Remind them that the sentence is written in the simple past tense. Depending on your group, you may wish to use this as an opportunity to develop their awareness of other forms of verbs such as the past continuous (*Bees were buzzing…*) and perfect tense (*Bees have buzzed…*). For further teacher guidance and explanations you should refer to the sections on verbs and tenses in the Grammar Bank.

- Tell the children that the author has given them extra information about how insects and characters move and act by adding in an extra word to some sentences. This special word is called an *adverb* because it adds information about how the verb (action) is done.

- Explain that the adverb tells us how the bees are buzzing. Ask the children to TTYP and decide which word is the adverb. Take feedback.

- Click 'Adverb' to reveal the adverb *gently*. Now click 'Root word' to show the root word and use MT/YT to share the root word and its definition.

- Finally, click 'My turn' to show a new sentence using the adverb.

- Ask the children to turn to Grammar: adverbs and word families on p.48 of the Pupils' Book and to look at the adverbs activity. Tell them to TTYP to compose their own sentence using the adverb *gently*. Take feedback and scribe a couple of good ideas onto the flipchart. (Note that children don't need to look at the 'Word families' section yet.)

- Click to the next slide to display the second sentence and repeat the process of identifying the verb, adverb, root word, etc. for the next three sentences. Note that on the fourth slide, the verb is made up of two words (*was complaining*) and there are two adverbs. If necessary, point out that *very* does not have a root word, but *loudly* does.

- Tell the children that it can be useful to think of words as belonging to different families. Explain that a human family called Smith will have lots of different people in it but they all belong to the Smith family; they are different kinds of Smiths!

- Explain that words that have the same root word belong to the same *word family*. Tell them that they are going to 'meet the families' of some of the words they have been looking at.

- Display **CD (file 3.2)** to show the first word family. Use MT/YT to read the first row aloud. TOL how to use the word *gentlest* in a sentence. Don't make it look too easy. Use MT/YT to say your sentence and then write it on the board or a flipchart.

- Navigate to the next slide and use MT/YT to read the row aloud. Ask the children to TTYP to think of a sentence using the word *curiosity*. Repeat the process for *breathlessly* and *loudest*.
- Remind them that words have different roles in the *word families*. They might be verbs, adverbs, nouns or adjectives.
- Navigate to the next slide to show the Word families grid. With the children, identify the word class of the word in the last four sentences you scribed on the board or flipchart. TOL to show how you have to think about the role of the word in the sentence, e.g. 'Gentlest *means the most gentle of all doesn't it? So it is describing how gentle something is here and that makes it an* adjective.'
- Now ask the children to turn to Grammar: adverbs and word families on p.48 of the Pupils' Book and to look at the Word families activity. Tell them to TTYP to take turns reading more word families from the *Smash and Grab!* story.

Homework Book p.17 provides further practice on word families.

<table>
<tr><td>

Curriculum link:
checking that the text makes sense, asking questions, drawing inferences

</td></tr>
</table>

Re-read a story 3

Purpose: for children to gain a deeper understanding of the story and to see the text for the first time

- Ask the children to read their copy of the story with their partners, alternate paragraphs each, and to read the words and phrases in bold with great expression! Explain that you will be listening in and looking out for particularly good reading.

Similes

Purpose: for children to become familiar with similes so they can visualise the images that the author creates

- Display **CD (file 3.3)** to explore the three similes from the story. If necessary, remind the children that a simile compares something with something else, giving the reader an image to help their understanding.
- Use MT/YT to read the first simile aloud and click on 'TOL' to show the think bubble to describe what picture the simile creates. Then click 'Image' to show a picture of what the simile makes you visualise in your mind and listen to the sound effect (this plays when you click on the artwork for the first two slides).
- Click to the next slide to display the second simile and repeat. Do the same with the third simile.
- Tell the children that you want them to close their eyes as you read each simile for a second time and visualise the images the similes create for them. After you have read each simile ask the children to TTYP and tell their partner what they saw. Take feedback.
- You may wish to print these similes from **CD (file 3.4)** to display on your Story wall. If possible, try to use these or other similes during the day. Encourage the children to use them too.

building a varied and rich vocabulary

Personal log

Purpose: for children to share the process of keeping a personal reading, writing and thinking log to record responses to texts and activities in a variety of forms

- Ask the children to read the sentence in the Pupils' Book p.49 ' "Well, you can see I'm not hiding those!" snapped the red-faced man, crossing his arms angrily.' and ask them to TTYP to identify the adverb that describes a verb. Take feedback. If necessary, explain that there are many verbs in this sentence, but only one adverb (*angrily*).

Fiction: Mystery

Curriculum link:
retelling stories
orally; discussing
and recording ideas

Personal log

Purpose: for children to keep a personal log for recording and reflecting on their exploration of stories

- Before the lesson print out copies of the picture prompt from **CD (file 4.3)**.
- Give one copy to each child. Tell them to take turns to re-tell the story of *Smash and Grab!* to their partner.
- Ask the children to TTYP and discuss how they could improve their re-telling (for example, by adding extra details about plot, characters, setting).
- Now ask them to annotate extra information or ideas onto their picture prompt and stick it into their Personal log.
- Ask the children to use their annotated picture prompt to take turns to re-tell the story a final time.

discussion; develop,
agree on, and
evaluate rules for
effective discussion

Big Question

Purpose: for children to develop their skills of argument and discussion through a mini enquiry session based on a philosophical question relating to the work of the day

- Display today's Big Question on **CD (file 4.4)**:

  Do things in museums belong to everybody?

- Follow the process as explained on Day 1.

Reading detective 2

Purpose: for children to explore how the author gives the reader clues about characters by showing what they do rather than telling the reader what they are like

- Display **CD (file 5.1)**. Explain to the children that sometimes the author tells us very directly how a character feels. For example, in the story when the children run after Mrs McCreevy it says, 'The children, perplexed, hurried after Mrs McCreevy.' This tells us how the children are feeling – perplexed (puzzled). Click on 'Telling' to show the sentence and a think bubble explaining how you might start to change this to a *showing* sentence.
- Explain that instead of *telling* us, the author could just *show* us instead. Click on 'Showing' to display a similar sentence. Use the think bubble to explain that now the author is not *telling* us that the children are perplexed but *showing* it in their faces.
- Click to the next slide to reveal descriptions of two of the suspects in the story. Click 'TOL' to show a think bubble and use it to explain to the children why this is a *showing* sentence. Click 'TOL' again and repeat the process for the second sentence.
- Explain that the author gives us clues about the characters by *showing* how they behave or act.
- Ask the children to look at the text on p.56 in their Anthology and TTYP to find other examples of the author *showing* us how the characters behave or act. Take feedback and write some of their ideas in the Class log.

Reading detective 3

Purpose: for children to explore how their knowledge of the character and the punctuation of the dialogue helps them create voices for the characters

- Remind the children that when they are reading the story they pick up clues about the different characters. Refer back to the last activity and ask the children to TTYP and discuss what they know about the red-faced man. Take feedback.

- Display his dialogue on **CD (file 5.2)**. Using the children's ideas about what they know of the red-faced man TOL about how this would help you read the dialogue. For example: '*We know he is angry. His red face helps us know he has a temper, so I imagine he might shout and have a waspish tone to his voice.*' (Demonstrate what you mean.)
- Tell the children that punctuation often gives clues as to *how* things are said. First draw attention to the inverted commas and remind the children that they show a character has started and finished speaking. Then point out that the comma after *Well* shows us that the character pauses after this word before he says the rest of the sentence. Explain that based on what you know about the character from the story, you can imagine that he barks out the *Well* crossly.
- Ask the children to TTYP and practise how they think the red-faced man says the first word of the sentence.
- Now point out the exclamation mark at the end of the speech. Explain that this means the character is saying something 'with feeling'. Say that whenever you see this punctuation you always ask yourself '*with what feeling?*' Ask the children to TTYP and discuss how the red-faced man is feeling as he says the sentence. Take feedback and use the children's ideas to say the dialogue in different ways, e.g. with anger, with indignation, mockingly.
- Now ask the children to TTYP and read the speech on the board to each other.
- Click to the next two slides and repeat the process for exploring the other characters' speeches.

What if not. . .? PB

Curriculum link: drawing inferences, participate in discussion about books

Purpose: for children to consider how character, setting and plot affect each other

- Ask the children to look at the What if not . . .? questions in the Pupils' Book on p.49. Model how you TOL about the first What if not . . .? What if not *a beehive . . .?* What if the thief hid the jewels *somewhere else in the castle grounds*?

  The beehive was a great place to stash the jewels because no one wants to go near bees. If I were the thief I might hide the jewels somewhere I could go back to when the museum was shut, perhaps in the garden, or in the compost heap – (that would be smelly!) or up a tree.

- Now ask the children to TTYP and discuss the other What if not...? questions. Collect feedback and develop answers.

Personal log PB

discussing and recording ideas

Purpose: for children to share the process of keeping a personal reading, writing and thinking log to record responses to texts and activities in a variety of forms

- Ask the children to choose one What if not . . .? question to explore further with their partner and write their ideas in a few sentences in their Personal log.

Big Question CD

discussion; develop, agree on, and evaluate rules for effective discussion

Purpose: for children to develop their skills of argument and discussion through a mini enquiry session based on a philosophical question relating to the work of the day

- Display today's Big Question on **CD (file 5.3)**:

  Can humans ever live together without laws and rules?

- Follow the process as explained on Day 1.

WRITING FICTION

DAY 6

What next?

Purpose: for children to explore alternative settings and descriptive phrases for their new story

- Tell the children that you have discovered the first part of a new mystery story for Adil and Katie to solve but that it doesn't have an ending. Display the first part of the story on **CD (file 6.1)** and read it to the children (it goes over three slides).
- Ask them to TTYP and talk about the setting and what they predict could have been stolen. Take feedback.
- Tell the children that you are going to write the moment in the story when Mrs McCreevy, Sergeant Pemberton and the children discover what has been stolen.
- Model writing three sentences that could be used in the new story. Guidance is provided in the form of a possible script on the printable **CD (file 6.2)**.
  - Use TOL to explain what you are doing and orally rehearse and change each phrase before you write. Focus on creating tension and pace and modelling how you use subordinate clauses to add extra information to the main clauses.
  - Explain how you are setting up the tone of 'excitement' by using accurate verbs and adverbs.
  - Ask the children to say each sentence as you compose it using MT/YT and then write it on a flipchart or the board.
- Once you have finished modelling the writing process, ask the children to turn to p.50 in their Pupils' Book. Encourage them to read each sentence in the paragraph with intonation and expression to show meaning.
- Now ask the children to write their own version of this paragraph in their Personal log, using three sentences based on the style of the original ones. Remind them to look at the prompts in their Pupils' Book. Encourage crossings out, switching words round, etc. Emphasise that this is writing in action, not a neat, finished piece of writing!
- Tell the children to take turns to read what happens next on p.51 of their Pupils' Book.

Build a character

Purpose: for children to work out which parts of an account are facts, and to infer other evidence about the characters from what they say

- Before the lesson, print out a copy of **CD (file 6.4)** for each pair of children.
- Tell the children that the police have surrounded the area and found three suspects for this crime. Display the **CD (file 6.3)**, which has images of the three suspects. Click on each suspect to hear their alibi.
- Click to the next slide to show the notes that Sergeant Pemberton made in his notebook, about the first suspect. Read through the facts and then the evidence, which shows what Sergeant Pemberton infers from these details.
- Click to the next slide to display the second suspect. Click on 'Audio 1' to hear her alibi again and 'Audio 2' to hear some additional questions from Sergeant Pemberton.
- Ask the children to TYYP to work out the facts. Take feedback. Click to the next slide to reveal the main facts about this suspect.
- Ask the children to TTYP and talk about what evidence there is of how the character acts. Take feedback, then click to the next slide to show the evidence you have listed.

- Give the children printed copies of the **CD (file 6.4)**, one between two. Read through the alibi for the third suspect again with the children, then ask them to read the interview in pairs, with one reading the words of Sergeant Pemberton and the other the words of Suspect 3.
- Ask the children to TTYP and work out the facts from the interview. Display the questions on **CD (file 6.5)** and encourage the children to use them. Take feedback and write some key facts onto the flipchart. For example: *the suspect had a connection to the house and especially to the nursery; the meeting with the Head Gardener is easy to prove.*

Curriculum link: inferring characters' feelings, thoughts and motives and justifying inference with evidence

Personal log

Purpose: for children to share the process of keeping a personal reading, writing and thinking log to record responses to texts and activities in a variety of forms

- Ask the children to re-read the transcript of the final suspect's interview on their printout of **CD (file 6.4)**. Ask them to TTYP to work out what evidence there is in the interview that shows us how the character might be feeling. Take feedback.
- Model using the one of the children's ideas and make a short sentence with it. For example: *The suspect might be feeling angry that his great grandfather was given the sack.*
- Ask the children to write up their evidence about the characters' feelings as short sentences into their Personal log.
- Now ask the children to TTYP and look for any evidence in the interview that shows us something about what the character is like. Take feedback.
- Model using the one of the children's ideas and make a short sentence with it. For example: *The suspect can remember some things in detail such as his meeting with the Head Gardener; he is less sure about other details such as what the figures in the garden looked like.*
- Ask the children to write up their evidence about what the character is like into their Personal log.

discussion; develop, agree on, and evaluate rules for effective discussion

Big Question (CD)

Purpose: for children to develop their skills of argument and discussion through a mini enquiry session based on a philosophical question relating to the work of the day

- Display today's Big Question on **CD (file 6.6):**

  Are adults always right?

- Follow the process as explained on Day 1.

DAY 7

plan writing by discussing writing that is similar

Build a story 1 (CD)

Purpose: for children to see a story grow through three stages of development

- Remind the children that they were given clues and evidence as background to the story *Smash and Grab!* before they heard and read the full story. It *prepared* them to read the full story.
- Explain that you are going to show them some questions that helped prepare you to write a full new episode of the story, called 'Queen Victoria's baby clothes are missing!' (Note that this is a continuation of the story started on Day 6.) Show the questions on **CD (file 7.1)** and ask the children to TTYP to discuss the questions.

- Take feedback and then click on 'Reveal' to show the answers. Use MT/YT to read through these answers.
- Click to the next slide to display the picture prompt for the story. Model telling your new mystery story using the picture prompt and the answers to your writer's questions. Your story might be something like:

The children and Mrs McCreevy looked in horror at the nursery. All the furniture was knocked over. Mr Masters went in and discovered that all the baby clothes belonging to Queen Victoria were missing. When Sergeant Pemberton arrived he got the police to surround the area and they found three suspects: Sam Shadowman – a concerned passer-by, Fareeha Malik – the toy expert, Jon Redman – great grandson of Queen Victoria's Head Gardener. When he interviewed them he found out that Fareeha Malik had been the room next door to the nursery at the time of the theft and she had seen a figure disappear with a bundle. Both Jon Redman and Sam Shadowman saw goings on in the vegetable garden and the evidence points to two people involved in stealing and hiding the clothes, probably somewhere in the vegetable garden.

<table>
<tr><td>

Curriculum link:
composing
and rehearsing
sentences orally;
creating settings,
characters, plot
</td></tr>
</table>

Write a story 1

Purpose: for children to plan their story using the picture prompt

- Print off a copy of the picture prompt for each child **CD (file 7.2).** Point out that this is the same setting as before, but you want the children to think about writing another version of the story, using the same characters, but with different objects stolen and different hiding places. For example, it could be a stolen tiara or robe from one of the other rooms along the first floor corridor. The compost heap or island could make a good hiding place, but the thief might get smelly hands or wet feet!
- Ask the children to turn to p.52 of the Pupils' Book and TTYP and read the questions.
- Model answering some of the questions using another stolen object and hiding place. TOL to explain how the place that is chosen for the hiding place will help the children catch the thief, e.g. *'If they went in the maze then they'd have to know the palace well – so that could be Fareeha Malik, the toy expert – she visits the palace a great deal; or Jon Redman because his great grandfather could have told him about the maze.'*
- TOL through the clues that the children should look for to work out who has done the crime, e.g. *'If they went in the maze they would have mud on their shoes or splashes of mud on their clothes.'* Tell the children to TTYP and talk about the crime and who they think has committed it.

<table>
<tr><td>

explore and collect
ideas; write for a
range of purposes
</td></tr>
</table>

Personal log

Purpose: for children to keep a personal log for recording and reflecting on their exploration of stories

- Tell the children to annotate their picture prompt, using ideas triggered by the questions, noting extra information about their mystery story. They should stick their story map into their Personal log.
- When they are ready, ask the children to start writing their own answers to the questions.

Curriculum link:
discussion; develop,
agree on, and
evaluate rules for
effective discussion

Big Question (CD)

*Purpose: for children to develop their skills of argument and discussion through a mini
enquiry session based on a philosophical question relating to the work of the day*

- Display today's Big Question on **CD (file 7.3):**

  Should we stop ourselves judging people before we know them?

- Follow the process as explained on Day 1.

DAY 8

plan writing by
discussing writing
that is similar,
recording ideas

Build a story 2 (CD)

Purpose: for children to see a story grow through three stages of development

- Display the **CD (file 8.1)**. Explain to the children that you have written a first
  draft of your story and you want the children to help you improve it and use it as
  a springboard for their own writing.
- Read the draft with the children using MT/YT. Note that the draft text covers
  two slides.
- Click on 'Showing' on Screen 1 to highlight how you have shown the reader
  something about different characters by their actions.
- Click on 'Similes' to highlight how your similes create vivid images and ideas for
  the reader. Point out that you borrowed the image of lemonade inside Katie's
  brain from the original story.
- Click on 'Verbs' to highlight some (not all) of your verb choices. Ask the children to
  TTYP and talk about which other verbs you could have used. Take feedback and write
  their ideas onto the board or flipchart.
- Click on 'Adverbs' to show how some actions are described in greater detail.
  Ask the children to TTYP and try to use one of the other verbs with an appropriate
  adverb. Take feedback, emphasising how verbs and adverbs work together to
  create a strong picture of what is happening. Again, note good examples on your
  board or flipchart.
- Ask the children to TTYP and talk about which ideas they would like to borrow
  for their story. Take feedback and encourage the children to say how they would
  change the ideas slightly so they fitted their story. (Make sure they don't lift your
  ideas wholesale!)

composing
and rehearsing
sentences orally;
creating settings,
characters, plot

Write a story 2

*Purpose: for children to add adverbs/verbs, showing not telling character sentences and
similes to their plan so they have a detailed plan to write from*

- Before the lesson, print out **CD (file 8.2)** for each pair of children.
- Tell the children that they need to start writing a detailed plan. Give out printed
  copies of **CD (file 8.2)** which will give them a structure to work within.
- Remind the children about the verbs and adverbs that you have gathered on your
  board or flipchart. Remind them how you used *darted* and *scurried* rather than
  ran to describe how the shadowy figures moved to the compost heap. Tell the
  children that they should add/change verbs as they write the information on to
  their plan.
- Tell the children that this is a great time to practise a simile or two to use in the
  story. It could be to describe how a character moves – *he darted like an arrow, he
  stood as still as a stone*, etc.

- Tell the children to TTYP and say and then write their own sentence using the adverb in their Personal log.

Big Question

Purpose: for children to develop their skills of argument and discussion through a mini enquiry session based on a philosophical question relating to the work of the day

- Display today's Big Question on **CD (file 3.5):**

Can an answer ever be the final one? *

- Follow the process as explained on Day 1.

  * This Big Question will be revisited on Day 11 – the first day of the Non-fiction week.

DAY 4

Reading detective 1

Purpose: for children to understand how the author puts clues into the story and makes some things purposely vague so that the reader can feel involved in solving the mystery alongside the characters

- Tell the children that the author has carefully planted clues in the story to interest the reader in the mystery. He has chosen words like *curious*, *odd* and *someone* to make the reader ask questions for example: What is curious? Why is it odd? Who is that someone?
- Display the first extract from the story on **CD (file 4.1)** and read it to the children. Make sure the children know where each extract comes from in the story. Click 'Highlights' to show the clues and then 'TOL' to talk about what clue the author is giving the reader or to explain how they are making a clue purposely vague to keep the reader guessing.
- Click to the next slide to display another extract and read it to the children. Click 'Highlights' to show the clues and then ask the children to TTYP and discuss what the author is doing – giving a clue or making the reader ask a question. Take feedback. Click 'TOL' to show what you think the author is doing.
- Repeat for extracts 3 to 5, taking feedback and using the TOL button to reveal what the author is doing.
- Print out **CD (file 4.2)** to display the clues that the author uses to make the reader ask questions.
- Tell the children to write down any other clues or questions that they find when they read the story on other occasions into their Personal log.

Re-telling the story

Purpose: for children to deepen their understanding and enjoyment of the story by increasing familiarity with the text

- Ask the children to turn to the story *Smash and Grab!* on pp.56–62 of their Anthology and to read the whole story silently to themselves.
- Display the picture prompt on **CD (file 4.3).** Model using the picture prompt to briefly tell the story to the children. Model annotating the picture prompt (using your whiteboard tools) so there is extra detail about the characters, settings or plot to help you tell the story better.
- Tell the story again using your notes to help you.

- Also ask the children to add extra information about the suspects. Encourage them to use the 'show not tell' technique when they describe the characters, so the reader gains an insight into their feelings and what they are like.

Solve the mystery (CD)

Purpose: for children to work out a suitable resolution for their story

- Tell the children that now you are going to work out how the mystery is solved. Display **CD (file 8.3).** Read it to the children. Make links between the clues that have been in the story so far and the place that Queen Victoria's baby clothes were found.
- Ask the children to TTYP and talk about what they know about the suspects and who they think might be the thief. Take feedback.
- Tell the children that you are going to write the ending for your story. TOL as you work through your ideas. For example:

The toy expert Fareeha Malik had the opportunity to get into the nursery and take the clothes and a reason to leave the palace with the bundle. So she could have taken the clothes to the compost heap. Jon Redman was waiting for her. He had a good reason to be in the garden waiting and he could signal to Fareeha when the coast was clear. She hid the clothes and when Redman was sure no one was looking he buried them in the vegetable plot. They could come back and get them later.

- Now explain how the children can find clues to work this out. TOL:

Katie had the right idea – she could sniff the suspects' hands and she would find that Fareeha smelled of compost! But Adil notices something else, he sees the other glove poking out of Jon's pocket. He realises that the two of them planned this audacious theft together.

- Ask the children to TTYP and work out who committed the crime in *their own* story and how Adil and Katie found them out. Remind them that they may have put clues into their story already, like having mud on their clothes, or wet feet.
- Ask them to add their ideas to their detailed plan about how their mystery is solved.

Curriculum link: discussing and recording ideas

Personal log

Purpose: for children to keep a personal log for recording and reflecting on their exploration of stories

- Remind the children that now the crime has changed, so should the title. Ask them to TTYP and discuss who or what should be the focus of the title.
- Model writing a few possible titles, using the children's ideas, on the flipchart. Ask the children to TTYP and discuss what the title of their story should be, then to write the title they have chosen in their Personal log.

discussion; develop, agree on, and evaluate rules for effective discussion

Big Question (CD)

Purpose: for children to develop their skills of argument and discussion through a mini enquiry session based on a philosophical question relating to the work of the day

- Display today's Big Question on **CD (file 8.4):**

Is it fair that one person might have to face the consequences of someone else's actions?

- Follow the process as explained on Day 1.

DAY 9

Build a story 3

*Purpose: for children to see an episode in a story grow through three stages of development
and to see the third stage of writing that will provide a model for their own story*

- Before the lesson print copies of the story from **CD (file 9.2)** for each child.
- Tell the children that you are going to show them how you completed your story.
- Explain that you are going to model writing the Build-up for this section of the story so that they can see how you developed your ideas and sentences. Display **CD (file 9.1)**. Click TOL and Think out loud about how you developed your Build-up section from your draft.
- Give out copies of the printed **CD (file 9.2)**. Explain that this contains the final version of 'your' story – you have developed the rest of the ending and the unveiling of the mystery. Ask the children to take turns to read the story, a paragraph at a time. Remind them to look out for similes, the use of the 'showing not telling' technique, adverbs and accurate verbs and complex sentences that they might like to borrow and adapt for use in their own story.
- Ask them to evaluate your story using the prompts on **CD (file 9.3)**. Take feedback.

Write a story 3 🔲

Purpose: for children to write their story using all the skills they have been exploring

- Tell the children that they are going to write their story now using their picture prompt, all their notes and the ideas in their detailed plans.
- Remind them to use the writing they have done in their Personal log to help them.
- Tell the children to look on p.52 of the Pupils' Book for some Top Tips for writing a page-turning mystery story!
- Children who need more support might focus on developing just one or two sections of their story. Others may be able to develop the whole story.

creating settings,
characters, plot;
monitor whether
their writing
makes sense

DAY 10

Write a story 3 (continued)

Purpose: for children to continue their writing story

- Ask the children to continue writing their story. Use the beginning of the session as a writer's workshop to help children with:
  - using *showing not telling* to give clues about a character
  - taking a phrase or sentence from another source and adapting it to fit their story
  - making sure that the solution to the mystery isn't given away too soon
  - laying out dialogue using the correct punctuation.

creating settings,
characters, plot;
monitor whether
their writing
makes sense

Share a story

Purpose: for children to read their story to a supportive critical partner

- Ask the children to take turns to read the first draft of their story to their partner. The listening partner should look out for any exciting verbs, any *showing not telling* or anything else that makes them enjoy the story.
- Ask the listening partner to feed back to the writer what they think worked really well in the story. This could be a comment about a simile or the choice of particular words, the portrayal of characters or the cleverness of the plot, for example.
- You may wish to spend longer at the Share a story/Edit stage of the writing process using teacher-led modelling to help children improve and polish their writing.

Curriculum link:
assessing the effectiveness of their own and others' writing

Evaluate and edit

Purpose: for children to evaluate their own and their partner's work against specific criteria and then discuss how they could improve their work

- Display **CD (file 10.1)** to show the evaluation prompts and read them together using MT/YT.
- As a model, select an example of work where the writing has met the criteria, and share this with the other children, explaining why it works well.
- Tell the children to take turns to read their partner's writing in pairs and discuss together how well they have met the criteria.
- Ask children to discuss at least two changes they could make to improve their work.

proofread for spelling and punctuation errors

Proofread

Purpose: for children to proofread their work and make changes to improve the accuracy of their grammar, punctuation and spelling

- Now ask children to proofread their work. If you have noticed that several children need to improve on a particular aspect of spelling, grammar or punctuation, use this as a focus for the Proofread activity. Write an example which includes common errors from the children's writing and use this as a model.
- The children should always be checking for standard use of punctuation and correct spelling of common exception words.
- The following points would be relevant as the particular focus for this Unit:
  - using correct punctuation for direct speech.

Further activity

- Publish: ask the children to type up their stories, making any changes from the Evaluate and edit and Proofread activities.

Non-chronological reports

In the Non-fiction reading and writing week, the focus is on developing children's understanding of the key features of non-chronological reports, using texts that focus on the possibility of humans colonising Mars and on space exploration in general.

See p.133 for the daily timetable for the Non-fiction week.

Non-fiction

Reading

Children will:

- think of questions about space for which they would like to find answers
- examine a non-chronological text, looking at its structure and features
- review their understanding of alphabetical order.

Writing

Key writing purpose to be shared with the children:

To write a non-chronological report and then present it to the class.

Writing evaluation to be shared with the children

My non-chronological report:

- includes some facts from my notes about space that the reader will find interesting
- is structured clearly to help the reader find information, e.g. *with headings and subheadings*
- includes extra information in diagrams and pictures with captions.

Grammar:

- includes conjunctions (*and, so, but*) to make the structure of my sentences varied, clear and interesting.

See the Planning section of the Software ('Timetables' tab) for a printable version of the Writing purpose and evaluation.

Non-fiction: Non-chronological reports

Curriculum link: reading for a range of purposes; learn the conventions of different types of writing

Think and link

Purpose: for children to become interested in non-chronological texts via one of the Big Questions they have explored

- Display the Big Question from Day 3 on **CD (file 3.5)**:

  Can an answer ever be the final one?

- Ask the children to TTYP to recall some of what they discussed before and take feedback.

- Tell the children that scientists are often looking for answers to very big questions such as, 'Where else could human beings live?' They do many experiments to try to find the answer. However, different scientists might still have different opinions on what the answers could be, and opinions change with time, so we may still feel they haven't found the final answer.

- Some scientists have been exploring the question 'Could human beings live on another planet, such as Mars?' Explain to the children that the distance between Earth and Mars is about 225 million kilometres (although it varies according to their orbits round the Sun). Scientists have been carrying out experiments for years with animals to see how they (and humans) might cope travelling long distances in space.

- Show the children the slide show of images of Mars and animals in space on **CD (file 11.1)**. Then ask the children to TTYP and discuss what they have seen (even though it will be all speculative at this stage). Take feedback and refer back to the images on the CD when possible.

Introduction

Purpose: for children to understand why we read non-chronological reports

- Tell the children that you would like to find out more about how scientists are exploring the question 'Could humans live on another planet such as Mars?' Ask the children to TTYP and talk about where you might be able to find out more information.

- Take feedback. Draw out that a book or a website article about space travel in general and travel to Mars in particular, would help you find out answers to the question.

- Model composing another question that you would like the answer to, such as *'I wonder how scientists could find out if humans can safely travel all the way to Mars because it is a really long way.'* Model making it more precise, such as *'How can scientists discover if humans can safely travel to Mars?'*

- Ask the children to TTYP and talk about any other questions that they would like to find the answers to, about space travel or making Mars a suitable place for humans to live on. Take feedback and model using the children's ideas to turn them into precise, specific questions and write them on the flipchart.

- Now ask the children to TTYP and think of key words that might help you search for information about space travel or life on Mars, on a search engine or website or book index. Take feedback and write the key words down.

opportunities to discuss language, including vocabulary, extending their interest in the meaning of words

Word power

Purpose: for children to understand technical language used in the non-chronological report before they read it for the first time

> imitation   simulated   habitable   atmosphere   microbes

- Tell the children you have found a text that tells you more about what scientists have been doing to find out if man could live on Mars. Explain that this text has got some special technical words in it.
- Show the children the words on **CD (file 11.2).** Read the words using MT/YT. Click 'Definitions' to show what the words mean. Read them using MT/YT. Then click 'Sentences' on the second slide to see the words in context in a sentence, and read these using MT/YT. Then ask the children to do the Word power activity in the Pupils' Book p.53.
- Print out the words and their definitions from **CD (file 11.3)** to display on the Report wall.

Read a non-chronological report

Purpose: for children to read the non-chronological report for the first time

- Tell the children that they can read about what scientists have been doing to find out if humans can live on another planet such as Mars, in the non-chronological report on pp.63–67 of the Anthology.
- Remind them to keep an eye out for any facts or information that will help answer the questions you wrote earlier during the Introduction activity. Tell the children to take turns reading 'Wanted: A New Planet!' a paragraph at a time.
- When they have read the report, ask the children to TTYP and talk about whether any of their questions have been answered. Take feedback.

<table>
<tr><td>

Curriculum link:
retrieve and
record information
from non-fiction

</td></tr>
</table>

Class log

Purpose: for children to share the process of keeping a class reading, writing and thinking log to record responses to texts and activities in a variety of forms

- Display the words and definitions on **CD (file 11.4).** Explain that these words are going to go in a glossary, so they need to be organised alphabetically.
- Ask the children to TTYP and work out which word would go first in the glossary. Take feedback and then drag and drop the word and its definition to the top of the list. Then repeat for all the remaining words.
- When you have finished, read through the glossary using MT/YT. Then print it so that it can be put in the Class log.

DAY 12

Key features of non-chronological reports

<table>
<tr><td>

discussing
non-fiction; learn
the conventions of
different types
of writing

</td></tr>
</table>

Purpose: for children to become familiar with some of the key language features associated with non-chronological reports.

- Display a page from the Anthology text on **CD (file 12.1).** Explain that you are going to look in detail at two pages of the non-chronological report and identify some of its key features.
- Point out the key features down the left hand side of the slide. Read each label, checking the children's understanding of the terms. You may need to remind them that proper nouns are names given to one particular place or thing, and they start with a capital letter.
- Ask the children to TTYP and decide where each of the key features appears in the text. Share their responses and use your whiteboard tools to draw a line to link the key feature to the correct place in the text.

- Click to the next screen which shows another section of the non-chronological report (p.65 of the Anthology) and repeat the process. Take feedback from the children, annotating the text onscreen with your whiteboard tools and clearing up any misconceptions. Make sure the children can understand that they could read the sections in any order and they would still make sense.
- Now tell the children to do the Key features of non-chronological reports activity in the Pupils' Book p.54. They need to find other examples of these key features in the full report in the Anthology pp.63–67.

Sentence starters

Purpose: for children to read a range of sentence starters and think about how they make the text more interesting to read

- Tell the children that the author gives us a clue about the purpose of each sentence by the way it starts. Some sentences tell us what other people think, others tell us facts, and others ask questions.
- Display the **CD (file 12.2)**. Point out the three different headings for the different purposes of the sentences. Read the different sentence starters using MT/YT.
- Then ask the children to TTYP and talk about the purpose of each sentence. Take feedback and drag and drop the sentence starters under the correct headings.
- Ask the children to turn to pp.63–67 of their Anthology and find the sentences. Then ask them to find one more example of each type of sentence.

<table>
<tr><td>

Curriculum link:

identifying main ideas drawn from more than one paragraph

</td></tr>
</table>

Class log

Purpose: for children to share the process of keeping a class reading, writing and thinking log to record responses to texts and activities in a variety of forms

- Display **CD file (12.3)**. Explain that you are going to look at some of the questions in the non-chronological report, and decide the purpose of these questions. Ask the children to look at the report in their Anthology.
- Read out the first question. Ask the children to work with their partner to find the question in the report in their Anthology.
- When they have found it (it is on p.63), ask the children to TTYP and to talk about the purpose of the question (it might be to introduce a new section, to introduce a new idea, to introduce some new facts, etc.) Take feedback and discuss what the question does. Repeat with the other questions.
- Ask the children to suggest where else questions could be used to engage the reader, to introduce a new section/idea/facts. Take feedback and scribe any of the children's ideas into the Class log.
- Print out the questions from **CD (file 12.4)** and stick them into the Class log.

<table>
<tr><td>

DAY 13

</td></tr>
</table>

Grammar: sentences

Purpose: for children to develop an awareness of compound sentences and subordinate clauses in complex sentences

<table>
<tr><td>

Year 3 Grammar
clause; subordinate clause

</td></tr>
</table>

- Tell the children they are going to explore some different types of sentences. During the following activities, keep each explanation as basic as possible at this stage. The point is to develop their awareness of different kinds of sentences over a longer period of time, not to confuse them or undermine their confidence when reading and writing at this early stage.
- Display **CD file (13.1)** to show a *simple sentence*. Use MT/YT to say it aloud. Explain that all sentences have at least one *clause*.

- Explain that a clause is a group of words that contain a *subject* and a *verb* and make up one part of a sentence. Click 'Next' and point to the relevant parts of the sentence (these are colour coded).
- Click on 'Next' to show a second simple sentence. Use MT/YT to say it aloud and say this also has one main clause. Point to the subject and verb.
- Click on 'Next' to show both sentences. Read them aloud and then say that we can use a conjunction to join them together to make a *compound* sentence. (Remind them that they looked at using conjunctions to make compound sentences in Unit 3.)
- Click on 'Next' to show the compound sentence. Use MT/YT to read it aloud. Point to the colour-coded part of the sentence as you read it, to show the children how the conjunction has replaced the first full stop.
- Explain that each part of a *compound sentence* is equally as important as the other and would make sense on its own. Tell the children that this compound sentence now has two main clauses.
- Explain that we can also have sentences where there is one main clause and another clause that gives us some extra information. Click on 'Next' to show a simple sentence and then read the think bubble aloud. Click on 'Next' again and use the TOL bubble to explain that this is additional information.
- Follow the on-screen prompts to show how the additional information forms a subordinate clause. Tell the children that this is called a *complex sentence*.
- The terms used in this activity should be used and revised at appropriate opportunities throughout the programme. When the children are confident using these terms, you may wish to point out that complex and compound sentences can also be called **multi-clause sentences**, because they have more than one clause in them.

Curriculum link: identifying how language, structure and presentation contribute to meaning

Deconstruction 1

Purpose: for children to read the source materials for a new part of the non-chronological report and learn how to take notes

- Before the lesson, print out copies of **CD (file 13.3)** for each pair of children.
- Tell the children that they are going to write a new non-chronological report about space exploration. It will be about NASA (the American organisation: National Aeronautics and Space Administration) research and manned and unmanned space exploration.
- Explain that you are going to look at some source material for this new section, and you will need to take notes about what you read. Display the web page on **CD (file 13.2)**. TOL about your ideas and thoughts about what the website will tell you as you read the headings of the different sections. Ask the children to TTYP and talk about what they think this web page will tell them. Take feedback and write some of their key ideas onto your flipchart.
- Read aloud the introduction 'About NASA', then click the heading 'Unmanned flights' at the top of the web page. TOL as you read, summarising the main idea in each sentence.
- Now click 'TOL' and use the think bubbles to model how to take notes about unmanned flights. You could also show how you could use abbreviations for longer words, etc.
- Give out printed copies of the material from the web site from **CD (file 13.3)** and ask the children to take turns to read the section: 'Manned flights'. Encourage them to underline key words and talk about what information it gives them, making notes in the way that you modelled with the first section.

Personal log

Purpose: for children to listen to the source materials for a new part of the non-chronological report and take notes

- Display **CD (file 13.4)** and click 'Play' to start an audio file of Professor Red talking about NASA's research in space. Listen all the way through once.
- Ask the children to TTYP and talk about the main points they remembered from the audio. Take feedback and write down their initial points. Try to draw out the main points so the children can use these as headings for their note-taking.
- Ask the children to take turns to read the Top Tips on p.55 of the Pupils' Book to remind them of note-taking skills.
- Remind the children of their task, to take notes about NASA's research. Tell the children to take notes in their Personal log as you replay the audio file, pausing the file at intervals so the children have time to think and write notes. You may wish to play the audio a third time.

<aside>
Curriculum link: discussing and recording ideas; write for a range of real purposes
</aside>

Class log

Purpose: for children to share the process of keeping a class reading, writing and thinking log to record responses to texts and activities in a variety of forms

- Show the children some images of the research on Mars and in space: **CD (file 13.5)**. Ask them to TTYP and discuss what caption could go underneath each picture. Take feedback.
- Print the pictures from **CD (file 13.6)** and stick them into the Class log. Write some of the children's ideas for captions under the pictures.

<aside>
DAY 14
</aside>

Deconstruction 2 📄 **PB**

Purpose: for children to read and identify where a non-chronological report could be improved

<aside>
discussing writing similar to that which they are planning to write
</aside>

- Before this activity, print out multiple copies of the report on **CD (file 14.2)**.
- Display the non-chronological report on **CD (file 14.1).** Explain that it is a first draft and needs a lot of checking and editing. Point out that it is all about manned flights in space. Remind them that on Day 13 they were looking at some information about manned flights.
- Give the children their copies of the report, printed from **CD (file 14.2)**. Remind them that in reports facts need to be checked carefully and ask them to take turns to read the report, looking out for any facts that are wrong. Take feedback. For example, 12 *men have walked on the moon, not 11; John F Kennedy was not an astronaut, but an American President; Neil Armstrong was the first man to walk on the moon in 1969, not 1961.*
- Ask the children to look on p.54 of the Pupils' Book at the key features of a non-chronological report. Model reading one of the key features, e.g. subheading, and look for it in the text. TOL as you discuss how all the headings and subheadings are missing and speculate where it should be and what it should be. For example:

  This first paragraph hasn't got a subheading so it needs one. It's about being a NASA astronaut. Maybe it could be 'So you want to work in space'? or 'Do you have what it takes to be an astronaut?'.

- Ask the children to TTYP and identify where other subheadings could be inserted, to show the reader that the information is divided into groups, so they can find what they are looking for easily. Ask for suggestions for new subheadings and scribe these onto the non-chronological report on screen.

- Go through some of the different key features. Model finding bad examples or lack of examples and talk about how you could introduce or improve them. TOL as you consider each feature. For example: '*The list of attributes needed to be a NASA astronaut could be bullet points – they would be much clearer to read through.*'
- Ask the children to TTYP and find other examples and write short annotations on their versions of the non-chronological report to show what they would do to make improvements. Take feedback and gradually improve the text.

Write 1

Curriculum link: explore and collect ideas

Purpose: for children to use their notes to plan a first draft of their non-chronological report

- Explain to the children that now they will be planning the first draft of their own report, by collecting together notes, checking facts and thinking about what technical language they could include.
- First, explain to the children that they need to check that their facts are correct. Ask children to look at their notes from Day 13 and TTYP to check their own and their partner's facts are correct. Take feedback and ensure that all children have correct content for their first draft.
- Next, remind the children that they might need to use some technical words in their non-chronological reports. Display the glossary on **CD (file 14.3)**. Use MT/YT to read the technical words and the definitions with the children. You can print out the glossary from **CD (file 14.4)** to display on the wall.
- Ask the children if they can see where they can use these technical words in their own non-chronological reports (which are still at note stage). Encourage the children to mark where they could add in the technical words. Take feedback.
- If possible, ask the children to research NASA, manned and unmanned flights using books from the library, or the Internet, and to collect notes that they would like to use in their final report.

Write 2 🅰 🅿🅱

recording ideas; using simple organisational devices such as headings

Purpose: for children to write a first draft of their non-chronological report, using their notes

- Now tell the children that it's time for them to write a first draft of their non-chronological report using the Anthology text, their notes from the audio, and any other sources of information available to them, such as the school library or Internet. Encourage them to include an introduction to explain what NASA is, then at least two other sections focusing on manned and/or unmanned space flight and research in space. Encourage them to draw on the features of non-chronological reports they've looked at to ensure their own report is clear and engaging.
- Remind them to use technical vocabulary where appropriate and to draw on the features of non-chronological reports that they have looked at, e.g. subheadings, pictures, captions, bullet points, including facts. Remind them to look at p.54 of the Pupils' Book for a list of these features.

Deconstruction 3

discussing writing in order to learn from its structure, grammar and vocabulary

Purpose: for children to see the first draft transformed into a non-chronological report

- When the children have completed their first draft, display **CD (file 14.5)**. Explain that it shows your final draft of a non-chronological report about manned space flights. Talk through some of the improvements that you made to the earlier draft they looked at. Point out the use of a title, subheadings, bullet points, present and past tense, the accurate use of facts.

- Tell the children that this draft is not quite finished. Ask them to help you identify what's missing. Tell them to TTYP and talk about what else could be included in this non-chronological report. Take feedback. Draw out that you could add some photos, diagrams, labels, captions, etc. Invite specific suggestions, e.g. *a photo of Neil Armstrong and a caption that says he died in 2012.*

Write 3

Curriculum link: organising paragraphs around a theme; drafting and re-reading to check their meaning is clear;

Purpose: for children to write their own sections of a non-chronological report

- Tell the children to complete their final draft of their own non-chronological report, bearing in mind all the features and improvements that they have just looked at and discussed.
- Encourage the children to make suggestions for images and diagrams that could be included, even if they don't have direct access to them. Remind them of the importance of captions to explain pictures, and labels to explain diagrams.

Personal log

discussing and recording ideas

Purpose: for children to consider the importance of titles and to choose one appropriate for a particular text

- When the children have written their final draft of the non-chronological text, ask them to think of a good title for it. This should be a title that all the subheadings come under. Ask the children to TTYP and discuss possible titles. Take feedback and write some ideas down on your flipchart.
- Ask the children to choose their favourite title and write it into their Personal log so they can use it tomorrow.

DAY 15

Evaluate and edit

assessing the effectiveness of their own and others' writing

Purpose: for children to evaluate their partner's work against specific criteria and then discuss how they could improve their work, in response to their partner's feedback

- Remind the children of the writing they did yesterday. They will now be evaluating and editing this writing to improve it, before turning a section of it into a radio broadcast.
- Display **CD (file 15.1)** to show the evaluation points and read them together using MT/YT.
- As a model, select an example of work from the children where the writing has met the criteria, and share this with the other children, explaining why it works well.
- Tell the children to take turns to read their partner's writing and discuss how well they have met the criteria.
- Ask children to discuss at least two changes they could make to improve their work.

Proofread

proofread for spelling and punctuation errors

Purpose: for children to proofread their work and make changes to improve the accuracy of their grammar, punctuation and spelling

- Now ask children to proofread their work. If you have noticed that several children need to improve on a particular aspect of spelling, grammar or punctuation, use this as a focus for the Proofread activity. Write an example which includes common errors from the children's writing and use this as a model.

- The children should always be checking for standard use of punctuation and correct spelling of common exception words.
- The following points would be relevant as the particular focus for this Unit:
  - checking correct use of conjunctions in compound sentences.

Broadcast

Note that you will need to have the children's non-chronological reports photocopied so they can annotate and alter them for this activity.

Purpose: for children to adapt their non-chronological reports into broadcast material

- Explain to the children that their non-chronological report can be turned into a broadcast for a radio science programme.
- Display **CD (file 15.2)** and click to play the broadcast based on a section of the non-chronological report. Ask the children to TTYP and find the section in their Anthology that it is based on (direct them to p.63). Play the broadcast again and tell the children to look out for how it has been changed from its written form. Ask the children to TTYP and talk about the changes, then take feedback.
- Display **CD (file 15.3)**. Explain that it is a writer's notes that show how a section of the non-chronological report was turned into a broadcast.
- Ask the children to re-read their section of the non-chronological report and TTYP and talk with their partner about how they would alter their writing to make it suitable for radio broadcast. Take feedback and write some of the ideas onto the flipchart.
- Display **CD (file 15.4)**. Explain to the children that this shows some images that could be used to illustrate this section of the report that you are turning into a broadcast. Ask the children to TTYP and discuss which images they think would fit best with different parts of the text. Take feedback, then model how you would write which image you wanted and where, onto the non-chronological report (i.e. using brackets to reference each picture at the correct place in the text).
- Ask the children to alter and annotate their non-chronological report, to transform it into a broadcast script. To support them, display **CD (file 15.5)** showing Top Tips for changing a text into a broadcast.

Make a broadcast

Curriculum link: read aloud their own writing to the class, using appropriate intonation so that the meaning is clear

Purpose: for children to rehearse reading out their broadcast script

- Give the children time to talk through how they are going to organise their broadcast, practising who will read each part of the script. Challenge partners to practise reading with expression to convey meaning and impact. If they wish, they could stand in front of the images from **CD (file 15.4)** to create a visual element to their broadcast.
- Ask the children to read the Top Tips for a good broadcast on p.55 of the Pupils' Book. Remind them to think about these tips when they rehearse and present their broadcast script.
- Confident partners could read out their broadcast scripts to the class.
- If you wish and have the equipment available, you could film the broadcasts using a digital camera. If children have access to computers individually, they could work with their partner in PowerPoint to organise the slide show of images on **CD (file 15.4)** into the order they want, then combine this with their voiceovers to create a television broadcast.

Fiction: Folktales
Non-fiction – Biography and autobiography

Timetable

WEEK 1 **Reading fiction** *The Enchantress of the Sands*

Day 1	Day 2	Day 3	Day 4	Day 5
The story store	Word power 📄	Special phrases 📄	Grammar: prepositions	Story climax
Think and link 📄	Read a story 1 – clues	Re-read a story 3	Settings	Dramatic reconstruction 📄
Key features of folktales 1 📄	Read a story 2 – evidence	Key features of folktales 2 📄	Personal log	What if not . . .?
Class log	Read a story 3	Personal log	Re-read a story 3	Personal log
Big Question	Class log	Big Question	Personal log 📄	Big Question
	Big Question		Big Question	

WEEK 2 **Writing fiction** *The Enchantress of the Sands*

Day 6	Day 7	Day 8	Day 9	Day 10
Story phrases 📄	Build a story 1	Build a story 2	Build a story 3 📄	Write a story 3 (continued)
Change the setting	Write a story 1 📄	Write a story 2	Write a story 3	Share a story
Build a sentence	Class log	Personal log		Evaluate and edit
Class log 📄	Big Question	Big Question		Proofread
Big Question				

WEEK 3 **Reading and writing non-fiction** Biography and autobiography

Day 11	Day 12	Day 13	Day 14	Day 15
Think and link 📄	Comparing biography and autobiography 2 📄	Taking notes 2 📄	Grammar: paragraphs	Write 3 (continued)
Introduction	Questions for research	Build a biography	Write 1	Evaluate and edit
Zoom in on key features of a biography	Taking notes 1 📄	Taking notes 3	Write 2 📄	Proofread
Comparing biography and autobiography 1 📄	Class log	Personal log	Write 3	Publish and present 📄
Class log				

📄: shows that a file should be printed out from the Software

Overview of the Unit

This Unit explores folktales, using the *The Enchantress of the Sands* by Jamila Gavin and other stories from a variety of cultures to explore the key features, settings, and dramatic language used in folktales.

In the Non-fiction week, the children will read an autobiography and a biography about Jamila Gavin, the author of *The Enchantress of the Sands*, and compare the two texts. The children will use audio and written sources to write biographies for a website of stories from people sharing their experiences of moving from one country to another. For more information about the Non-fiction week and the Non-fiction writing evaluation criteria, see p.177.

Where appropriate, the children will be encouraged to develop an awareness of audience and purpose in relation to the fiction and non-fiction texts they are reading and writing.

Teacher modelling is provided in the teaching notes, Software and the Pupils' Book, supporting the children's writing at every stage in the Fiction and Non-fiction weeks.

The Homework Book provides a homework activity related to the content of this Unit for each of the three weeks.

Fiction

Reading

Children will:

- explore the structure of folktales, and the archetypes that make up the plot and characters in *The Enchantress of the Sands*
- analyse how Jamila Gavin uses rich language to depict the setting
- use drama to explore the suspense in the climax of the story.

Writing

Key writing purpose to be shared with the children:

To write a new folktale with a vivid setting, atmosphere and an exciting climax.

Writing evaluation to be shared with the children

My new folktale:

- has a vividly described setting that the reader can imagine
- includes dialogue and action that moves the story on
- is tense and suspenseful, because my characters have secrets.

Grammar:

- includes adverbs and adverbials to explain when and where things happened (*The next evening… On the far side…*).

See the Planning section of the Software ('Timetables' tab) for a printable version of the Writing purpose and evaluation.

Fiction: Folktales
The Enchantress of the Sands by Jamila Gavin

READING FICTION

Resources

PB Pupils' Book pp.56–64

A Anthology pp.68–80

CD CD on Interactive whiteboard Unit 6

GB Grammar Bank on CD

HB Homework Book pp.20–23

DAY 1

Curriculum link: listening to and discussing a wide range of fiction, identifying themes

The story store

Purpose: for children to explore stories that introduce archetypal characters and themes to be explored in the main study text

- Use **CD (file 1.1)** to listen to two stories: *A Crocodile Named Rain Cloud* (a Burmese folktale) and *Baba Yaga* (a Russian folktale).
- Tell the children that these are stories that have been passed on from generation to generation through storytelling and that they have only been written down in the last few hundred years. Some of these folktales are what we know as fairy tales.
- Tell the children where the two tales they have heard are from and make links to a few of the key features in the geography/culture of the area (e.g. the wide river in Burma in *A Crocodile named Rain Cloud*, the dark forest in Russia in *Baba Yaga*).
- Ask the children to TTYP (Turn to your partner) and tell their partner about any folktales or fairy tales they know. Take feedback and if possible tell the children where their story is from.

recognise themes and use of magical devices in folk tales

Think and link

Purpose: for children to understand the main themes and archetypes associated with folktales

- Display **CD (file 1.2).** Explain that many folktales have very similar features. These features are traditional and have been used in lots of stories all over the world. The features can be themes, objects, characters and even the structure of the story. Show each slide and ask the children to TTYP and discuss the traditional folktale features on that slide.
- Can they think of any stories that have similar features, e.g. similar characters or objects? Collect feedback. TOL (Think out loud) to explain further any of the features that the children may not have experiences of. Link the slides to fairy tales/folktales that you know.
- You can print off a list of these features from **CD (file 1.3)** to put up on your Story wall for this unit.

identifying conventions of different types of writing

Key features of folktales 1

Purpose: for children to identify the main features of a folktale

- Before the lesson, print off the Folktale grid **CD (file 1.7)** and the story of *Baba Yaga* **CD (file 1.8)**, one for each pair of children.
- Tell the children that you are going to look for key features of a folktale in the two stories they heard earlier in the Story store.
- Display **CD (file 1.4)** and read *A Crocodile Named Rain Cloud*.
- Display **CD (file 1.5)** and explain that you are going to think about the key features of the story you have just read.
- Read the heading of each row and make sure the children understand what it means/refers to and then ask the children to TTYP and see if they can find an example of the first heading: a hero/heroine or good man/woman. Take feedback. Click 'Complete' to fill in the first row of the grid.

- Continue in this way until you have filled the whole grid: note that it uses two slides. TOL so the children can see you model finding answers. Not all headings will have an example in the story.
- Now display **CD (file 1.6)** and read the second folktale *Baba Yaga* to the children.
- Hand out the Folktale grid for this folktale printed off from **CD (file 1.7)** and ask the children to work with their partner to fill it out. You may wish to give the children printed copies of this story, from **CD (file 1.8)**. You could fill out the grid as a group with children who need more support.
- Take feedback on the children's responses. Encourage them to spot any similarities and differences between the stories.

Class log

Curriculum link: discussing and recording ideas; predicting

Purpose: for children to share the process of keeping a class reading, writing and thinking log to record responses to texts and activities in a variety of forms

- Ask the children to TTYP and talk about the two folktales they have just read. Can they remember some of the key features of folktales that appear in these stories? Take feedback and scribe their ideas into the Class log.
- Ask the children to TTYP and talk about what happened in the stories they have just read. Take feedback and write their ideas into the Class log. The children may come up with specific examples, but try to turn them into generic events, e.g. if a child says 'Vasilisa has to get coal,' say *'Yes that's right. The heroine has to find something special. Often the hero or heroine in a folktale has to find something, or solve a problem, or save someone.'*
- Ask the children to TTYP and discuss whether any of the characters either learn a lesson or change because of what happens in the story. Take feedback and write their ideas into the Class log.
- Review the log and explain that these ideas and thoughts will help the children to make predictions about what might happen in folktales and even help them to write their own folktale later.

Big Question ⓒⒹ

discussion; develop, agree on, and evaluate rules for effective discussion

Purpose: for children to develop their skills of argument and discussion through a mini enquiry session based on a philosophical question relating to the work of the day

- Display today's Big Question on **CD (file 1.9)**:

  What do stories tell us about the world and ourselves?

- Ask the children to TTYP to talk about this question. Collect feedback and scribe some responses on the board or flipchart.
- Click 'Prompts' to show some statements that may help to encourage discussion.

DAY 2

Word power

discussing words and phrases that capture the reader's interest and imagination

Purpose: for children to become familiar with vocabulary specific to traditional stories

> *enchantress   herdsman   begone   rejoiced*

- Display **CD (file 2.1)** to focus on some specific words in the story. Explain that these are words that we rarely use in our everyday talk, but they are often used in traditional stories such as folktales. Tell the children that looking at these words now will help them to understand the story when they hear it for the first time.

- Use MT/YT (My turn/your turn) to read the first word aloud. Click on 'TOL' to show the think bubble that explains its meaning and gives an example of its use in a sentence. Go through all the slides to focus on all four words: *enchantress*, *begone*, *herdsman* and *rejoiced*.
- Now ask the children to look at the Word power activity on p.56 of their Pupils' Book.
- You may wish to print these words from printable **CD (file 2.2)** to display on your Story wall for this unit. Let the children hear you using them in your conversation and teaching throughout the day and praise them if they use one of them.

Curriculum link:
predicting

Read a story 1 – clues (CD)

Purpose: for children to be motivated to read the new story. To make links between the new story and those in the Story store

- Explain to the children that you have found some clues about the new story and you need their help to find out more. Convey your own eagerness and enthusiasm and draw them into your excitement. Perhaps tell them that they are 'story detectives'.
- Explain to the children that you will use these clues, along with the ideas from the Story store, to work out more about the new story. Display **CD (file 2.3)**. Click 'Reveal' on each slide to reveal the clues. (Note that there are two clues on the first two slides, and one clue on the final slide.)
- After each clue has been revealed ask the children to TTYP and talk about what it means and how it might relate to the story. Then take feedback from the class. Make sure you do not reveal the ending at this stage!

predicting,
identifying how
language, structure,
and presentation
contribute to
meaning

Read a story 2 – evidence (CD)

Purpose: for children to hear more about the new story, to make links with their own experiences and to make predictions before they hear the full version

- Tell the children that as well as the clues some more evidence has come to light about the story. Display **CD (file 2.4)** to show the evidence. Say that you are really excited about what the evidence might be.
- Click on 'Reveal/Hide' to reveal the evidence (an image of a golden drum) and then click on 'Audio 1' to make it speak.
- Ask the children to TTYP to make a prediction about the story.
- Click on 'Audio 2' to hear the audio again, and at the end, to hear the golden drum pose some questions. Ask the children to TTYP to discuss the questions and then take feedback.

checking that the
text makes sense,
asking questions,
drawing inferences

Read a story 3   (teacher only) (CD)

Purpose: for children to hear and enjoy the full version of the story for the first time

- Tell the children that they are now going to hear the whole story for the very first time. TOL about which parts you can't wait to hear about. Ask the children to TTYP to share what they are looking forward to in the story.
- Say that you need to switch your Storyteller voice on! Make it a special moment as if you are getting ready for a performance.
- Now read aloud the full story from the Anthology pp.68–73 with great enjoyment, enthusiasm and intonation to show meaning.
- At the end of the story, display **CD (file 2.5)** which shows a list of questions. Ask the children to TTYP to discuss the questions, then share feedback with the whole class.

Class log

Purpose: for children to share the process of keeping a class reading, writing and thinking log to record responses to texts and activities in a variety of forms

- Explain to the children that the story is a traditional one, set in Botswana, long ago. Show them the slide show **CD (file 2.6)** which includes a map of the country and some information about Botswana today. Point out that much of Botswana is still rural (explain that *rural* means unchanged by humans) – there are still savannah lands, stretches of dry desert and wetlands around the rivers and deltas, like the settings depicted in the story.
- Ask the children to TTYP and discuss each slide. Take feedback and scribe any questions that the children have about Botswana into the Class log.
- You can find child friendly information about Botswana online at sites such as http://kids.nationalgeographic.com
- You could ask the children to find more pictures or information about Botswana and the Kalahari Desert (on which the setting is based) at an appropriate time in the week. You may need to explain that the Kalahari is actually a semi-desert, with some rainfall each year, so it does have some vegetation in most parts, including grasses and trees.

Big Question

Purpose: for children to develop their skills of argument and discussion through a mini enquiry session based on a philosophical question relating to the work of the day

- Display today's Big Question on **CD (file 2.7)**:

  Is it good to know about different places and traditions? *

- Follow the process as explained on Day 1.

  * This Big Question will be revisited on Day 11 – the first day of the Non-fiction week.

DAY 3

Special phrases

Purpose: for children to explore powerful phrases used in the story and increase their knowledge of how imagery can be used to create vivid pictures in the reader's mind

> *...where the sound of one step upon the shining white grains can be heard a hundred miles away... He thought his heart would break. As soft as a heartbeat, he crossed the Singing Sands. She gave a crocodile smile. ...but before she could say a word, she crumbled into a pile of dust.*

- Tell the children that there were some phrases in the story they heard yesterday that the writer used in order to create powerful pictures in the reader's mind. Display the Special phrases on **CD (file 3.1)**.
- Read out the phrases one by one using MT/YT. TOL explaining the images and ideas that they conjure up for you. Link each phrase to where it appears in the story.
- Once you have made a firm link between the first phrase and the story, explain to the children how all those ideas are going to help you say that phrase with the expression that brings the scene to life. Read the phrase as you would in the story.
- Ask the children to TTYP and discuss the part of the story the first phrase comes from and how they will read it in the story. Repeat for each of the phrases.
- You may wish to print these phrases from **CD (file 3.2)** to display on your Story wall for this unit.

Fiction: Folktales

Curriculum link:
checking that the
text makes sense,
asking questions,
drawing inferences

Re-read a story 3 🅐

Purpose: for children to gain a deeper understanding of the story and to see the text for the first time

- Ask the children to read the story on Anthology pp.68–73 with their partners, reading alternate paragraphs each. Remind them to read the words and phrases with expression that will help their partner gain a deeper understanding of the story. Explain that you will be listening in and looking out for particularly good reading.

Key features of folktales 2 🆑 🖨 🅐

Purpose: for children to identify the main features of a folktale

- Before the lesson, print off the folktale grid from **CD (file 3.4)**, one for each pair of children.
- Tell the children that you are going to look for key features of a folk/fairy tale in *The Enchantress of the Sands*. Ask them to turn to the story on pp.68–73 of the Anthology.
- Display **CD (file 3.3)** and explain that you are going to see what key traditional features the story has.
- Read the heading of the first row and model finding the answer in the story. TOL as you do, so the children are aware of the processes you are using to locate the answer. Click 'Complete' to show the answer. (There are only answers for the first three rows – the father is the hero, the enchantress is the 'baddie' and the wise man gives the father the drum.)
- Model finding the answers for the next two rows. Encourage the children to race you to find the answers. Take feedback. Then give the children their folktale grids from **CD (file 3.4)** to complete in pairs.
- You may want to fill out the grid as a group with children who need more support.

discussing and
recording ideas

Personal log

Purpose: for children to keep a personal log for recording and reflecting on their exploration of stories

- Ask the children to TTYP and tell their partner the favourite part of the story and how it made them feel. Then ask them to write their thoughts in their Personal log.

discussion; develop,
agree on, and
evaluate rules for
effective discussion

Big Question 🆑

Purpose: for children to develop their skills of argument and discussion through a mini enquiry session based on a philosophical question relating to the work of the day

- Display today's Big Question on **CD (file 3.5)**:

  Why are some people unkind or hurtful to others?

- Follow the process as explained on Day 1.

DAY 4

Year 3 Grammar
prepositions

Grammar: prepositions 🅐

Purpose: for children to develop their awareness of the function of prepositions in a text

- Tell the children that there are lots of words that we use a lot when we are speaking or writing that are really useful because they show us how events, people and places are connected.
- Say that these words are called *prepositions*. Write the word on the board and say it using MT/YT.

- Explain that the writer of *The Enchantress of the Sands* has used prepositions to show us the connections between the settings, characters and events in the story. Tell the children that you have picked out a section of the story that contains prepositions. Use MT/YT to say: *'But one day the evil enchantress came and sat in the shade of the acacia tree.'* Explain that the word *in* is needed to help us to understand the connections between the evil enchantress, her actions and the acacia tree.
- Write the sentence on the board and underline the preposition *in*. Explain that a preposition usually shows where something or someone is, or where they are 'positioned'.
- Say that the next sentence in this section contains two prepositions. Use MT/YT to say: *'She knew that above her head, three pairs of eyes gazed down at her.'*
- Explain that the words *above* and *at* are needed to help us to understand the connections between the enchantress (pronoun she here), where she is, where the brothers are (represented by the three pairs of eyes here) and what is happening.
- Write the sentence on the board or a flipchart and underline the prepositions *above* and *at*.
- Now ask the children to write the heading *Prepositions* in their Personal log and write the words *in*, *above*, and *at* under the heading.
- Explain that you have found some more prepositions in the story *The Enchantress of the Sands*. Tell them to add these words to their list of prepositions in the Personal log: *upon, under, towards, into.*
- Ask the children to look at pp.70–71 of the Anthology story *The Enchantress of the Sands* and to TTYP to find examples of sentences containing any of the prepositions in their list.
- Choose different sets of partners to share their examples, making sure that they identify the whole sentence and not just the preposition in isolation. Correct and clarify where necessary.
- Ask the children to TTYP to make up two sentences using any two prepositions chosen from their list and to write them in their Personal log. Choose two or three to share their sentences. Correct and clarify where necessary.

Settings ⓒ 🅐

Purpose: for children to look at settings in detail before writing their own

- Display part of the story text on **CD (file 4.1)**. Tell the children that you are going to scan the text to find descriptions of three settings so that you can collect them. (The settings are the desert, the tree house and the enchantress's hut.)
- Model how you scan the first section of text on the first slide. TOL looking for key words that might lead to a description of the setting, e.g. *sands, shining white grains, a hundred miles away.*
- Click 'Zoom in' to show the description of the desert setting. TOL as you describe what the description makes you see. Click 'Collect' and the description will automatically go into the Settings collector bag.
- Ask the children to TTYP and describe to each other how they imagine the setting of the desert – what picture does it create in their mind? Encourage them to describe how they imagine it might smell and what sounds there would be. If you feel the children need to reinforce their ideas, ask them to read the relevant paragraph in their Anthology.
- Click to the text on the next slide and repeat the process with the description of the tree house. After scanning this text, click 'Zoom in' to show the tree house setting. Click 'Collect' and the description will automatically go into the Settings collector bag.

- Ask the children to take turns to read the same paragraph in their Anthology p.68. Then ask them to TTYP and describe the setting of the tree house to each other.
- Click to the next slide, which describes the enchantress's hut. Ask the children to scan it for a description of the setting. Take feedback and click 'Zoom in' to show the description of the inside of the enchantress's hut.
- Click 'Collect' and the description will automatically go into the Settings collector bag.
- Ask the children to TTYP to describe the enchantress's hut setting to each other. Note, keep **CD (file 4.1)** open for the next activity too.

Curriculum link:
composing
and rehearsing
sentences orally;
building a varied
and rich vocabulary

Personal log (CD) (PB)

Purpose: for children to keep a personal log for recording and reflecting on their exploration of stories

- Click on the 'Reveal' button on the fourth, fifth and sixth slides in **CD (file 4.1)** to display the three settings in the story. Ask the children to TTYP and take turns to use the information to describe the three different settings – the desert, the tree house and the enchantress's hut.
- Take feedback and model turning the children's descriptions into complete sentences. Use additional words and phrases to create more detailed description that adds atmosphere. If necessary, encourage the children to shut their eyes and imagine the settings in detail. Use the prompts below to help you model your sentence.
  - Have you described what you can see?
  - Have you described how hot or cool the setting is?
  - Have you made your setting seem safe or full of danger?
  - Have you described the sounds that you could hear if you stood in the setting?
- Ask the children to go to p.57 of the Pupils' Book and use the prompts to write their own descriptive sentence about one of the settings in their Personal log.

checking that the
text makes sense,
asking questions,
drawing inferences

Re-read a story 3 (A) (CD)

Purpose: for children to deepen their understanding and enjoyment of the story by increasing familiarity with the text

- Ask the children to look at *The Enchantress of the Sands* on pp.68–73 of their Anthology and to read the whole story silently to themselves.
- Display the story map on **CD (file 4.2).** Model using the story map to tell the story to the children. Then model annotating the story map so there is extra detail about the characters, settings or plot to help you tell the story better. (Use interactive whiteboard tools to make your annotations.)
- Tell the story again using your annotations to help you.

discussing and
recording ideas

Personal log (CD) 📄

Purpose: for children to keep a personal log for recording and reflecting on their exploration of stories

- Before the lesson starts, print off the basic story map on **CD (file 4.3)** for each pupil.
- Give the children their own copy of the story map to take turns to retell the story of *The Enchantress of the Sands* to their partner. Ask the children to TTYP and discuss how they could improve their retelling – adding extra details about plot, character and settings.
- Now ask them to annotate extra information or ideas onto their own map and stick it into their Personal log. Ask the children to use their annotated story map to take turns to retell the story to each other a final time.

Big Question

*Purpose: for children to develop their skills of argument and discussion through a mini
enquiry session based on a philosophical question relating to the work of the day*

- Display today's Big Question on **CD (file 4.4)**:

  Can you change your life story?

- Follow the process as explained on Day 1.

DAY 5

Story climax

Purpose: for children to understand how the climax of the story relies on character as well as plot

- Display the story map onscreen **CD (file 5.1)** and retell the story. Explain
  that this story can be broken into sections: the beginning and build up (at
  the tree house), the problem (the enchantress stealing the children and the
  father visiting the wise man and crossing the singing sands), the climax (in the
  enchantress's hut) and the ending (the family returning to the tree hut with
  much rejoicing).
- Tell the children that they are going to focus on the climax of the story. Click to
  the next two slides to display the climax of the story onscreen.
- Explain that there is particular tension in this part of the story because the
  father and the enchantress are both pretending to be something they are not,
  and it's very important the father isn't discovered because he needs to trick the
  enchantress to get his children back.
- Ask the children to TTYP and discuss what the father knows about the enchantress.
  Take feedback and write their ideas on a flipchart. Then ask the children to TTYP
  and discuss what the enchantress thinks she knows about the old man and what she
  is hiding from him. Take feedback and write their ideas on the flipchart.
- Say to the children that these hidden ideas are underneath the words that the
  characters are saying to each other in the climax.
- Move to the next slide to reveal the dialogue for the climax. Model saying the
  father's first lines, then say what he might be thinking first: '*I hope the enchantress
  doesn't see through my disguise. I am desperate to get to my boys*' and then say the
  father's line.
- Ask the children to TTYP and tell each other what the characters are thinking
  whilst they are saying each line. Take feedback and write their ideas down.

Dramatic reconstruction

Purpose: for children to explore the tension and suspense in the climax of a story

- Before the lesson, print off the dialogue sheet **CD (file 5.3)** for each child.
- Ask the children to work in pairs to act out the dialogue prepared in the previous
  activity. Move around observing.
- Tell the children to act out the same scene but this time they should say what
  their characters are thinking. The characters will react as they did before, as if
  they are hearing the correct words. Move around observing.
- Feed back to the children. Explain to them that the disguise and the secrets that the
  two characters are keeping help to give the story tension. The father is pretending
  to be old and the enchantress is pretending to be harmless.

- Display **CD (file 5.2)** to show the characters' dialogue with their actions written in. You can also give the children a printable copy on **CD (file 5.3)** to use in their role-play. Tell the children that they now need to add in the idea of disguise to their role-play. They need to convince the other character that they are harmless but when they think they are not being watched they should try to show who they really are. The father could look desperately for his sons, the enchantress could rub her hands with glee or smile a wicked smile.
- As the children act and rehearse, move through the room giving advice and encouragement.
- Ask the children to TTYP and decide which moment of the role-play was the most tense and exciting. When was the moment that the outcome of the story could go either way? Discuss where the actual climax is and how the children could make this moment seem the most dramatic and exciting in the role-play. (For example, they could freeze for a moment and then move in slow motion, or make a sound effect for the snap of the magic stick.)
- Give the children time to incorporate this into their role-play.
- Make sure that the children have time to watch each other's performances if they wish to.

What if not...? PB

Curriculum link: drawing inferences, participate in discussion about books

Purpose: for children to consider how character, setting and plot affect each other

- Ask the children to look at the What if not...? questions in the Pupils' Book p.58. Model how you think out loud about the first What if not...? What if not *the Singing Sands?* What if the obstacle were *a deep river?*

  In folktales the hero often has to cross difficult land. Sometimes he or she has to get through brambles and thorns that guard somewhere. Sometimes he or she has to get past terrible beasts such as dragons or four-headed dogs. If I were to keep this story in Botswana, the father might have to cross a huge river or the Okavango Delta and not disturb the vicious crocodiles or enormous water snakes …

- Now ask the children to TTYP and discuss the other What if not . . .? questions. Collect feedback and develop answers.

Personal log PB

discussing and recording ideas

Purpose: for children to keep a personal record of their responses to texts and activities in a variety of forms

- Ask the children to choose one What if not . . .? to explore further with their partner, for example talking about what effect the change might have on the story. Encourage them to write their ideas in a few sentences in their Personal log.

Big Question CD

discussion; develop, agree on, and evaluate rules for effective discussion

Purpose: for children to develop their skills of argument and discussion through a mini enquiry session based on a philosophical question relating to the work of the day

- Display today's Big Question on **CD (file 5.4)**:

  Is it always physical things that stop us from doing something or getting somewhere?

- Follow the process as explained on Day 1.

WRITING FICTION

DAY 6

Curriculum link:
discussing words
and phrases
that capture the
reader's interest
and imagination

Story phrases

Purpose: for children to understand how language can be used to show the relative passing of time and to link events in the story together

> *On the far side   It was because   Every day,   So every day, when   And every evening,*
> *But one day   But because   The next evening   The next day   When the herdsman*
> *When he got to   On the other side   For a moment   ...but before she...*

- Print out **CD (file 6.2)** before the lesson starts. It contains example sentences that you might want to use when you model retelling the story using specific phrases.
- Tell the children that you have collected words and phrases from the story *The Enchantress of the Sands*, that help to link the story together by:
  - showing the passing of time
  - explaining cause and effect (why things happen)
  - describing location (where things happen).
- Tell the children that these phrases could be useful for their own writing, because they help to link the story together and to control its pace and tension.
- Ask the children to turn to p.59 of their Pupils' Book to see the list of story phrases and use MT/YT to read them out.
- Display the story map **CD (file 6.1)**. Tell the children that the phrases are in the order that you found them in the story and that you are going to try telling the story using as many of them as you can. Model retelling the story of *The Enchantress of the Sands* using the phrases. See **CD (file 6.2)** for a printable example (the focus phrases are in bold italics and followed by paraphrases of the story text, for context).
- Ask the children to TTYP and discuss which of the phrases give a sense of time passing in the story. Take feedback.
- Now ask the children to listen out for phrases that explained *why* something happened in the story or *where*, as you retell the story a second time. Take feedback.
- Challenge the children to retell the story using as many of the phrases as they can. They should use the list on p.59 of the Pupils' Book and their copy of the story map in their Personal log. Move around the room observing and quietly helping out.
- Now ask the children to TTYP and tell their partner which of the sentences they used they liked the most and why. Choose two and explore the feedback by analysing what the story phrase is doing to the sentence, e.g. showing *when* things happened, showing *what* happened or *where* it happened.

Change the setting

Purpose: for children to explore alternative settings and descriptive phrases for their new story

- Tell the children that they will be writing their own folktale set in another part of Botswana. Remind the children of the What if not...? activity from Day 5, e.g. 'What *if not* the Singing Sands? What *if the obstacle were* a deep river?' and refer back to some of the children's ideas from that activity.
- Display the story map on **CD (file 6.3)** and talk through the three settings: the tree house, the Singing Sands and the enchantress's hut. (Note that the setting of the herdsman in the desert has been deleted as it plays only a minor part in the story and the main focus is on the other three settings.) Click to the next slide to show the alternative setting of the story in the Okavango Delta. This slide shows three places in the Delta where the action could take place.

- Click 'TOL' to give some initial ideas about each of the three settings in the Okavango Delta and share them with the children.
- Ask the children to TTYP and take turns to describe the three different parts of the new setting of the Okavango Delta to their partner. Take feedback and write some of the best descriptions and ideas on your flipchart. These can be individual words, phrases, similes, etc.
- Click to the next three slides, to show individual images of the new settings. Invite children to offer some suitable descriptions – then click 'Reveal' to show more descriptions. Use MT/YT to share them with the children and TOL to make links between the words and phrases and the images they conjure up.
- Ask the children to TTYP and work together to come up with their favourite phrase to describe each of the settings. Take feedback and write some of the phrases up on your flipchart or on cut-up card to display on the Story wall.

Build a sentence

Curriculum link: discussing writing similar to that which they are planning to write; composing and rehearsing sentences orally

Purpose: for children to compose a complex sentence that includes a simile

- Explain you are going to look at some sentences that combine the setting with action, which create a vivid picture for the reader. Then you are going to change them so that they show the new setting of the story.
- Reveal the two sentences on **CD (file 6.4)**. Read them aloud and comment on how the author shows the passing of time, e.g. using *when* and *before*. The first part of the sentence evokes the setting, the middle part describes the action, and the final part gives us a description and information.
- Click to the next screen which shows the first two clauses of the sentence again, but with gaps and a choice of alternative wording suitable for the new setting in the Okavango Delta.
- Re-read the first clause, using substitutions for *the shining white place* that reflect the new setting. Get feedback from the children about the different choices and comment on their effect on the atmosphere of the setting.
- Do the same for the middle part of the sentence. Write the complete new sentence on the flipchart or board.
- Click to the next screen to reveal the second sentence. Read it aloud and comment on how the author uses a simile to give us an image of how the father walks upon the sands. (You may need to remind the children that a simile compares one thing with another, using the words *like* or *as…as*.)
- Draw attention to the alternative sentence, which has a gap and a choice of similes that could be used to show how the father crosses the marshes of the Okavango Delta. Use MT/YT to share the choices with the children.
- Ask the children to TTYP and discuss which option they prefer. Take feedback and then write one version of the complete new sentence on the flipchart or board.
- Ask the children to compose their own version of the two sentences. If necessary, display the suggestions on the screens again, but give the children the option of thinking up their own descriptions.

Class log

building a varied and rich vocabulary

Purpose: for children to share the process of keeping a class reading, writing and thinking log to record responses to texts and activities in a variety of forms

- Display the images of the Okavango Delta **CD (file 6.5)** and TOL as you link the images with the descriptive work you did in the Change the setting activity earlier.
- Point out to the children that slide 5 shows a group of hippos – called a *hippo pod*.

- Ask the children to TTYP and compose some phrases/words to describe each image. Take feedback and scribe good words and phrases into the appropriate page in the Class log. (These images or similar ones could be printed and pasted into the Class log.)

Curriculum link:
discussion; develop, agree on, and evaluate rules for effective discussion

Big Question CD

Purpose: for children to develop their skills of argument and discussion through a mini enquiry session based on a philosophical question relating to the work of the day

- Display today's Big Question on **CD (file 6.6)**:

  Should we always help other people get what they want?

- Follow the process as explained on Day 1.

DAY 7

Build a story 1 CD PB

discussing writing in order to understand and learn from its structure, grammar and vocabulary

Purpose: for children to see a story grow through three stages of development

- Explain that you are going to build up your new version of the story, keeping the same story structure as *The Enchantress of the Sands,* but that you are going to make some changes.
- Tell the children that the characters will stay the same but the enchantress is now the enchantress of the Endless Marsh. The main plot will stay the same – the children are stolen and the father rescues them but some keys things will change, such as the warning and secret signal the father makes; the person who helps the father; the magical item he is given; how he crosses the difficult terrain without the enchantress seeing or hearing him.
- Display the first slide on **CD (file 7.1)**. Explain that this shows a story map for your new story, but it is slightly different from the previous one because as well as showing the house on stilts, the marshland and the enchantress's hut it also includes the home of the helper or wise person. Explain that you have included the home of the wise person because there are some changes that you want to make to the story in that setting.
- Click to the next slide to show the image of the house on stilts. Click on 'Reveal' to display the first choices. These focus on the father's warning and the secret signal. Use MT/YT to go through the options for the father's warning. TOL as you make a choice and note it on a flipchart or board.
- Ask the children to TTYP and decide which warning they like best and why. Take feedback.
- Then focus on the choice of secret signals. Ask the children to TTYP and decide which secret signal they like best and why. Take feedback.
- TOL as you model turning those two choices orally into the first part of the story. For example:

  Once there was a father with three motherless boys, who lived in the Endless Marshes of the Okavango Delta. At the edge of those wild marshes lived an evil enchantress who snatched children, so the father made sure his children were safe by keeping them in a house on stilts high above the marshes with only a rope ladder to get in or out of the house.

  Every day the father warned his boys, 'Never let down the ladder when I'm away fishing unless you hear me hoot three times.'

- Ask the children to TTYP and take turns to tell their partner how they will use the warning and secret signal to start their story. Listen in and share some good examples with the class.

- Now click to the next slide to show a small house on stilts. Explain that this is where the father's helper lives. Click 'Reveal/Hide' to show the choices of who can help the father and the advice he or she gives him.
- Model making your own choices and noting them on the flipchart or board. TOL to show the children your thought processes. Ask the children to TTYP to make their choices and take feedback.
- Click to the next slide to reveal the picture of the marshlands. Explain that you are now going to choose the magical object that was given to the father to help him cross the marshlands, and the transport he will use. Click on 'Reveal' to view the options.
- Use MT/YT to go through the options with the children. Explain which choice you would make and TOL to show how you would use this information in the story. Then ask the children to TTYP to make their choice.
- Go back to your story map and flipchart, listing the choices you have made. Remind the children of the phrases you used on Day 6 to help retell the story *The Enchantress of the Sands* (see Story phrases activity, on p.59 of the Pupils' Book).
- Model telling your new story using the story map on the first screen of **CD (file 7.1)** with all your new choices and the story phrases to ensure the story flows fluently and logically.

Curriculum link: composing and rehearsing sentences orally; creating settings, characters, plot

Write a story 1

Purpose: for children to plan their story using the interactive story map

- Before the lesson starts, print a story map for each child from **CD (file 7.2)**.
- Give each child a copy of the new story map containing the new images.
- Go back to **CD (file 7.1)**, displaying the slides which have choices for the father's warning, signal, etc. Tell the children to decide on their choices to change their story. They don't have to stick to the choices they discussed in pairs. Tell them if they have an idea of their own for any of the choices they can use that idea instead.
- Explain that you want them to write their choices as short notes onto their story map printout. When they are happy with their choices they can use the story phrases on p.59 of the Pupils' Book and the story map to tell their new story to their partner.
- You may want to write a shared plan with a group of children who need more support. If so, print out the story map onto an A3 sheet and give the children separate sticky notes to write on for annotating the story map. Once the children are confident about the story, ask them to annotate any other information or story phrases they want to use onto their story map.

explore and collect ideas; compose sentences orally

Class log

Purpose: for children to keep a personal log for recording and reflecting on their exploration of stories

- Show the children the image on **CD (file 7.3)** of the Endless Marshes (the equivalent of the Singing Sands in the Anthology story).
- Use MT/YT to describe the picture, e.g. say you think the swamp's waters are:
  'not just *murky* … but *deep deadly dark waters, cold cloudy pools*'
  'not just *scary* … but *horrifying, shiver-making, petrifying*'
  'not just *dangerous places* … but *treacherous streams, hidden wild places*.'
- Ask the children to TTYP to create their own Not just… sentences to describe the Endless Marshes. Take feedback and add some of them to the Class log.

Big Question (CD)

Curriculum link: discussion; develop, agree on, and evaluate rules for effective discussion

Purpose: for children to develop their skills of argument and discussion through a mini enquiry session based on a philosophical question relating to the work of the day

- Display today's Big Question on **CD (file 7.4)**:

  Where would you be afraid to go?

- Follow the process as explained on Day 1.

DAY 8

plan writing by discussing writing that is similar, recording ideas

Build a story 2 (CD)

Purpose: for children to see a story grow through three stages of development, to develop their ability to write an exciting climax using dialogue and describing actions to create tension

- Note that the children will need to refer to the story maps that they annotated on Day 7 for this activity.
- Remind the children of the role-play they did to explore the climax of *The Enchantress of the Sands* on Day 5. Talk briefly about how they explored what the two characters were hiding, what they were really thinking and who they really were.
- Explain that you want to use that idea and the same mix of dialogue and action to create a gripping climax for your new story.
- TOL as you describe what you imagine will happen at the end of your story. For example:

The father has used mud to disguise himself as a swamp man and the enchantress is going to pretend to be a healer. He will come hobbling in to her for help to heal his sore legs. The enchantress sees his magical reed flute and lets him in. She will pretend to make a healing soup – but actually wants to poison him. Just as before the father will see his sons hidden in the hut. He will take the chance to grab the enchantress's magic stick as she puts it down to pour 'herbs' into her boiling pot.

- Ask the children to TTYP and tell each other the ending of their own story using their story map to help them plan. (This is the story map printed from **CD (file 7.2)** which they annotated in Day 7.) Remind them to decide on:
  - a made-up excuse for the father to come to the enchantress
  - how he is disguised
  - who the enchantress is pretending to be
  - how the father will snatch the magic stick to break it and kill the enchantress.

Dramatic reconstruction

- When the children are sure of what they are going to do, ask them to take turns to act out their story climax in role as the father and enchantress.
- Observe what they do and say, and write any good dialogue or actions that you see onto the flipchart.
- Use some of the dialogue you have collected to remind the children how to set out dialogue. Show them how to use synonyms for *said* to tell the reader exactly how the character is speaking.
- Ask the children to act out their endings a second time, this time thinking very carefully how they speak their dialogue – do they mutter, wheedle, cajole, beg, plead?
- After the second role-play, ask the children to feed back some of their dialogue and how they were saying it. Model writing some of this up for the children, and TOL as you choose the right synonym for *said*.
- Let the children write some notes in their Personal log – noting the dialogue for the character and how they are speaking.

- Now ask the children to act out their climax a final time – this time thinking about their gestures and how they move – do they hobble, stumble, grin slyly, beckon, grab, snatch, tremble?
- After the final role-play ask the children to feed back some of their actions. Write up their feedback so you have a list of verbs. Model writing a couple of sentences using the verbs.
- Let the children write some notes in their Personal log – noting the verbs they would use to show how the characters move for different parts of the climax.

Curriculum link:
composing
and rehearsing
sentences orally;
creating settings,
characters, plot

Write a story 2

Purpose: for children to create an exciting climax using dialogue to create tension and tell the story

N.B. In this unit the focus is on the children writing an effective, exciting climax. In order to achieve this, children will write this part of the story in depth, with plenty of support and a sound model, before they write the rest of the story, which will be an adaptation of the original story.

- Tell the children that they are ready to write the climax of their story. Remind them of the role-play they have just done and the notes they have written in their Personal log.
- Display **CD (file 8.1)** to show your introductory sentence. TOL as you describe how it gives the setting and describes the father arriving at the enchantress's hut.
- Click to the next slide to show the dialogue that you want to use in your re-telling. Read it aloud and TOL to describe how each piece of dialogue moves the story on.
- Click to the next two slides to show the action added into the dialogue, so that the whole climax is complete. Read it to the class. Click 'Highlights' to highlight some of the verbs and TOL to explain how they add to the tension, e.g. *enticed, cajoled*
- Ask the children to read the Write a story 2 prompts on p.60 of the Pupils' Book to help them write their story climax and ending in their Personal log.

discussing and
recording ideas

Personal log

Purpose: for children to keep a personal log for recording and reflecting on their exploration of stories

- Remind the children that the setting has now changed so their story needs a new title. Ask the children to TTYP and discuss who or what should be the focus of the title: the father, the enchantress, the boys or the Endless Marshes? Take feedback.
- Model writing a few possible titles onto the flipchart using the children's ideas.
- Ask the children to TTYP and discuss what the title of their story should be. Tell them to write their title in their Personal log.

discussion; develop,
agree on, and
evaluate rules for
effective discussion

Big Question

Purpose: for children to develop their skills of argument and discussion through a mini enquiry session based on a philosophical question relating to the work of the day

- Display today's Big Question on **CD (file 8.2)**:

  Do all stories need unkind characters?

- Follow the process as explained on Day 1.

DAY 9

Curriculum link:
understand the
skills and processes
that are essential
for writing

Build a story 3

Purpose: for children to see a story grow through three stages of development and to see the third stage of writing that will provide a model for their own story

- Print out a copy of **CD (file 9.2)** for each pair of children, before the start of the lesson.
- Tell the children that they are almost ready to write the rest of their story. Remind them that they have worked on the climax of the story, but they need to think in more detail about the other sections of the story – the Beginning, the Build up, the Problem, all of which come before the Climax.
- Display your story map on **CD (file 9.1)**. Point out the four main locations: the house on stilts, the swamp, the wise man's hut and the enchantress's hut. Very briefly, talk through what happens at each location, pointing out which place is the Beginning, Build-up, Problem and Climax section of the story. Mention where you will use some of the key features that you have explored about folktales: the warning, three things, magical objects, hero, villain, wise person.
- Explain to the children that you are now going to read (together) the new version of the story that you have written. Click to the next slide to show the Beginning of your story. Read it aloud and TOL to explain your language choices to describe the setting. Draw attention to the highlighted phrases that you have borrowed from the original story.
- Click on the other slides to go through the same process for the Build up and Problem sections of your story. TOL explaining your language choices and in particular anything you have borrowed from the original story.
- Distribute printed copies of **CD (file 9.2)** to pairs of children. Explain that this printout contains your new text for the climax and ending of your new story. Ask the children to take turns to read the text, a paragraph at a time, and to look out for any words, phrases or dialogue they might like to borrow for their own story. (This text is similar to the story climax you wrote on Day 8.)

creating settings,
characters, plot;
monitor whether
their writing
makes sense

Write a story 3

Purpose: for children to write their story using all the skills they have been exploring

- Tell the children that they are going to write their story now using the ideas in their Personal log and their story map from Day 7. (The story can be completed on Day 10.) Remind them of the sentences they composed on Day 6 in their Personal log that they could adapt and use to describe the beginning of the father's journey.
- Tell the children to take turns to discuss with their partner what they want to change in their story.
- Ask the children to write a plan for their story, by building up notes under the headings *Build up, Climax, Resolution,* and *Ending.* Then ask children to share their plan with their partners.
- Some children might not write a complete story, but the process of planning and building their episodes is the important thing here.
- Display **CD (file 9.3)** which shows some Top Tips to help the children write a gripping story.

Write a story 3 (continued)

Purpose: for children to continue writing their story

- Ask the children to continue writing their story. Use the beginning of the session to remind the children to:
  - use dialogue to make the story move on, and also to create tension and suspense
  - borrow a phrase or sentence so it fits their story
  - choose suitable phrases to show the passage of time (e.g. *That night...*, *After a long...*); where things happened (e.g. *On the other side, Under the tree...*); why things happened (e.g. *because..., which made...*).

Curriculum link:
creating settings, characters, plot; monitor whether their writing makes sense

Share a story

Purpose: for children to read their story to a supportive critical partner

- Ask the children to take turns to read the first draft of their story to their partner.
- Tell the partner who is listening, to look out for good use of dialogue that moves the story on, description that gives vivid images and a gripping ending.
- Ask the partner to feed back to the writer what they think worked really well in the story and to make one suggestion for improving it further.

assessing the effectiveness of their own and others' writing

Evaluate and edit

Purpose: for children to develop a willingness to make changes to their writing in the light of evaluation

- Display the list of questions on **CD (file 10.1)**. Explain that this list is to help the children to think about how well they have written their story.
- Tell them to evaluate their own stories and TTYP to discuss one or two things that they would change to improve the story.
- Ask them to re-write one or two sentences incorporating their changes.

proofread for spelling and punctuation errors

Proofread

Purpose: for children to proofread their work and make changes to improve the accuracy of their grammar, punctuation and spelling

- Now ask the children to proofread their work. If you have noticed that several children need to improve on a particular aspect of spelling, grammar or punctuation, use this as a focus for the Proofread activity. Write an example which includes common errors from the children's writing and use this as a model.
- The children should always be checking for standard use of punctuation and correct spelling of common exception words.
- The following points would be relevant as the particular focus for this Unit:
  - punctuating direct speech correctly
  - checking spelling of high-frequency adverbs of time, e.g. *soon, suddenly.*

Further activity

- Publish: ask the children to type up their stories, making any changes from the Evaluate and edit and Proofread activities.

Biography and autobiography

The Non-fiction week links to the fiction week through a focus on biographies and autobiographies of Jamila Gavin, the author of *The Enchantress of the Sands*. Children then make notes from audio and written sources to write their own biography for a website of stories that people have shared about moving from one country to another.

See p.159 for the daily timetable for the Non-fiction week.

Non-fiction

Reading

Children will:

- explore information about Jamila Gavin
- think about how biographies are structured, and examine their key features
- compare biography with autobiography.

Writing

Key writing purpose to be shared with the children:

To write a biography using notes taken from audio accounts and fact files.

Writing evaluation to be shared with the children

My biography:

- includes interesting information, developed from my notes, about journeys people have made from one country to another
- organises information clearly, e.g. *using headings and subheadings.*

Grammar:

- uses paragraphs to help the reader follow my biography easily.

See the Planning section of the Software ('Timetables' tab) for a printable version of the Writing purpose and evaluation.

Curriculum link:
reading for a range
of purposes

Think and link

Purpose: for children to become interested in biography and autobiography via one of the Big Questions they have explored

- Display the Big Question from Day 2 on **CD (file 11.1)**:

  Is it good to know about different places and traditions?

- Ask the children to TTYP to recall some of what they discussed before for this Big Question and take feedback.

- Tell the children that many people live somewhere different from where they were born. Ask the children to TTYP and talk about where they were born or where their parents were born. Take feedback and write the different places on your flipchart.

- Explain that many people enjoy finding out where their families have come from and that Jamila Gavin, the author of *The Enchantress of the Sands,* was born in India but now lives in England.

- Tell the children that the story of a real person's life is called a *biography* and if the person writes the story of their own life it is called an *autobiography*. Click to the next slide on the CD to display the definitions. Print these out from **CD (file 11.2)** to display on your Non-fiction wall.

Introduction

Purpose: for the children to understand why we read biographies and autobiographies

- Find two comparative websites (biography and autobiography) about Jamila Gavin. The following website is currently available: www.Jamilagavin.co.uk (autobiography) and you could also refer to http://www.walker.co.uk and find her in the list of authors and artists (biography).

- Go to the autobiography section of the website. Draw attention to the types of information that can be found on this website, e.g. information about Jamila, how her travels inspired her writing. Tell the children that this website is *autobiographical* because Jamila wrote it about herself.

- Then show the biography that you have found and read the information to the children. Explain that this is a *biography* because it is about Jamila but written by someone else.

- Ask the children to TTYP and talk about how they think the two websites are different and take feedback. Make sure they see that Jamila is able to talk about things that are personal to her, how her travels inspire her, her diaries, etc. on her website, whereas the Walker site does not do this.

- Write up the differences you have found and place them under the headings *Biography* and *Autobiography* on the Non-fiction wall.

discussing non-fiction; learn the conventions of different types of writing

Zoom in on key features of a biography

Purpose: for children to read a biography and understand what its key features are

- Display **CD (file 11.3)** to show the subheadings from the Jamila Gavin biography in the Anthology. Read the headings aloud and TOL as you predict what information you expect to find under each heading. For example: 'She never thought she would be a writer . . . *I think this paragraph will talk about why she is a writer now and why it was a surprise.*'

- Ask the children to turn to pp.74–75 of the Anthology where they will see the text with the subheadings. Ask them to take turns to read each paragraph aloud to their partner. Use TTYP to discuss and clarify the information that they have read.

- Display **CD (file 11.4)** and explain that it shows *part* of the text on the webpage. Point out the labels down the left hand side of the slide, which note some of the key features of a biography. Choose one key feature and TOL to explain what that feature is. Then identify an example of the relevant feature in the text and use your whiteboard tools to draw a line from the feature label to the relevant place in the text.
- Use TOL and TTYP to involve the children in identifying the other key features of the biography and continue to use your whiteboard tools to link the labels to the relevant places in the text. Note that some labels are relevant to more than just one place in the text.
- Click to the next slide to display another extract of the text, and do the same with the new key feature labels. Note that many of the key features appear on both pages, so encourage children to talk about these as well. For example, the use of the third person throughout.

<table>
<tr><td>**Curriculum link:**
asking questions to improve their understanding of a text</td></tr>
</table>

Comparing biography and autobiography 1

Purpose: for children to understand the differences between biographical and autobiographical texts

- Tell the children that there is a part of Jamila Gavin's autobiography for them to read – the opening of a chapter called 'Boasting' on pp.76–80 of the Anthology. Ask the children to TTYP and tell their partner what an autobiography is. (Remind them to look at the information on the Non-fiction wall if necessary.)
- Explain to the children that they are going to be 'detectives' as they read the autobiography. Display **CD (file 11.5)** which lists some questions about autobiography. Read them to the children and TOL to explain what the questions mean and what you'd be looking for if you were reading the text. For example:

  What style of writing is used in the autobiography? *This is about the way the author writes, for example in the first person using 'I' and 'we' or in the third person using 'she' or 'he'. I'll have to look out for these pronouns in the text…*

  What is the main purpose of the autobiography? *I would wait until I've read the whole of the autobiography before I tried to answer this one. I would think … what age is Jamila here? What is she doing? What is she thinking? Why is she saying this? These sort of things would help me work out what the purpose is.*

- Ask the children to read the opening of the chapter 'Boasting' in their Anthology and to note down in their Personal log any clues that will help them to answer the detective questions. Take feedback and make notes on your flipchart.
- Click to the next slide to display the key features of an autobiography. Choose one key feature and model finding an example of it on pp.76–80 of the Anthology. Ask the children to TTYP and find another example of that feature (when possible!).
- Go through the list of key features on the CD, using TOL and TTYP to involve the children in identifying the features in the Anthology autobiography. Then ask the children to TTYP and discuss how autobiography and biography are similar and different. Take feedback.
- Click to the next slide to display the lists of key features of biographies and autobiographies side by side. Discuss them with the children. Is there anything they missed or were surprised about?
- You can enlarge and print out the key feature lists from **CD (file 11.6)** to display on the Non-fiction wall.

Non-fiction: Biography and autobiography

Curriculum link:
retrieve and
record information
from non-fiction

Class log

Purpose: for children to share the process of keeping a class reading, writing and thinking log to record responses to texts and activities in a variety of forms

- Write *Jamila Gavin* at the top of a clean double page of your Class log. Ask the children to TTYP and talk about two things that they have found out about Jamila Gavin. As you take feedback, turn the children's ideas into statements, e.g. '*Jamila was born in 1941.*'
- Give each pair two blank sticky notes. Ask them to write one piece of biographical information about Jamila Gavin on each note and to stick them into the Class log. (You may need to direct some children to focus on different pieces of information if they are likely to duplicate the same information as other pairs.)
- Read some of the statements the children have written and model linking them so that you have similar information together, e.g. all the information about India together, all Jamila's birth details together.
- Ask the children to TTYP and discuss, '*What do we know about Jamila?*' Take feedback referring back to the Class log.

DAY 12

discussing their
understanding
and explaining the
meaning of words
in context

Comparing biography and autobiography 2

Purpose: for children to consolidate their understanding of the differences between biographical and autobiographical writing

- Ask the children to TTYP and discuss the main differences between biographies and autobiographies. Take feedback and encourage them to look at the key feature lists on the wall if they are unsure. If you have not put the lists on the wall, they can be displayed from the third slide on **CD (file 11.5)** or printed out from **CD (file 11.6)**.
- Tell the children that you are going to read out some phrases from the two Jamila Gavin texts and they have to decide whether they are from the biography, the autobiography or both.
- Display the different phrases on **CD (file 12.1)** and read them aloud. Ask the children to TTYP to decide where the phrases are from. Take feedback and drag and drop the phrases into the boxes suggested by the children. Ensure that they understand the difference between the use of the first and third person.
- Now ask the children to turn to the activity on p.61 of the Pupils' Book, called Comparing biography and autobiography. Tell them to take turns with their partner to read the phrases and to decide whether they are from a biography or an autobiography. Take feedback and discuss which types of information can be in both types of text (e.g. *facts*).

Questions for research

Purpose: for children to understand how to compose research questions

- Tell children that they will be writing biographical information for a website about people who have migrated from one country to another. (If the children are unfamiliar with the word *migrated*, explain that it means that people have moved from one place to another.) Tell them that they will be listening to two people's stories about moving from Bosnia and Ivory Coast to the UK and explain that a good researcher has a list of questions they want answered *before* they start their research. This is what you are going to draw up now.
- Remind the children of the types of information they gathered about Jamila Gavin. Show them the Class log from Day 11 and draw their attention to the way the information they gathered was grouped.

- Display the question words *(Where? When? How? Who? Why? What?)* on **CD (file 12.2)**. Tell the children that they can use these words when they write their questions.
- TOL as you model composing a question. For example, *'I want to ask a question about where the people were born. This is basic information to start with. I could say:* When and where were you born?' Write your final question onto the flipchart.
- Now ask the children to TTYP and compose a question. Display **CD (file 12.3)** to help them. Take feedback, improve their ideas where necessary and write a couple more questions onto the flipchart.
- Tell the children to use the Questions for research prompts to help them write three research questions into their Personal log.

Taking notes 1

Purpose: for children to understand how to take notes by listening to an audio file; for children to find key words and make summaries

Note that the source material used in this and subsequent activities is based on accounts from people who have shared their experiences of moving to the UK from other countries, although some details have been altered to suit the activities.

- Before the lesson, print out one copy of **CD (file 12.5)** and cut it up.
- Tell the children that together you are going to listen to one of the accounts and make notes using your research questions.
- Explain that the first story is told by a woman from Bosnia-Herzegovina. Show the children where this is on the map of Europe on **CD (file 12.4)**.
- Show them your questions from the printable **CD (file 12.5)**. Stick them to the flipchart allowing plenty of space so that you can add notes around them later.
- Ask the children to TTYP and talk about any questions in their Personal log that they would like to add to the ones you have on display. Take feedback and add in any further questions on the flipchart.
- Play the audio on **CD (file 12.6)**. Listen to it all the way through.
- Afterwards, TOL as you explain your initial thoughts and ideas linking the woman's story to the questions on the flipchart. Play the audio a second time. Add some information to the flipchart. Make sure that you write the information in note form, rather than full sentences. Use key words and phrases only at this stage.
- Review the information you have gathered. Ask the children to TTYP and discuss what additional information you need to gather and where in the audio that might be. (Note that not all the answers to your questions will be in the audio.)
- Play the audio a third time, pausing it to add any more information to your notes.

Curriculum link: using non-fiction, know what information they need to look for; asking questions

Class log

Purpose: for children to share the process of keeping a class reading, writing and thinking log to record responses to texts and activities in a variety of forms

- Ask the children to briefly TTYP to say whether you wrote whole sentences when you took your notes. Take feedback and if necessary remind them that you only wrote down key words and phrases, not whole sentences.
- Ask the children to look at the list of questions and decide which of those were not answered fully or not answered at all. Take feedback.
- Write the questions that you need more information for into the Class log. (You will need to refer back to this later, when looking at additional sources of information.)

Taking notes 2 (CD)

Purpose: for children to take notes independently by listening to an audio file

- Before the lesson, print off the research questions note-taker from **CD (file 13.1)**, one copy for each pair of children.
- Tell the children that they are going to take notes from another account, using their research questions for guidance. This account is about a man from Ivory Coast in Africa. They can write their notes on a copy of the research questions note-taker.
- Remind them of any additional research questions that you wrote on the flipchart on Day 12 and tell them to add these to their question sheet.
- Display **CD (file 13.2)** to show the children where Ivory Coast is on a world map.
- Play the audio on **CD (file 13.3)**. Remind the children that they are listening in order to answer their research questions.
- Ask the children to TTYP and discuss any answers they have so far. Take feedback and note any key ideas onto your flipchart for the children to refer to later.
- Play the audio a second time, pausing to gather new information and giving the children time to write the information down, next to the appropriate question. Note that you may have to guide this to start with.
- Ask the children to TTYP to review the information they have gathered and to discuss what additional information they need. Take feedback and try to help the children work out where in the audio the answer might be. (Note that they will not be able to gain answers to all their questions from this audio file. They will be given an additional source later on.)
- Play the audio a third time. Make sure you give the children enough time to add to their notes.
- Give the children time to finish and review all their notes.

Build a biography (CD)

Purpose: for children to understand how to take notes from an additional source

- Explain to the children that you are going to model (with their help) how to make notes from another source – this time a written source. This source gives more detailed information about the woman from Bosnia, who they heard about in the audio on Day 12. Show the questions and notes that you gathered on your flipchart on Day 12 Questions for research.
- Remind the children that there were some questions that you weren't able to answer, and these were noted in the Class log. Ask children to TTYP and talk about which questions weren't answered or were not answered fully.
- Display the fact file on **CD (file 13.4)**. (Note that it extends over two slides.) Explain that this is a fact file about the same woman who emigrated from Bosnia. Model how to skim quickly through the text looking for key words and ideas that will help answer one of the questions. Add the notes to the appropriate question on your flipchart.
- Choose another question and ask the children to work with their partner and scan the fact file for key words and ideas to answer it. Take feedback and add notes to the flipchart.
- Continue to do this until all the information possible has been found in the fact file.

Curriculum link: discussing writing similar to that which they are planning to write; use skills they have learnt earlier to find out information

DAY 13

Taking notes 3 🅿🅱 Ⓒ🅓

Purpose: for children to take notes from an additional source independently

- Note that in this activity the children will need to refer to their research questions note-taker that they worked on in Taking notes 2.
- Tell the children that it is now their turn to make notes from a written source, in preparation for writing a biography. Ask them to turn to the fact file on p.62 of the Pupils' Book. Explain that this fact file gives more information about the man from Ivory Coast that all the children took notes about.
- Ask the children to look at their research questions note-taker and then TTYP and discuss which of the research questions they still need to answer or find extra information for. Take feedback.
- Display **CD (file 13.5)** which shows some Top Tips for note-taking and explain that this should help the children as they read the fact file and write notes onto their research questions note-taker.
- Note that some children may need to work with adult support in this note-taking activity from a written source.

Curriculum link: discussing and recording ideas; write for a range of real purposes

Personal log

Purpose: for children to keep a personal reading, writing and thinking log to record thoughts and ideas for their own writing

- Ask the children to TTYP and discuss the person (or one of the people) they have been finding out about. Ask the children to think of three things that really stand out about the experiences of the person that they have been researching. Ask the children to write them down in their Personal log.

DAY 14

Grammar: paragraphs Ⓒ🅓 🅿🅱 🅷🅱

Purpose: for children to develop their awareness of the function of paragraphs in a text

Year 3 Grammar introduction to paragraphs to group related material

- Remind the children that in her biography, Jamila Gavin wrote about her experience with tigers in India (Anthology p.80). Explain that if she saw a tiger in England, it would probably be in a zoo (which is why the other children found her stories about being near wild tigers in India very exciting).
- Ask the children to TTYP and briefly tell their partner if they've been to a zoo or seen one on TV. How do they feel about zoos? What kinds of animals might live in a zoo? Take feedback.
- Tell the children that they are going to explore why and how we use *paragraphs*, focusing on a main topic about zoo animals.
- Ask them to imagine that the main topic is a very large box containing all the information about the different zoo animals. Display **CD (file 14.1)** to show a labelled box and explain that this represents the main topic. Tell them that if the information about the different zoo animals were all jumbled up inside that one big box, it would very disorganised and confusing. Explain that it would be much better if smaller, separate boxes of information about each kind of animal were inside.
- Click on 'Next' to show the container again and then click three times on the screen to show the smaller boxes. Remind them that the big box represents the main topic and the smaller boxes are the mini topics. These smaller boxes have grouped the information about different types of animals.

- Tell the children that you are going to turn the boxes into a written text. Click on 'Next' to show the title and topic sentences. Explain that the title and the topic sentence sets out what the *main topic* is (zoo animals). Read it chorally with the children. Explain that the first *mini topic* (mammals) will begin on a new line. Click on 'Next' to show the example. Read it out chorally with the children.
- Click on 'Next' again to show the second mini topic (birds) and repeat the process. Ask the children to TTYP to say what they think the next mini topic will be and then ask for a choral response. Check that they all say *reptiles*.
- Explain that each section of writing is called a *paragraph*. Explain that a paragraph is a section of writing that tells us there is a new focus on something to do with the main topic.
- Click on 'Next' to show the full text with new labels showing how it is divided into paragraphs. The mini topic sentences for reptiles have also been added.
- Explain that in a normal text, the paragraphs would not be shown in different colours. Ask the children to discuss how we would know when a new paragraph began and ended if we didn't have the colour code. Choose two to feed back and check they understand about the change of focus and the spacing between paragraphs. Keep the colour-coded text on your screen for the next activity.
- Now ask them to look at the Grammar: paragraphs activity on p.63 of their Pupils' Book. Ask them to TTYP to take turns to read the sentences.
- Model how you decide to which one of the colour-coded paragraphs the first sentence belongs, making links between the information contained in the sentence and the most appropriate paragraph on your screen.
- Tell the pupils to TTYP to decide to which one of the paragraphs they would add the next sentence. Choose two to feed back and ask them to give reasons for their answer. Repeat the process for the rest of the sentences.

Homework Book pp.22–23 provides further practice on paragraphs.

Write 1 ⓒⒹ

Curriculum link: explore and collect ideas; organising paragraphs around a theme

Purpose: for children to understand how to group information into paragraphs

- Remind the children how you grouped information together about Jamila Gavin into topics in the Class log on Day 11.
- Remind the children that they used questions to make notes about the stories they have read and heard. This means that much of the information they have gathered will already be grouped into broad topics. Each topic can be developed into a paragraph. The next task is to decide what order the topics/paragraphs should be put in, and then the order of the ideas within each paragraph.
- Display the research questions on **CD (file 14.2)**, and use TTYP and TOL to bring children into your thought process as you drag and drop them into a logical order for the structure of the biography. Explain that each of these questions represents a paragraph of information. Explain that the order is now like a plan for the full text.
- Tell the children that now you are going to look at how to organise information within each paragraph. Click to the next slide on the CD file. It displays notes for the research question 'What was your journey like?' TOL as you drag and drop the notes into a logical order for a paragraph.
- Point out the bank of adverbs of time at the bottom of the screen. Tell the children that you could use these to link your ideas and sentences together to help turn your notes into full sentences in each paragraph.

- Model using some of the words as you orally build the notes into sentences, e.g. 'First *Amela and her family travelled along the river to get to the sea.* Then *they took a small boat along the coast – they travelled at night.* After that *they crossed Europe using trains and buses.*'
- Give each pair several small sticky notes. Ask the children to TTYP and choose one of their research questions from Taking notes 3 on Day 13. Then tell them to write each of their notes onto a small sticky note and to decide in which order they would use them in a paragraph. Encourage them to orally link the notes together to make a full paragraph. Take feedback.

Write 2 ⓒⒹ 🖹 🄿🄱

> **Curriculum link:** discussing writing in order to learn from its structure, grammar and vocabulary

Purpose: for children to see a model of the writing process

- Before the lesson, print out a copy of **CD (file 14.3)** for your reference.
- Tell the children that you are going to turn your plan from today's activity and notes from Days 12 and 13 to write a biography about Amela for a webpage.
- Go through the checklist of key features for a biography (this can be found on Pupils' Book p.64 and on your Non-fiction wall).
- Model the writing process using the teacher's script from printable **CD (file 14.3)**, one paragraph at a time. Intersperse the children's writing sessions, Write 3 (see below), with each of your modelled paragraphs so that they can base their own paragraph on the biography as soon after modelling as possible.
- Remember to TOL as you amend your writing to show the children that the writing process is a bit messy and requires changes! (You can, of course, adapt the script to suit your notes.)
- Display your completed biography on **CD (file 14.4)** and discuss it with the children.

Write 3 🄿🄱

> organising paragraphs around a theme; drafting and re-reading to check their meaning is clear

Purpose: for children to write their biography as independently as possible

- Tell the children that they are going to write their own biography about the account that they have written notes for from the audio account and fact file in the Pupils' Book p.62.
- Make sure that you give the children the opportunity to write each paragraph following you modelling your own paragraph, as outlined above, so that the writing is done in stages, rather than in one go.

Write 3 (continued)

Purpose: for children to write their biography as independently as possible

- Continue the process as explained on Day 14. Once the children have written their biographies, ask them to TTYP and to read their biography aloud.
- Encourage the children to make any changes to their work that they feel are necessary at this time.

Evaluate and edit ⓒⒹ

> assessing the effectiveness of their own and others' writing

Purpose: for children to evaluate their own and their partner's work against specific criteria and then discuss how they could improve their work

- Display **CD (file 15.1)** to show the evaluation points and read them aloud using MT/YT.
- As a model, select an example of work where the writing has met the criteria, and share this with the other children, explaining why it works well.

- Tell the children to take turns to read their partner's writing in pairs and discuss together how well each piece of writing has met the criteria.
- Ask children to discuss at least two changes they could make to improve their work.

Curriculum link: proofread for spelling and punctuation errors

Proofread

Purpose: for children to proofread their work, and make changes to improve the accuracy of their grammar, punctuation and spelling

- Now ask the children to proofread their work. If you have noticed that several children need to improve on a particular aspect of spelling, grammar or punctuation, use this as a focus for the Proofread activity. Write an example which includes common errors from the children's writing and use this as a model.
- The children should always be checking for standard use of punctuation and correct spelling of common exception words.
- The following points would be relevant as the particular focus for this Unit:
  - using the past tense correctly and consistently
  - using the third person correctly and consistently
  - spelling high frequency adverbs of time correctly.

Publish and present

Purpose: for children to publish their biographies

Note that it would be good for the children to have access to computers to publish their writing.

- Make sure that all children have either a copy of the webpage template on a computer or printed out onto paper **CD (file 15.2)**. (You might want to encourage children who need less support to make their own template.) Note that this template can be adapted to suit the children's needs, for example you could replace the photograph with another paragraph, add more paragraphs, etc.
- Remind the children that they need to make their biography easy to read so suggest they add at least a couple of subheadings to help guide the reader through the information.
- Ask the children to TTYP and discuss a good subheading for the first paragraph of the biography. Take feedback.
- Give the children time to write or type in the final version of their biography webpage.

Curriculum coverage chart

England	*Literacy and Language* Year 3 is closely matched to the Programmes of study for the new *National Curriculum in England* from 2014 and the Year 3 grammar requirements listed in its Grammar appendix.
	See the overview chart on p.18 and the curriculum link boxes in the teaching notes for details.
	Literacy and Language is suitable for children working at National Curriculum level 2a and above and aims to take children to level 5 and beyond. See **www.oxfordprimary.co.uk** for curriculum updates.
Scotland	Primary 4 *Curriculum for Excellence* First level
Wales	*Literacy and Language* enables children to become accomplished in
	oracy across the curriculum
	reading across the curriculum
	writing across the curriculum.
	See **www.oxfordprimary.co.uk** for further details and a free downloadable correlation chart when the new *National Literacy and Numeracy Framework* is introduced.
Northern Ireland	Primary 4/Year 4
	The following points from the *Language and Literacy* curriculum are covered in each unit of *Literacy and Language*:
	Unit 1
	Talking and listening: 1, 2, 3, 5, 6, 7, 8, 9, 10, 11, 12, 13, 14
	Reading: 1, 3, 4, 5, 6, 7, 8, 9, 10, 11, 12, 16
	Writing: 1, 2, 3, 4, 5, 6, 7, 8, 9, 11, 12
	Unit 2
	Talking and listening: 1, 2, 3, 5, 6, 7, 8, 9, 10, 11, 12, 13, 14
	Reading: 1, 3, 4, 5, 6, 7, 8, 9, 10, 11, 12, 16
	Writing: 1, 2, 3, 4, 5, 6, 7, 8, 9, 11, 12
	Unit 3
	Talking and listening: 1, 2, 3, 5, 6, 7, 8, 9, 10, 11, 12, 13, 14
	Reading: 1, 3, 4, 5, 6, 7, 8, 9, 10, 11, 12, 16
	Writing: 1, 2, 3, 4, 5, 6, 7, 8, 9, 11, 12
	Unit 4
	Talking and listening: 1, 2, 3, 5, 6, 7, 8, 9, 10, 11, 12, 13, 14
	Reading: 1, 2, 3, 4, 5, 6, 7, 8, 9, 10, 11, 12, 16
	Writing: 1, 2, 3, 4, 5, 6, 7, 8, 9, 11, 12
	Unit 5
	Talking and listening: 1, 2, 3, 5, 6, 7, 8, 9, 10, 11, 12, 13, 14
	Reading: 1, 3, 4, 5, 6, 7, 8, 9, 10, 11, 12, 16
	Writing: 1, 2, 3, 4, 5, 6, 7, 8, 9, 11, 12
	Unit 6
	Talking and listening: 1, 2, 3, 5, 6, 7, 8, 9, 10, 11, 12, 13 ,14
	Reading: 1, 3, 4, 5, 6, 7, 8, 9, 10, 11, 12, 16
	Writing: 1, 2, 3, 4, 5, 6, 7, 8, 9, 11, 12